Anthropologies and Futures

Anthropologies and Futures

Researching Emerging and Uncertain Worlds

EDITED BY JUAN FRANCISCO SALAZAR, SARAH PINK, ANDREW IRVING AND JOHANNES SJÖBERG

Routledge
Taylor & Francis Group

LONDON AND NEW YORK

First published 2017 Bloomsbury Academic

Published 2020 by Routledge
2 Park Square, Milton Park, Abingdon, Oxon OX14 4RN
605 Third Avenue, New York, NY 10017

Routledge is an imprint of the Taylor & Francis Group, an informa business

Cover design: Adriana Brioso
Cover image: Entrance to Global Seed Vault, Svalbard, Norway (© Cultura RM Exclusive/ Tim E White/Getty Images)

A catalogue record for this book is available from the British Library.

Library of Congress Cataloging-in-Publication Data
Names: Salazar, Juan Francisco, editor.
Title: Anthropologies and futures : researching emergingand uncertain worlds / edited by Juan Francisco Salazar, Sarah Pink, Andrew Irving and Johannes Sjberg.
Description: London ; New York, NY : Bloomsbury Academic,an imprint of Bloomsbury Publishing, Plc, [2017] | Includes bibliographical references and index.
Identifiers: LCCN 2016047945 (print) | LCCN 2017019648(ebook) | ISBN 9781474264877 (pb) | ISBN 9781474264884 (hb)
Subjects: LCSH: Ethnology–Research. | Applied anthropology–Methodology. | Applied anthropology–Philosophy.
Classification: LCC GN345 (ebook) | LCC GN345 .A5785 2017(print) | DDC 301–dc23
LC record available at https://lccn.loc.gov/2016047945

Typeset by Fakenham Prepress Solutions, Fakenham, Norfolk NR21 8NN

ISBN13: 978-1-474-26488-4 (hbk)
ISBN13: 978-1-474-26487-7 (pbk)

Contents

List of Figures

Acknowledgements

This book was inspired by the formation of the EASA (European Association of Social Anthropologists) Future Anthropologies Network, established in 2014. We would like to thank all of our network colleagues and collaborators who worked with us in the development of our collective Future Anthropologies Manifesto, which is available online and published as Chapter 1 as a reminder of our intent. We also thank Bloomsbury's editorial team for their support of our project, especially Jennifer Schmidt, Commissioning Editor, Food Studies and Anthropology and Clara Herberg, Editorial Assistant, Anthropology and Food Studies.

Notes on Contributors

Simone Abram is Reader at the Anthropology department at Durham University UK, where she is also a Director of the Durham Energy Institute. She has published widely, including books, *Culture and Planning* (2011) and *Rationalities of Planning* (2002 with Jonathan Murdoch), and edited volumes including, *Elusive Promises* (2013 with Gisa Weszkalnys), *Media, Engagement And Anthropological Practice* (2015 with Sarah Pink) and *Tourism Ecologies in the European High North* (2016 with Katrìn Anna Lund). Simone has been a visiting Professor at the University of Paris and at Tromsø University, and a visiting researcher at the universities of Oslo and Gothenburg and at l'EHESS, Paris.

Yoko Akama is an award-winning design researcher in the School of Media and Communication and co-leads the Design+Ethnography+Futures research program (http://d-e-futures.com/) at RMIT University, Australia, where she is Associate Professor. She also established the Design for Social Innovation and Sustainability in Asia-Pacific network (http://desiap.org/). Her Japanese heritage has embedded a Zen-informed reflexive practice to carve a 'tao' (path) in human-centred design. Her practice is entangled in complex 'wicked problems', shaped by working with regional communities in Australia in strengthening their resilience for disaster preparedness and with Indigenous Nations to enact their sovereignty and self-determination. She is an Adjunct Fellow of an ecosystem innovation studio, Re:public Japan and Visiting Fellow at the Centre of Excellence in Media Practice, Bournemouth University. She is a recipient of several major research grants in Australia and the UK and winner of the prestigious Good Design Australia Awards (2014). For more information please go to www.rmit.edu.au/staff/yokoakama.

Elisenda Ardèvol is Associate Professor in Social Anthropology and Cultural Studies at the Department of Arts and Humanities, at the Universitat Oberta de Catalunya. Current Director of mediaccions Digital Communication and Culture Research Group at UOC, she participates in different Masters and PhD programs in Media, Digital and Visual Anthropology and has been Visiting Scholar at the Centre for Visual Anthropology of the University of Southern California, Los Angeles, and EU Visiting Fellow at the Digital Ethnography

Centre at the RMIT, Melbourne. Her main research is related with ethno-graphic methodologies, digital culture, visuality and media in everyday life. Recently, she is also exploring design, creativity and collaborative practices in digital technologies.

Alexandra D'Onofrio is in her final stage of her practice-based PhD in AMP (Anthropology Media and Performance) at the University of Manchester. She is a photographer, filmmaker and community theatre facilitator and has been working on experiences and narratives of migration since 2005. Her previous work includes the audio-visual documentary 'Caught in Between Darkness and Light' (2008, winner of the Richard Werbner award), which was the outcome of her MA in Visual Anthropology at the University of Manchester, and 'La Vita che non CIE' (2012, a trilogy of short documentaries on detention and repatriation centres in Italy, of which 'Luck will save me' was winner of Lavori in Corto Festival 2012 – Turin) in collaboration with journalist Gabriele Del Grande (Fortress Europe).

Annie Fergusson completed her PhD using the methodological approach of the ethnography of communication to understand how meaning and social value is created in a speech community in Mexico. As a polyglot she brings multi-faceted experiences to her applied intellectual work which centres on the ways in which communicative practices are responsive to context. Theoretically, she subscribes to Bourdieusian notions of social theory and practice and Hymesian notions of diversity which situate man-made units of meaning within inter-actional exchanges. Geographically she is fascinated with emergent paradigms of the Global South. She currently works as a User Experience Designer working on digital technologies. In this work, she applies her methods for understanding broad social contexts, localized communities of practice and individual micro practices in order to enhance human-computer interactions.

Faye Ginsburg is David B. Kriser Professor of Anthropology at NYU where she is also founder and director of the Center for Media, Culture and History, and the Council for the Study of Disability. Her work focuses on cultural activism and social transformation, from her early work on abortion activism to her current book in progress (in collaboration with Rayna Rapp) *Disability Worlds: Cripping the 'New Normal' in 21st Century America*. A multiple award-winning author, she is also a recipient of Macarthur, Guggenheim and other awards for her research. Ginsburg is President of the Dysautonomia Foundation.

Andrew Irving is Director of the Granada Centre for Visual Anthropology at the University of Manchester. His research areas include sensory perception, time, illness, death, urban anthropology and experimental methods. Recent books include *Whose Cosmopolitanism?* (with Nina Glick-Schiller, Berghahn 2014); *Beyond Text? Critical Practices and Sensory Anthropology* (with Rupert Cox and Chris Wright, Manchester University Press 2016) and *The Art of Life and Death* (University of Chicago, 2016). Recent media works include the play *The Man Who Almost Killed Himself* (2014) in collaboration with Josh Azouz and Don Boyd, which was premiered at the Edinburgh Film Festival and was concurrently live-streamed to Odeon Cinemas and BBC Arts. Other recent media works include the *New York Stories Project* (2013), which is currently hosted on more than thirty websites, including Scientific American, the Smithsonian, Wenner Gren and National Public Radio.

Magdalena Kazubowski-Houston is an anthropologist, performance theorist, and theatre director. She is Associate Professor of Theatre and has graduate appointments in Theatre & Performance Studies and Social Anthropology at York University. Her research explores performance ethnography, ethnographic storytelling and ethnographic (non)fiction as collaborative, reflexive, and affective research methodologies in the study of future, migration, interiority, violence, and ageing. She has collaborated on imaginative ethnography projects with Romani minorities in Poland, Nazi-Holocaust survivors in Poland and Canada, and low-income residents in Vancouver's Downtown Eastside. She has also worked as a professional theatre director, performer, and playwright, both nationally and internationally. Her book, *Staging Strife* (2010), was awarded the International Congress of Qualitative Inquiry (ICQI) Outstanding Qualitative Book Award and the Canadian Association for Theatre Research (CATR) Ann Saddlemyer Book Prize (2011). She is the co-founding member of the Centre for Imaginative Ethnography (CIE), a project committed to advancing critical and politically conscious research.

Tony Knight is as an environmental anthropologist completing his PhD thesis at the University of Kent following a successful career in international management consulting. His research focuses on the relationships that exist between humans and 'wild' nature, specifically at the interstices of modern pastoralism and a contested landscape in the process of being rewilded by charismatic large predators in the French Pyrenees. Tony's transdisciplinary approach draws heavily on ethnographic fieldwork and political ecology, dealing with multispecies actors who dwell in different overlapping ontological landscapes. Tony has a particular interest in a public anthropology that contemplates the Anthropocene and future imaginaries.

Débora Lanzeni is a junior researcher at the Universitat Oberta de Catalunya and member of *mediaccions* Digital Culture Research Group, and holds a visiting fellowship in Information and Media Studies in Aarhus University,

Denmark. She holds a PhD in Information & Knowledge Society. Her publications include 'Digital Visualities and Materialities: Paths for an Anthropological Walk' (2014); 'Technology and Visions of the Future: Imagination in the Process of Digital Creation from an Ethnographic Approach' (2014) and 'Smart Global Futures: Designing Affordable Materialities for a Better Life' in Pink, Ardévol and Lanzeni, *Digital Materiality: Anthropology and Design* (2016).

Annette Markham is Professor of Information Studies at Aarhus University in Denmark & Affiliate Professor of Digital Ethics in the School of Communication at Loyola University, Chicago. She holds a PhD in organizational communication (Purdue University, 1998), with a strong emphasis in interpretive and ethnographic methods. She researches how identity, relationships, and cultural formations are constructed in and influenced by digitally saturated socio-technical contexts. Her pioneering work in this area is well represented in her first book *Life Online: Researching Real Experience in Virtual Space* (Altamira 1998). Annette is internationally recognized for developing epistemological frameworks for rethinking ethics and methods in twenty-first-century networked contexts. Her writing can be found in a range of international journals, handbooks, and edited collections.

Sarah Pink is Distinguished Professor and Director of the Digital Ethnography Research Centre at RMIT University, Australia. She is Visiting Professor at Halmstad University, Sweden and Loughborough University, UK, and Guest Professor at Free University, Berlin, Germany. Her recent works are usually collaborative and include the books *Theoretical Scholarship and Applied Practice* (2017), *Digital Materialities* (2016), *Digital Ethnography: Principles and Practice* (2016), and *Screen Ecologies* (2016). Less conventional works include *Un/Certainty* eBook (2015), *Laundry Lives* documentary film (2015) and the *Energy and Digital Living* website www.energyanddigitalliving.com

Rayna Rapp is Professor of Anthropology at New York University. Her areas of research are gender, reproduction, health and culture and science and technology in the U.S. and Europe. She is the author of *Testing Women, Testing the Fetus: The Social Impact of Amniocentesis in America* (Routledge, 2000). Her recent articles include 'Genetic Citizenship' and 'Gender, Body, Biomedicine: How Some Feminist Concerns Dragged Reproduction to the Center of Social Theory' in *Medical Anthropology Quarterly*. She is currently working on a book with Faye Ginsburg entitled *Disability Worlds: Cripping the 'New Normal' in 21st Century America*.

Juan Francisco Salazar is Associate Professor in Media Arts at Western Sydney University. For over a decade, he worked with Indigenous media organizations and cultural activists in Latin America on communication rights and citizens' media practices. His current research interests are on life in extreme environments, human-soil relations and futures. He has conducted ethnographic research in Antarctica since 2011 where he produced the Antarctic Digital Storytelling Project (2012–13) and filmed the documentary *Nightfall on Gaia* (2015), which premiered at the 14th RAI Ethnographic Film Festival (Bristol 2015) and has screened at numerous international film festivals. Since 2011 he has been a member of the executive committee of the Humanities and Social Sciences Expert Group (HASSEG) of the Scientific Committee for Antarctic Research (SCAR). He is co-author (with H. Cohen and I. Barkat) of the award-winning *Screen Media Arts: Concepts and Practices* (Oxford University Press, 2008) and has been a visiting fellow at University of Sussex (UK); Universidad de Las Américas (México); Universidad de Valparaíso (Chile).

Johannes Sjöberg is a lecturer in Screen Studies at The University of Manchester. He specializes in film practice as research and more specifically in the boundaries between artistic and academic forms of research and representation. His approach is based on the combination of extended ethnographic fieldwork and improvisational art forms, mediating complex cultural understanding within a reflexive context. This approach has developed as a research interest through previous professional work with theatre improvisation and as a documentary filmmaker. Sjöberg was awarded a PhD in Drama for his practice-based research on the ethnofictions of Jean Rouch, focusing on the use of projective improvisation in ethnographic filmmaking and applied on identity, performance and discrimination among transgendered Brazilians. He is currently convening the PhD programme in Anthropology, Media and Performance at The University of Manchester and conducting research on psychodrama and play in fieldwork research, and 'ethno science fiction' as an ethnographic film method.

Paul Stoller is Professor of Anthropology at West Chester University and has been conducting anthropological research for more than thirty years in West Africa (Niger) and among African immigrants in New York City. This body of research has resulted in the publication of fourteen books, which include ethnographies, memoirs, novels, a biography and collections of academic essays. His most recent work, published in October 2014, is *Yaya's Story: The Quest for Well-Being in the World*. In April 2013, the King of Sweden, Carl XVI Gustav, awarded him the 2013 Anders Retzius Gold Medal to honor his significant scientific contributions to anthropology. In 2015, The American Anthropological Association awarded him the Anthropology and Media Award (AIME) in recognition of his longstanding The Huffington Post blog that brings an anthropological perspective to politics, higher education, culture and media. His latest book, *The Sorcerer's Burden*, a novel, was published in the Fall of 2016.

Karen Waltorp is an anthropologist and filmmaker. She is the director of *Manenberg* (2010) building on her long-term fieldwork in the South African township, which received the Royal Anthropological Institute's Basil Wright Film Prize. A follow-up film is currently in production. She is part of the Danish Research Council funded research group *Camera as Cultural Critique* at the Department of Anthropology at Aarhus University, where she also teaches design anthropology, as well as in the experimental visual master program *Eye & Mind*. Previously, she taught at the Department of Anthropology, University of Copenhagen and at the Royal Danish School of Design. She spent the spring semester 2016 as visiting scholar at the Department of Anthropology, UC Berkeley. Her fourteen-month PhD-fieldwork and filmmaking was with young Muslim, second-generation women in Copenhagen, and focused on place-making with smartphones, moral experimentation, and on anthropological knowledge-making processes.

1

Futures anthropologies manifesto

EASA future anthropologies network

Introduction

The ten-point manifesto laid out below was written over the course of three days at the Conference of the European Association of Social Anthropologists (EASA) in Tallinn, August 2014. More than twenty participants in the Anthropology at the Edge of the Future: Forward Play Lab[1] contributed lines, which were cut and moulded by Juan Francisco Salazar, Jude Robinson and Lydia Nicholas, then presented to the attendees of the Media futures panel.[2] The Manifesto incorporates feedback from dozens of anthropologists, and it has been established as the starting point for the continued collaborative work of a network of engaged, creative and bold practitioners.

Future anthropologies manifesto

1 We are critical ethnographers engaged with confronting and intervening in the challenges of contested and controversial futures.

2 We are stubbornly transdisciplinary and transnational: we collaborate, hybridize and compromise. We break boundaries and network without fear of incapacity or contamination.

3 We de-centre the human, embracing larger ecologies and technological entanglements.

4   We probe, interrogate and play with futures that are plural, non-linear, cyclical, implausible and always unravelling.

5   Anthropology of the future is accretive. It builds on traditions, reflects on pasts.

6   We are bold enough to engage with complexity and stay with differences and uncertainties. We traverse the macro, mundane and minute and embrace the chaotic, multisensory, performative and material dimensions of social life in the Anthropocene.

7   We understand and are understood. We foster a politics of listening attuned to a diversity of voices and we tell stories that are imaginative, illustrative and informative. We create and design a variety of materials and processes that are provocative, disruptive, adaptable and reflexive.

8   We get our hands dirty. We are ethical, political and interventionist, and take responsibility for interventions.

9   We may be epistemologically filthy, improvisational and undisciplined. We may struggle, and fail and transform.

10   Anthropology of the future supports current and future members to be part of a strong and recognizable community of practice.

Notes

1 See http://www.nomadit.co.uk/easa/easa2014/panels.php5?PanelID=3230 (accessed 22 May 2016).
2 See http://www.nomadit.co.uk/easa/easa2014/panels.php5?PanelID=3070 (accessed 22 May 2016).

2

Anthropologies and futures: Setting the agenda

Sarah Pink and Juan Francisco Salazar

*A*nthropologies and Futures calls for a renewed, open and future-focused approach to understanding the present, anticipating the unknown, and intervening in the world. It is aligned with the movement toward a critical anthropological ethnography whose practitioners are engaged with confronting and intervening in the challenges of contested and controversial futures, and it advances the agenda to depart from the constraints of conventional mainstream anthropological practice, as stated in the critical manifesto of the Future Anthropologies Network (this volume Chapter 1). Collectively, its contributors are determined to refigure anthropology: beyond its reliance on documenting and analysing the past; its dependence on long-term fieldwork; and its tendency to close itself off in critical isolation. Such approaches have paralyzed the discipline in a world where the insights of creative, improvisational, speculative, and participatory techniques of a renewed anthropological ethnography have the potential to make a significant contribution in the making of alternative futures.

This book, as a collective action, seeks to derail mainstream social and cultural anthropology from an insular and inward looking single-discipline route that threatens to exacerbate its isolation and incapacity to participate and intervene in the major worldmaking activities of our times. At the margins of anthropology, applied, interdisciplinary, futures, and interventional strands have long since militated for a useful and engaged anthropological practice, and have gained traction. Yet, as a discipline, anthropology has been on track to arrive late on the futures research scene. By opening our scholarship, practice, and intentions to other disciplines, techniques, and aspirations, we have the opportunity to bring to the study and making of futures an approach inflected by the ethical and participatory principles of anthropology. The benefits are both the contribution that anthropology can offer to world making *and* a renewed anthropology that nevertheless maintains its critical core, its ethnographic origins and its capacity to engage with the world and people at a depth and moral perspective. These characteristics of an anthropological commitment to attempt to comprehend the world in a way that cares are fundamental to our discipline and to the practice of Futures Anthropology. Yet we call for an anthropology that is more daring, open, and interventional: that faces futures and our role in shaping them, full on, while retaining a critical perspective. This book sets the ground for this movement in anthropology, as a shared concern.

The critical manifesto developed collectively by the Future Anthropologies Network (this volume Chapter 1) states ten principles established collectively by a group of about thirty anthropologists in Tallinn, Estonia, after our founding workshop at the conference of the European Association of Social Anthropologists (EASA) in 2014.[1] The manifesto is ambitious and intentionally provocative. While this book may not achieve its call in full, it takes a step towards, and argues for the Futures Anthropology that we believe the network envisages. Likewise, the chapters are not all equally radical. However, the spirit of the book lies in a desire to move on, beyond what anthropology conventionally does, and to lay the foundations to advance towards a new state of the discipline. While it could be argued that these foundations already exist in the fields of applied anthropology and design anthropology, and to some extent in STS (Science and Technology Studies) anthropology, and environmental anthropology, we propose something different; we argue for an interventional anthropology that puts at its core a theoretical and practical consideration of futures, and the possible ways they might be conceptualised and played out.

This is not to say that attention to futures has been absent in anthropology as a discipline, or in the work of individual anthropologists. As we outline below, the notion of future has been pondered from a variety of perspectives within anthropology. It is therefore surprising that in place of a dynamic set of critical debates, and a field of practice enthused by a concern with futures, instead (as we show below), we encounter a history of truncated pathways, which have never sustained a coordinated field of future-focused anthropological enquiry. Establishing techniques for researching futures sits at the core of the work of this book, and is played out in the work of the contributors. By techniques we do not simply refer to practical methods, detached from their users or communities that can be transferred from one project to another. Rather, drawing on Tim Ingold, we understand that 'technique is embedded in and inseparable from the experience of particular subjects in the shaping of particular things' (2000: 315); a method or approach is always situated and emergent from within the particular circumstances through which it plays out. The techniques we are concerned with should not be confused with ways of doing anthropological fieldwork. Rather we are interested in the application of future-oriented theoretical, methodological, and practical techniques of research and intervention as part of a renewed anthropological agenda. In this endeavour we are not alone. Some applied anthropologists, design anthropologists, and anthropologists engaged in public-oriented activities likewise seek to join up the anthropological and ethnographic cores of their theory and practice, to make change in the world. Where our agenda is different is that rather than attaching our work to one specific discipline that we might then blend with anthropology to make change in the world, we are committed to making futures in ways that diverge from conventional anthropology. This could involve coupling our endeavours with those of, for example, design, STS, geography, policy-making, creative practice, planning, and the life sciences. This task also requires us to account for the contested politics of uncertain, emerging, and as yet unknown worlds. In a context where it is claimed that 'numerous tools and methods have been developed to study not just probable and possible but also preferred futures' (Adam and Groves 2007: 32) an engaged futures-oriented anthropology needs to redress the fact that ethnography has been to date a neglected method for studying futures. In an interdisciplinary context we need to make futures ethnographically thinkable, and to demonstrate how an anthropological ethnography can put this into practice.

In this chapter we have chosen to use the label Futures Anthropology to denote the field of practice that we wish to nurture. The plural in this label refers to the multiplicity of futures and modes of future thinking that fall into this category. We refer to anthropology in the singular rather than in the plural, not because we wish to speak of a unified and homogeneous discipline, but because we would like the see the field of Futures Anthropology as a movement that consolidates a number of principles and ideals, as called for in the manifesto. We also differentiate our deliberations from those concerned with the future of anthropology. While the latter is of course at the core of our concerns too, it is however, an outcome, rather than the motive for our discussions. The chapters of this book suggest a number of ways to realize a Futures Anthropology, and advance what we believe is viable and possible. Yet to understand how to proceed we benefit from learning from past limitations. We next explore anthropologists' past attempts to engage with futures, to explain how futures research was, in the past excluded from the anthropological mainstream.

Being in the wrong temporality at the wrong time

The temporalities and timings of anthropology as they emerged during the twentieth century, and have persisted into the present, have had related problematic dimensions for a Futures Anthropology. The first is the temporality of ethnographic practice with its past orientation and the second is that attempts to develop future-focused anthropologies have always been badly timed, since theoretical turns in the discipline never seem to have worked in their favour. Thus the anthropological method itself is embedded with a past orientation, and the theoretical canons of the discipline have not accommodated a future-focused shift. Below we propose that the current theoretical and methodological environment of an interdisciplinary anthropology opens up possibilities for Futures Anthropology to emerge. First we outline how being in the wrong temporality at the wrong time has inhibited the making of Futures Anthropology.

We begin our story in the 1970s, when the futurist Alvin Toffler famously published *Future Shock*, a best-selling book concerned with the accelerating changes in post-industrial societies (Toffler 1970). This book marked a period in the 1970s when the future as an object of forecast and technological manipulation, David Valentine argues, 'seemed to most fully capture the imaginations of the lay public, politicians, policy makers and forecasters, including some anthropologists' (Valentine 2015: 110). Shortly after Margaret Mead wrote 'A Note on Contributions of Anthropology to the Science of the Future' (1971) and along with some other anthropologists began a focus on the future as a matter of scholarly interest and engaged research. As Samuel Collins notes, Mead began to conceptualize the future in a way that remains unique, by outlining a robust architecture for anthropological contributions to the future (Collins 2007: 1184), which attempted to show the importance of studying the possible and desired sociocultural futures of human civilization, as well as other future oriented topics strange to anthropology, such as the existence of aliens and the colonization of outer space. In the wake of Mead's work, anthropologists Magoroh Maruyama and Arthur Harkins wrote *Cultures Beyond the Earth* (1975) and *Cultures of the Future* (1978). Both books suggested the role anthropology could play in the search for extra-terrestrial intelligence or the study of the future in anthropology in relation to the 1980s sustainability debate, but went largely unnoticed in anthropology and other disciplines at the time. Theirs and Mead's work on anthropological futures was largely dismissed as populist by a generation of anthropologists concerned with developing a 'scientific' anthropology (Collins 2007: 1183) and an interpretive anthropology bound by the study of non-western cultural symbols and meanings.

Around the same time, an 'anticipatory anthropology' began to emerge as a more applied futures approach. Pioneered by Robert Textor, Reed Riner and others (Riner 1987; Textor 2005) this approach influenced a small number of applied anthropologists in the 1980s. In developing a critique of the field of futures research at the time, these researchers sought an integration of anthropological and futures research theories by adopting the assumptions, aims and methods of futures research, but enveloping these within an anthropological understanding of concepts such as 'culture, time, holism, and cross-cultural perspectives' (Riner 1987: 317) to develop grounded work towards anticipating middle-range futures within existing local, regional, national, and global socio-cultural systems (Textor 2005). This move involved theorizing futures by starting from empirical phenomena as the basis from which to develop general statements about the future that could be verified by data. It used the perspective, theories, models, and methods of anthropology in an anticipatory manner, so that individuals, citizens, leaders, and governments could better make informed policy decisions, thereby improving the community's or society's chances of realizing preferred futures and avoiding undesired ones (Razak 2000). Nevertheless, this form of anticipatory anthropology was restrictive because it situated anthropology's contribution at a micro-level, whereby available information plus ethnographic inquiry would be used to anticipate and visualize possible alternative futures for a given cultural group at a very particular moment in time. Thus, it would prohibit its contribution to wider macro-level debates or theory building either in anthropology itself or in applied research fields.

As the 1980s progressed, some of the most significant turns in the history of the discipline emerged, as anthropologists increasingly bought into the 'writing culture turn' (Clifford and Marcus 1986), and the discipline was gripped simultaneously by the political critique of an emerging feminist anthropology and the influence of postmodernism and continental philosophy. Within this environment the anthropological focus on the particular, reinforced further by Johannes Fabian's (1983) opportune exposition of the ethics of ethnographic temporalities, meant that anthropological ethnography would for some time yet remain fixed in the past tense and in a representational idiom. Anthropologists interested in futures have commented on the past temporality of anthropological ethnography ever since. For example, Riner pointed out three decades ago that anthropology's forte has always been disciplined hindsight' (Riner 1987: 311), while in the 1990s Nancy Munn observed that in anthropology 'futurity is poorly tended as a specifically temporal phenomenon', attributing this to a tendency by anthropologists to view the future in 'shreds and patches' in relation to the close attention given to 'the past in the present' (1992: 115–16). This point is raised in different ways by a range of anthropologists. Jane Guyer protested, that 'the anthropology of time settles so quickly into the "past in the present" and memory' (2007: 10), while Matthew Hodges has argued that anthropologists have mostly operated within the constraints of spatialized conceptions of linear time (Hodges 2008). Daniel Rosenberg and Susan Harding in the introduction to their edited volume *Histories of the Futures* assert that futures seem always to be haunted by the 'semiotic ghosts' of futures past (2005), a point also raised by Collins (2008) in his attempt to propel anthropology's engagement with the future as a reaction against the hegemonizing impulses of 'mass-produced homogeneity' (Collins 2008: 8). Similarly, David Valentine observes that 'the very idea of "the future" provokes suspicion in anthropologists because of its suturing to the teleologies of modernity and capitalism' (2012: 1064). Most recently Peter Pels (2015) has brought ethics back into the discussion, by suggesting that anthropologists have long neglected the future as an object of study as a result of an unfinished project of postcolonial reflexivity. Indeed it is not surprising, given the ethical weight of anthropology's colonial past, and the use of a reflexive past-tense to redress this, that there have never been too many openings to contest this past-orientation, since it had been the basis upon which anthropology as a whole discipline had re-validated its moral and ethical worth. In this line Ulf Hannerz has argued for the relevance of a subjunctive anthropology that might develop in the public domain and reveal the stance that anthropologists could adopt towards the abundant variety of macro-scenarios at play today and contribute to an informed citizen's understanding of the contemporary world – and to the debate over both present and future worlds (Hannerz 2003: 174, 184). Below we explain how new ethical horizons relating to our responsibility for shaping global futures shift this perspective. First we reflect on the theoretical contexts that constrained further attempts at Futures Anthropology.

Turning theory out of time

Since the early 1990s an anthropology of time has addressed questions of how people in different cultural contexts orient themselves in relation to known and unknown futures, and of how such futures are envisioned and acted upon. As Nielsen (2011) notes, detailed ethnographic accounts have often been employed to show how possible worlds unfold and how 'the future emerges as anticipation inscribed in the present' and how 'hopes and aspirations reorient individual life trajectories' (Nielsen 2011: 398. See also Appadurai 2013; Miyazaki 2006; Nielsen and Pedersen, 2015). These works represent a wide range of different theoretical commitments and disciplinary priorities. While it is not our concern here to unpack their debates and trajectories, we argue that this diversity of approaches has militated against the formation of an anthropological theory of the future, and reveals how anthropologies of futures have been influenced by theoretical turns, rather than themselves being the basis for theory building. This is something that needs to change, as argued below. First, we interrogate two examples of how attempts at anthropologies of futures clashed with anthropologies of time, in order to understand how this occurred.

In the 1990s and 2000s new anthropological approaches to futures emerged, yet these were not coherent with the most popular theoretical developments in mainstream anthropology. For example, Sandra Wallman's volume *Contemporary Futures* (1992), which examined the future in classi-cally framed ethnographic case studies, was published in the same year as Alfred Gell's monograph (1992) *The Anthropology of Time*, which has had an enduring influence in anthropology. While Wallman and her contributors argued for ethnography's capacity as a technique for 'knowing' the world, this was precisely one of the assumptions that Gell developed a critique of. For Wallman, anthropological perspectives were not really about the future as it will be, could be, or ought to be, but were concerned with futures visualized in our own or others' cultures in the present. Wallman's approach concurred more with George Herbert Mead's view of a future that is only possible and revocable as a dimension of the present, and simultaneously endorsing a Geertzian-type strategy for the 'interpretation of futures' through a framework that attended to the role of symbols in the construction of meaning. Her proposal 'to interpret the way we and others picture the future, and then to understand the effects of our (or their) picturing it as we/they do' (1992: 2), was therefore already anachronistic at the time, and thus slipped out of view, as new theoretical perspectives led anthropology's mainstream debates in another direction.

Similar interpretations can be made of more recent attempts to put futures on the anthropological agenda, such as Arjun Appadurai's lament that 'in spite of many important technical moves in the understanding of culture, the future remains a stranger to most anthropological models of culture' (Appadurai 2013: 5). Following a broadly culturalist and representational approach Appadurai identified that 'there is still an underlying pull in the core concepts of anthropology – such as culture, diversity, structure, meaning and custom – toward persistence, stability, fixity'. He has argued that '[t]his tendency has limited the anthropological contribution to the study of how different human societies organize the future as a cultural horizon' (Appadurai 2013: 5). While a focus on stability would most likely limit the anthropological study of where future lies in different cultures, we arrive at a different expla-nation. That is, we argue, that interpreting Futures Anthropology as the study of how future figures in models of culture, in itself limits anthropology as a field of study. Contemporary departures from a representational anthropology

offer alternatives that broadly refigure the focus whether towards phenomenological and ontological approaches, questions of materiality and agency, or
towards an 'anthropology of emergence' (Maurer 2005) that does not 'settle
in mere descriptive adequacy but that uses its objects to unsettle anthropological claims to knowledge' (2005: 1).

Interdisciplinary parallels

While the future-focused anthropologies outlined above emerged during
the twentieth and early twenty-first centuries, in other social science and
humanities disciplines, parallel and perhaps more impactful investigations
of futures began to develop. We do not encompass this whole history, but
refer to selected contributions from sociology and human geography. These
works reveal further the limits of a traditional anthropology of futures, form
backdrops to the anthropological discussions of future developed by contributors to this book, and endorse the need for a renewed and interdisciplinary
Futures Anthropology.

A core difference between anthropological attempts to bring a focus on
futures that built up from the particularity of ethnographic examples, and
sociological approaches to future lies in the capacity of the latter to generalize about society. This difference between anthropological and sociological
approaches to the world is frequently revealed in the tendency of anthropologists to chip away critically at grand sociological theories that are belied by
the specificity of ethnographic investigation. However in the case of futures,
where the specific is unknowable, sociologists have been more successful
in establishing an agenda (Bell 2009; Adam and Groves 2007). Wendell Bell
suggested that the study of the future, offered social researchers 'both a
scheme for organizing and analysing the social realities that confront us, and a
way of orienting and directing our efforts' (Bell 1971: 328), and Barbara Adam
and Christopher Groves's work has been particularly influential in offering an
analysis of how futures are not merely imagined but also made, told, traded,
tamed, transformed and traversed through uneven approaches to the future
which they frame as doing, knowing and caring, that is, between action,
knowledge and ethics (Adam and Groves 2007: 11). Bell's work also had an
applied strand since he sought to engage these categories to assist social
scientists as responsible change agents in future-knowing and future-shaping
processes. Recent future geographies analysis has also been influential,
tackling questions such as 'how life is now governed under conditions of an
uncertain unfolding of events and networks of relations' (Anderson and Adey
2012: 1529) and pursuing an analytical framework to better understand how
geographies are made and remade through processes of governing the future

as these futures 'are brought into the present and take on some form of presence' (Anderson and Adey 2012: 1529). There, the future is not an object of study, but the focus is on those 'measures, registers, apprehensions, engagements and movements that appear to be important for understanding the unfolding of many events' in the present (Merriman 2012: 24).

Anthropology's commitment to cultural relativism, the study of the particular, and moral investment in the ethics of situating knowing in a past temporality has thus been both its saviour and its limitation. Anthropologists committed to this approach have scorned those whose work involves the development of universal theories, arguing, for instance, for attention to indigenous epistemologies and for honouring other ways of knowing, beyond modern western theory, as being owed equal weight. This creates a complex minefield for anthropologists working with futures to navigate, since we have two possible fates: either to be constrained by the inability to generalize about where futures lie in whole societies; or see futures as an universal element of human ways of being in the world; or to be criticized for advancing theories of futures that do not prioritise the critique that the very study of futures is derived from a modern western paradigm, that claims to identify its own definition of futures in the lives of others who might see things rather differently.

If we contrast this impasse with how sociologists and geographers have successfully integrated the study of futures into their disciplines, there are lessons to be learned. For example, the geographer Ben Anderson has influentially argued that people anticipate and act on futures through assemblies of what he terms styles, practices and logics (Anderson 2010). As such, in cultural geography, theory has been advanced to provide ways to 'see' how futures are articulated and activated in society. Effectively Anderson has constructed a set of concepts that can then be employed to refer to how futures emerge performatively and discursively. However for us as anthropologists these typologies and conceptual frameworks for futures lack attention to the messy ways a detailed exposition of how such futures play out and are imagined and experienced would reveal. They offer interpretations and typologies of societal phenomena but do not engage them to understand how change happens on the ground or better put, how futures emerge as complex configurations of things and processes of different qualities and affordances that coalesce and change, and the relationalities and contingencies through which this happens. As anthropologists we would argue here, that at least in part this means that an ethnographic approach is needed, but, as the examples developed in this book also demonstrate, by this we do not mean a recourse in the very ethnography of the last century that as argued above has impeded the emergence of Futures Anthropology within the mainstream. We also do not mean an anthropology that simply chips away at the theories proposed by sociologists and geographers. Instead, we call for the development of more productive dialogues between ethnography and theory to produce more adventurous approaches for making Futures Anthropology including inventive and affective methodologies. We next outline how future-focused anthropologies have more recently begun to develop, before arguing for the need to develop techniques for future-focused anthropologies – ways of doing Futures Anthropology that are theoretical, methodological and that attend to an anthropological way of doing ethnography *with* others, and that are based in dialogues between ethnography and theory (where theory might not always originate in anthropology), rather than being strictly led by one or the other.

Has futures anthropology at last arrived in time?

Rosenberg and Harding's edited volume mentioned earlier was an important volume in that it invited readers to speculate about possible pasts that never eventuated, and open up speculation as an approach for exploring more radical future possibilities that may confound those of predictions and forecasting. It was an innovative volume as it included a series of interludes – including a game, a short story, a timeline and, as in our case, a manifesto. This volume marked a renewed engagement with futures surging in the mid-2000s in anthropology and cognate disciplines and led to a series of contemporary anthropological endeavours that have increasingly incorporated a focus on the modalities through which the future – as a contingent set of possibilities – is made present and decided upon (Rabinow 2008). This includes contexts such as urban planning (Abram and Weszkalnys 2013), scientific modelling of climate change (Hastrup and Skrydstrup 2013; Taddei 2013), biotechnology and the life sciences (Helmreich 2009), finance (Maurer 2002), economentality (Mitchell 2014) religious time (Guyer 2007), HCI (Human-Computer-Interaction) and ubiquitous computing (Dourish and Bell 2011), contemporary environmental politics (Mathew and Barnes 2016; Hastrup and Skrydstrup 2013), cosmos and outer space (Battaglia 2005; Valentine et al. 2012) and design anthropology (Gunn et al. 2012).

For example, Abram and Weszkalnys show how urban planning is an inherently optimistic and future-oriented activity that entails 'a broad set of tactics, technologies and institutions' for both imagining the future and preparing in advance, but also for 'managing the present' (Abram and Weszkalnys 2013: 2) (see also Abram, this volume). They have thus characterized planning as 'a key material practice through which we attempt to project ourselves into the future' (Abram and Weszkalnys 2013: 9). Likewise Mark Nuttall's 'anthropology of anticipation' in the Arctic has demonstrated the role of anticipation in climate change studies, while outlining the possibilities for ethnography as an approach to understanding anticipation multiplies, as a form of knowledge, as ontology, as foresight and insight, as engagement, as orientation, as self-realization, and as a consideration of potential (Nuttall 2010: 33). A similar future-focused anthropology is also emerging beyond the study of the future in the present, for instance in the collaborative work of David Valentine, Valerie Olson and Debbora Battaglia who have turned to the notion of extreme spaces, to propose a future oriented ethnography that explores forms of sociality that cannot yet be fully imagined, but which humans strive for (Valentine et al. 2012: 1008). The concept of the extreme here postulates a new way to convey practices and visions of the future, and to move beyond the limits of Earthly politics. In focusing on the cosmos and outer space, Valentine et al. have effectively asked what anthropology's stakes are in this field.

While these recent works do not together represent a field of established practice in Futures Anthropology, they collectively signify a readiness, an openness and a demand for engagement with futures in anthropological theory and practice. There is however a greater role for Futures Anthropology, which we argue defines its possibility as an expanded field of practice. While the study of future as imagination in the present is important to Futures Anthropology research (Crapanzano 2004), it is limited in the extent to which it can participate in interdisciplinary theory building and in significant debates of our time. As Marilyn Strathern has observed, 'people's actions are all the time informed by possible worlds which are not yet realized' (2005: 51). Other initiatives have pushed further to identify a role for anthropology in developing new practices of imagining futures, for new perspectives on anticipatory action 'which takes seriously those 'possible worlds' which, although not yet realized, inform people's everyday actions' (Nielsen 2011: 399). Hence, as anthropologists we mustn't lose sight, as Anna Tsing insists, of 'imagining the about-to-be-present' (2005: 269) in ways that avoid the 'shadow of inevitability' of neoliberal globalization and attend 'to states of emergence – and emergency … [where] hope and despair huddle together' (2005: 269).

Such a path can be complicated for anthropologists – particularly given the trajectories we outlined above. For example, the predictive stances of future scenarios as built by economists, or climate change scientists, or the objectifying models of future personas offered by design researchers, are equally valid as topics for anthropological deconstruction (like examples of planning and environmental anticipation discussed above). Yet, if we let these tendencies constrain us, anthropologists will be unable to make the important contributions we can offer fields including environmental research, synthetic biology or outer space exploration. In such fields, we argue, anthropological investigation of future social, political, legal, economic and ethical impacts is needed. A Futures Anthropology project therefore involves a step in anthropological practice, whereby anthropologists might become participants in processes of anticipating futures.

Tim Ingold has argued that anthropology is an enterprise 'energized by the tension between speculative inquiry into what life could be like and a knowledge, rooted in practical experience, of what life is like for people of particular times and places' (Ingold 2014: 393). As noted above, some possibilities for thinking differently about futures are enabled through a phenomenological approach that takes ongoing processes of change as its starting point, where what is next is continuously unfolding, and where anticipation and imagination equally emerge, as part of the embodied and experiential ways we live in the world – as researchers, participants and collaborators in research. However, while Ingold's vision of anthropology perched between practical experience and speculative inquiry is enticing, it is an optimistic rendering of what much of anthropology has been and still is. *Anthropologies and Futures* proposes how the discipline can proceed towards playing out Ingold's vision as a core enterprise, but in practical-methodological ways that Ingold has been criticized for not laying out (Shryock 2016). It seeks to dissolve this impasse whereby anthropology is stuck between a desire to understand futures and an inability to advance this field of inquiry as a collective pursuit. In part, we argue, this has come about because the question of techniques for researching futures has not been adequately confronted.

A contemporary example of an anthropological practice that drawing on Ingold's work involves making possible futures is design anthropology (Gunn et al. 2013). The project of design anthropology is a future-oriented concern, through which the discipline's past-orientation is directly challenged. While design anthropology is theoretically diverse, theories of human activity as a forward moving process have been taken up by some leading design anthropologists, to offer a vision of design that is emergent, slipping over into the future as it progresses. Subsequently design anthropology becomes not just a way of using ethnography to imagine futures, or to study how futures are imagined in the present lives of participants in research or in design practice. Rather, it can be seen as a theoretical and methodological proposition that argues for a particular understanding of futures that builds from a theory of how human life and the configurations of things and processes of which it is part are on-goingly emergent. By bringing together design and anthropological techniques to interrogate, make and intervene in future possibilities and scenarios, design anthropology offers a practical way forward, and a ground where future ethnographies are already being tested, in the form of, for example, 'ethnographies of the possible' (Halse 2013: 180).

One more relevant instance for thinking about a Futures Anthropology that we would like to bring into account is the context provided by the so-called ontological turn in anthropology and related disciplines. The expediency of this theoretical method and its particular mode of practicing ethnography is manifold for thinking futures anthropologically. First, as a reaction against the 'writing culture' focus on culture as representation and the emphasis on the textual and social construction of cultural accounts it allows us to think about futures beyond the discursive aspects of cultural representations of the future to allow for a more speculative engagement with the existence of multiple futures existing simultaneously. The implications are manifest for how we in this edited volume propose that worldviews about the future be challenged in support of an emphasis on future worlds and worldmaking practices that take into account human as well as more than human agencies. As Holbraad, Pedersen and Viveiros de Castro (2014) argue, the politics of an ontologically inflected ethnography or 'ontography' resides 'not only in the ways in which it may help promote certain futures, but also in the way it "figurates" the future in its very enactment' (2014). Or, in other words, and to paraphrase Elizabeth Povinelli (2012), how the future 'otherwise' can be accounted for ethnographically. The counterpoint to this approach as Bessire and Bond (2014) have rightly observed, is that this paradigm's analytical focus on the future redefines the coordinates of the political as well as anthropology's relation to critique. As they suggest, an ontological approach 'shifts the insurgent front lines of ethnography from located descriptions of resistance, suffering, and governance to anticipatory evocations of heterogeneous assemblages' (Bessire and Bond 2014: 441). Yet, while the ontological turn has invited anthropologists to consider alternative futures, Bessire and Bond prompt us to not overlook that a project on futures in anthropology has to begin 'with the recognition that our futures are contingent because our present is as well. If ontological anthropology fails to account for such contingencies, then it assumes the form of a modern myth and the only image it reflects is its own' (Bessire and Bond 2014: 450).

Techniques for an engaged futures anthropology

We are at a moment where some of us, as outlined in our Manifesto, are moving toward a renewed, experimental anthropology, which is also involved in the theoretical turns of its time. This version of Futures Anthropology is moreover an engaged anthropology that actively responds to the moral obligation for us to implicate ourselves in futures. As Appadurai (2013) has discussed there is increasingly a moral responsibility to be mindful of and prepared for doing cultural research that accounts for the future – to create anticipatory and interventionist public/applied anthropologies of the future. The challenges this poses have been recognized by others such as James Ferguson who has warned that 'if anthropology is to contribute to the work of creating better human futures, it will need to demonstrate the relevance of anthropological knowledge and anthropological ways of thinking to the great practical and political issues that today confront our increasingly intercon-nected but unequal world' (Ferguson 2014: n.p.).

The ethics of responsibility are thus complex. Indeed, to quibble with Strathern, it is not simply that possible worlds are not yet realized, rather, possible worlds are precisely merely possible, and might not be realized in the forms that they are 'possible'. The ontological status of possible worlds is that they are emergent from a particular way of imagining through contingent configurations of the present. Future worlds will likewise be emergent, but constituted through different configurations of things, processes and the contingencies that are part of them. We are therefore, all in different (but poten-tially complementary) states of expert *not knowing*. The challenge becomes how we might form such expertise, both for ourselves as researchers, and in collaboration with others, whose possible futures or everyday alterities we wish to comprehend. The types of futures expertise that ethnographic not knowing can generate are distinctly anthropological. Here we differ from those who take predictive approaches, such as economists and others who analyse and model future scenarios, as experts in this (in fact unknown and uncertain) terrain. While it might be that as anthropologists we share with other 'experts' a world where 'one defining quality of our current moment is its characteristic state of anticipation, of thinking and living toward the future' (Adams et al. 2009), as anthropologists our stance is to never be the expert. Instead we learn about and with other people's expertise, accredit this expertise to them as collaborators in shared endeavours. In futures research this means creating generative forms of *not knowing* with others, which might involve imagining, planning, designing, enacting, intervening or anticipating the future on an everyday basis.

The techniques for researching the future developed by the contributors to this book are theoretical, analytical and methodological. Some are more conventional in their encounters with participants. Others, as discussed later, develop novel methods. All, in a typically anthropological way are reflexive.

As the contributors to this book show, what will happen next can be under-stood as contingent on the relatedness of different scales of global events. Indeed, contingency is at the core of understanding how futures play out. For instance, Andrew Irving examines how people's future selves, experiences and modes of expression are intertwined with and affected by the globally dispersed contiguous actions of others. Similar global entanglements emerge in Karen Waltorp's account of how dreams, digital technologies and religious attitudes of patience figured in how a young Palestinian-Jordanian woman in Denmark narrated the kidnapping of her daughter. This is also something that Alexandra D'Onofrio addresses through her research with Egyptian migrants in Milan to show the existential possibilities of certain imagined futures through which migrants often redefine who they are and ascribe new meanings to their past and present circumstances. These two chapters link back to Irving's emphasis on contingency, which reminds us both that we cannot know what will happen and of the tendency for logics to be constructed not only around what *will* happen, but also around the narration of what has happened. Similarly, by examining critically the way that futures are manifested in planning in the UK, Simone Abram shows not only the many kinds of futures always at play in urban planning, but the many ways of these futures are negotiated and contested future, of seeking to secure the passage from now to then, of securing action today that ensures desired futures or avoids undesired futures. Abram's political critique of how futures are forged in ways that unveil the silence and exclusion of those who do not figure in neoliberal visions of the future is also taken up by Faye Ginsburg and Rayna Rapp who present an inspiring case of a politically entangled ethnography of ubiquitous disability in the United States. Ginsburg and Rapp's work is an example of an emergent, future-oriented form of anthropologically informed longitudinal ethnography that illustrates how disabilities are produced by mediated relations on the part of both producers and audiences with invest-ments in embracing particular understandings of disability. Critiques about neoliberal figuring of the future are also implicit in Anthony Knight's account of how the multispecies worlds of 'traditional' pastoralists, conservationists, wolves and bears in the French Pyrenees, contest future macro-scenarios of ecomodernist projects of rewilding Europe. Thus suggesting how antici-patory ethnography could usefully inform policy-making and planning in such contexts.

Other contributors, while maintaining theoretical and contextual under-standings, have sought to develop interdisciplinary methods for encountering futures, thus militating for new ways of doing future ethnographies. Sarah Pink, Yoko Akama and Annie Ferguson introduce a future-oriented ethno-graphic practice where future is an alterity of the present. They examine how possible alterities are sensed, imagined and 'felt' through a blended practice of design, ethnography and video methodologies. Débora Lanzeni and Elisenda Ardèvol also focus on design processes to tackle how the notion of the future is made and fixed in mundane social and digital-material life and the vernacular futures of smart technology designers. The engagement with the future as experiential, sensory and embodied is also advanced by

Magdalena Kazubowski-Houston who together with Roma communities in Poland creates ethnographic experiments situated at the intersections of imagination, performance-centred research, and storytelling to that generate 'affective interiorities' that may act upon futures. Juan Francisco Salazar similarly experiments with making a speculative documentary film, *Nightfall on Gaia*, as a generative ethnography through which to speculate futures with, blurring fact and fiction to develop a critical description of how distinctive forms of sociality and subjectivity are unfolding and coalescing in Antarctica. Like Salazar, Johannes Sjöberg and Alexandra D'Onofrio also use film as a technique for engaging with futures. Sjöberg for instance examines how to apply projective improvisation in ethnographic film – what he calls ethno science fiction, a co-creative genre of ethnographic film – to explore how fieldwork young people in the UK relate to their imagined environmental futures future. And finally, Annette Markham invites us to think of remix as an ethical literacy for anthropologies of futures. Markham acknowledges that remix as a metaphor for anthropologies of futures is more attitudinal than formulaic as a way of emphasizing the generative and playful aspects of anthropological research.

These proposals for researching the future anthropologically respond to the earlier lament that anthropology 'has designed relatively few methods to analyze or speculate about the future' (Heemskerk 2003: 932) and re-examine the basis and nature of the tools we speculate or imagine with and the contexts we imagine in, especially considering (like Pink 2015), how sensory or mythical concepts become part of this (Connor and Marshall 2015: 7). As the following chapters attest, the future is never a *tabula rasa* of endless possibilities. Futures are already crowded with fantasies, paranoias, traumas, hopes, and fears of the past and the present (Rosenberg and Harding 2005). A Futures Anthropology requires a set of techniques that support or initiate the work outlined in our manifesto. However, in a Futures Anthropology, techniques do not refer simply to methods for collecting 'data' or learning about how futures are sensed or mythologized. Our techniques need to be theoretical, methodological, and interventional, to provide ways of researching futures that attend to the particular in dialogue with theoretical concerns about how futures unfold, and in relation to an interventional and engaged impulse to work towards claiming back alternative futures.

Future-focused anthropologies have always been lurking at the margins. As we have shown there are several reasons why they have not grown out of the anthropological centre or mainstream. But that is perhaps a good thing, since often the more interesting accounts emerge at margins. This is thus a call for anthropology to engage at its edges, with other disciplines and with future temporalities.

Note

1 After the workshop, about thirty participants went to a pub, divided into three groups to each produce a set of points, which were synthesized by four volunteers from our group into the collective manifesto, to state a vision for Future Anthropologies.

References

Abram, S. and M. Lien, 2011. 'Performing nature at world's ends'. *Ethnos: Journal of Anthropology* 76 (1): 3–18.

Abram, S. and G. Weszkalnys. 2013. *Elusive Promises: Planning in the Contemporary World*. Oxford and New York: Berghahn.

Adam, B. and C. Groves, 2007. *Future Matters: Action, Knowledge, Ethics*. Leiden: Brill.

Anderson, B., 2010. 'Preemption, precaution, preparedness: Anticipatory action and future geographies'. *Progress in Human Geography* 34 (6): 777–98.

Anderson, B. and P. Adey, 2012. 'Future geographies'. *Environment and Planning A* 44 (7): 1529–35.

Appadurai, A., 2013. *The Future as Cultural Fact*. London and New York: Verso.

Battaglia, D. (ed.), 2005. *E.T. Culture: Anthropology in Outerspaces*. Durham, NC: Duke University Press.

Bell, W., 1971. 'Epilogue'. In W. Bell and J. Mau (eds), *The Sociology of the Future. Theory, Cases, and Annotated Bibliography*, 324–36. New York: Russell Sage Foundation.

Bell, W., 2009. *Foundations of Futures Studies: Histories, Purposes and Knowledge*, 5th edn. New Brunswick, NJ: Transaction Publishers.

Bessire, L. and D. Bond, 2014. 'Ontological anthropology and the deferral of critique'. *American Ethnologist* 41 (3): 440–56.

Clarke, A. J., 2011. *Design Anthropology: Object Culture in the 21st Century*. New York: SpringerLink.

Clifford, J. and G. Marcus (eds), 1986. *Writing Culture: The Poetics and Politics of Ethnography*. Berkeley, CA: University of California Press.

Collins, S. G., 2007. 'Le temps perdu: Anthropologists (re)discover the future'. *Anthropological Quarterly* 80 (4): 1175–86.

Collins, S. G., 2008. *All Tomorrow's Cultures: Anthropological Engagements with the Future*. Oxford and New York: Berghahn Books.

Connor, L. H. and J. P. Marshall, 2015. 'Ecologies, Ontologies and Mythologies of Possible Futures'. In L. H. Connor and J. P. Marshall (eds), *Environmental Change and the World's Futures: Ecologies, Ontologies and Mythologies*. New York: Routledge.

Crapanzano, V., 2004. *Imaginative Horizons: An Essay in Literary-philosophical Anthropology*. Chicago: University of Chicago Press.

Dourish, P. and G. Bell, 2011. *Divining a Digital Future: Mess and Mythology in Ubiquitous Computing*. Cambridge, MA: MIT Press.

Fabian, J., 1983. *Time and the Other: How Anthropology Makes its Object*. New York: Columbia University Press.

Ferguson J., 2014. *A Rightful Share: Beyond Gift and Market in the Politics of Distribution*. Keynote address at The Future with/of Anthropologies, Japanese Society of Cultural Anthropology (JASCA) 50th Anniversary Conference, Tokyo 15–18 May.

Fischer, M. J., 2007. 'Four genealogies for a recombinant anthropology of science and technology'. *Cultural Anthropology* 22 (4): 539–615.

Gell, A., 1992. *The Anthropology of Time: Cultural Constructions of Temporal Maps and Images*. Oxford: Berg.

Gunn, W., Otto, T. and R. C. Smith (eds), 2013. *Design Anthropology: Theory and Practice*. London: Bloomsbury.

Guyer, J. I., 2007. 'Prophecy and the near future: Thoughts on macroeconomic, evangelical, and punctuated time'. *American Ethnologist* 34 (3): 409–21.

Halse, J., 2013. 'Ethnographies of the Possible'. In W. Gunn, T. Otto and R. C. Smith (eds), *Design Anthropology: Theory and Practice*, 180–97. London: Bloomsbury,

Hannerz, U., 2003. 'Macro-scenarios. Anthropology and the debate over contemporary and future worlds'. *Social Anthropology* 11 (2): 169–87.

Hastrup, K. and M. Skrydstrup (eds), 2013. *The Social Life of Climate Change Models. Anticipating Nature*. London and New York: Routledge.

Heemskerk, M., 2003. 'Scenarios in anthropology: Reflections on possible futures of the Suriname Maroons'. *Futures* 35 (9): 931–49.

Helmreich, S., 2009. *Alien Ocean: Anthropological Voyages in Microbial Seas*. Berkeley and Los Angeles: University of California Press.

Hodges, M., 2008. 'Rethinking time's arrow: Bergson, Deleuze and the anthropology of time'. *Anthropological Theory* 8 (4): 399–429.

Holbraad, M., M. A. Pedersen and E. Viveiros de Castro, 2014. 'The politics of ontology: Anthropological positions. Theorizing the Contemporary'. Cultural Anthropology website, 13 January. Available online: http://culanth.org/fieldsights/462-the-politics-ofontology-anthropological-positions (accessed 25 January 2016).

Ingold, T., 2000. *The Perception of the Environment*. London: Routledge.

Ingold T., 2013. *Making*. London: Routledge.

Ingold, T., 2014. 'That's enough about ethnography!', *HAU, Journal of Ethnographic* Theory 4 (1). Available online: http://www.haujournal.org/index.php/hau/article/view/hau4.1.021 (accessed 22 May 2016).

Maruyama, M. and A. M. Harkins (eds), 1975. *Cultures Beyond the Earth: The Role of Anthropology in Outer Space*. New York: Vintage Books USA.

Maruyama, M. and A. M. Harkins (eds), 1978. *Cultures of the Future*. Berlin: Walter de Gruyter.

Mathews, A. S. and J. Barnes, 2016. 'Prognosis: Visions of environmental futures'. *Journal of the Royal Anthropological Institute* 22 (1): 9–21.

Maurer, B., 2002. 'Repressed Futures: Financial Derivatives. Theological Unconscious'. *Economy and Society* 31 (1): 16–36.

Maurer, B., 2005. 'Introduction to "ethnographic emergences"'. *American Anthropologist* 107 (1): 1–4.

Mead, M., 1971. 'A note on contributions of anthropology to the science of the future'. *Human Futuristics* 3 (Social Science Research Institute). Honolulu: University of Hawaii.

Mead, M., 2005. *The World Ahead: An Anthropologist Anticipates the Future.* Robert B. Textor (ed.). New York: Berghahn Books.

Merriman P., 2012. 'Human geography without time-space'. *Transactions of the Institute of British Geographers* 37: 13–27.

Mitchell T., 2014. 'Economentality: How the future entered government'. *Critical Inquiry* 40: 479–507.

Miyazaki, H., 2006. 'Economy of Dreams: Hope in Global Capitalism and Its Critiques'. *Cultural Anthropology* 21 (2): 147–72.

Munn, N. D., 1992. 'The Cultural Anthropology of Time: A Critical Essay'. *Annual Review of Anthropology* 21: 93–123.

Nielsen, M., 2011. 'Futures within: Reversible time and house-building in Maputo, Mozambique'. *Anthropological Theory* 11 (4): 397–423.

Nielsen, M. and M. A. Pedersen, 2015. 'Infrastructural Imaginaries: Collapsed Futures in Mozambique and Mongolia'. In M. Harris and N. Rapport, *Reflections on Imagination: Human Capacity and Ethnographic Method*, 237–62. Surrey: Ashgate.

Nuttall, M., 2010. 'Anticipation, climate change, and movement in Greenland'. *Études/Inuit/Studies* 34 (1): 21–37.

Pels, P., 2015. 'Modern Times: Seven Steps toward an Anthropology of the Future'. *Current Anthropology* 56 (6): 779–96.

Pink, S., 2015. *Doing Sensory Ethnography,* 2nd edn. London: Sage.

Povinelli E., 2012. 'The will to be otherwise/the effort of endurance'. *South Atlantic Quarterly* 111: 453–75.

Rabinow, P., 2008. *Marking time: On the Anthropology of the Contemporary.* Princeton, NJ: Princeton University Press.

Razak, V. M., 2000. 'Essays in anticipatory anthropology'. *Futures* 32 (8): 717–28.

Riner, R. D., 1987. 'Doing futures research anthropologically'. *Futures* 19 (3): 311–28.

Rose, M., 2010. 'Envisioning the Future: Ontology, Time and the Politics of Non-representation'. In B. Anderson and P. Harrison (eds), *Taking-place: Non-representational Theories and Geography,* 341–61. Farnham: Ashgate.

Rosenberg, D. and S. Harding (eds), 2005. *Histories of the Future.* Durham, NC: Duke University Press.

Shryock, Andrew. 'Ethnography: Provocation'. Correspondences, Cultural Anthropology website, 3 May 2016. Available online: http://culanth.org/fieldsights/871-ethnography-provocation (accessed 9 May 2016).

Sillitoe, P., 2007. 'Anthropologists only need apply: Challenges of applied anthropology'. *Journal of the Royal Anthropological Institute* 13 (1): 147–65.

Strathern, M., 2005. *Kinship, Law and the Unexpected: Relatives Are Always a Surprise.* Cambridge: Cambridge University Press.

Taddei, R., 2013. 'Anthropologies of the Future: On the Social Performativity of (Climate) Forecasts'. In H. Kopnina and E. Shoreman-Ouimet (eds)., *Environmental Anthropology: Future Directions,* 246–65. New York: Routledge.

Textor, R. B., 1978. 'Cultural futures for Thailand: An ethnographic enquiry'. *Futures* 10 (5): 347–60.

Toffler, A., 1970. *Future Shock.* New York: Amereon.

Tsing, A. L., 2005. *Friction: An Ethnography of Global Connection.* Princeton, NJ: Princeton University Press.

Valentine, D., 2012. 'Exit strategy: Profit, cosmology, and the future of humans in space'. *Anthropological Quarterly* 85 (4): 1045–67.

Valentine, D., 2015. 'What happened to the future?' *Anthropology Now* 7 (1): 110–20.

Valentine, D., V. A. Olson and D. Battaglia, 2012. 'Extreme: Limits and horizons in the once and future cosmos'. *Anthropological Quarterly* 85 (4): 1007–26.

Wallman, S. (ed.), 1992. *Contemporary Futures: Perspectives from Social Anthropology.* London and New York: Routledge.

3

The art of turning left and right

Andrew Irving

FIGURE 3.1 *11 September 2001 (Photo by Andrew Irving) (Photo by Spencer Platt/Getty Images)*

I would like to begin by inviting the reader to look at the two photographs above in order to ask: what is the connection between these two images? I am particularly interested in *the imaginative space* that exists between the images and how this is filled with possible events and scenarios. It is almost as if the mind cannot help but establish a connection between the photographs and is compelled to construct a narrative, filling the gap with storyline, content and meaning. The process of forming a connection between the images also places them in time, given that the content and character of their relationship is not revealed in the moment of perception but like all relationships unfolds over time towards a future not yet known. A narrative bridge is built through our capacity to make creative associations across space and time, to combine elements into new forms and patterns based in resemblance, contiguity and the imaginary rather than what is present to the eye, attesting to our species-wide facility for metaphorical thinking, alchemy and montage.

It was Aristotle who suggested 'thinking' was 'part imagination' and 'part judgement', and that 'the soul never thinks without a mental image [phantasma]' (1936: 177/431a 15–20). His Law of Contiguity states that things or events proximate in time or space become intertwined and associated in the mind and imagination, and implies a temporality where, relative to each other, one event exists in the past and the other in the future. However, according to Aristotle, it is also possible for the imagination to establish relationships with events that have not yet happened and he suggests that it is by means of 'images or thoughts in the soul' that a person 'calculates and plans for the future in view of the present' (1936: 179/431b 5–10). Many centuries later, Hume similarly recognized that the imagination is not only necessary for comprehending things such as cause and effect – and thus how relationships are established between past and future events – but also the development of complex ideas and the understanding of art and literature. Hume argued that thinking encompasses three principles of association, namely (i) *resemblance*, (ii) *contiguity in time and place,* and (iii) *causation,* which combine to establish links between our past and present experiences and expectations of the future. For Hume, contiguous and associative thinking is necessary for all forms of learning and understanding. However, he also warned of its dangers, noting how one can make erroneous causal connections and predictions about the future, or take two things such as 'gold' and 'mountain' and combine them to construct false, fantastical notions of golden mountains that exist in make-believe and not in reality.

When approaching the two photographs from a practical and ethnographic perspective, critical questions emerge concerning the embodied and empirical relationship between the images, including how connections are made between individual persons and global events in the contemporary social, political and global landscape. Persons and cultures throughout the world have long been interconnected by language, stories, ideas and technology, as well as trade, migration, travel and war, but perhaps never with quite the same intensity as over the last few decades, as graphically evidenced by 9/11. People's lives and future possibilities are now routinely affected on an individual and collective basis by small- and large-scale actions, events and occurrences that happen in proximate and far-away places. Daily life, from rural Afghanistan to downtown New York, has become increasingly inter-connected through terror, technology and political events that reveal the complex global and economic relationships that shape people's perceptions, experiences and understandings of the contemporary world.

People's future selves, future experiences and future modes of expression are inextricably intertwined with the contiguous small- and large-scale actions of others whose understanding exists beyond the limits of our current theories and methods. Our collective disciplinary approaches and epistemologies are often trivialized by the complex interrelation of actions and events that take place at scales, densities and distances unknown to both Aristotle and Hume. This leads us to ask how we might research or represent the relationship between people's current and future lives and interactions from an empirical, ethnographic or corporeal perspective, when the life of a person or social group can be radically affected and shaped by ordinary and extraordinary events which take place in distant lands.

In response, this chapter seeks not an answer but attempts an ethnographic consideration of the temporal and spatial interconnection of global events both large and small from a fieldwork-based perspective. More specifically, it investigates how simple everyday acts, movements and decisions of the kind that are performed on a continuous basis – such as turning left or right, deciding to stop for a coffee, walking down one street rather than another – have radical consequences for a person's future life. By considering how such commonplace actions do not exist in isolation but are necessarily intertwined and contiguous with large- and small-scale events around the world, this chapter aims to offer an ethnographically grounded exploration of the relationship between action, contingency and the future. In doing so, it follows William James's argument that there is always some form of practical, as opposed to merely theoretical or conjectured, connection between present and future events. This reinforces how understanding the future in an increasingly interconnected world is not only a theoretical, philosophical or scientific problem but a profoundly ethnographic and anthropological one insofar as people around the world from all walks of life are continuously linked through actions that define the possibilities and constraints of their own and other people's futures.

As such, I would now like to return to the two images from the start of the chapter to consider their practical, embodied and ethnographic connection in more detail.

I took this photograph (Figure 3.2) outside the Hotel Africana in Kampala, Uganda, in May 2009. The subject of the photograph is Sandra Kyagaba, an HIV+ Ugandan activist who has been open about her HIV status since being

FIGURE 3.2 *Sandra in 2009 holding picture of herself taken on the same spot on 11 September 2001. Photo by Andrew Irving*

diagnosed at nineteen years old. The photograph shows Sandra holding a photograph of a younger woman. The woman in the photograph is none other than Sandra herself taken eight years previously on the morning of 11 September 2001, shortly after she had been informed she did not have long to live. In my photograph from 2009, she is standing on the very same piece of grass she was originally standing on when she posed for the earlier photograph on 11 September 2001. A complex temporal interplay emerges whereby Sandra faces my camera and carries a photograph of her younger self, as seen from the perspective of an unknown and unforeseeable future that she never thought she would be alive to see.

The photograph of the Twin Towers was taken on the same day on the other side of the world, and became one of the most famous and widely circulated images in human history. It captures the exact moment the second hijacked plane hit the World Trade Center on the morning of 11 September 2001. The photographer, Spencer Platt, woke up hungover, switched on the news and heard about the first plane hitting the North Tower. A professional photographer who lived close to Brooklyn Bridge, he grabbed his camera and ran to the bridge to get a good vantage point. Unbeknown to him as he stood on the bridge taking pictures, the second plane was travelling towards the South Tower, striking in the same instant he pressed his shutter.

In the photograph of Sandra that was also taken on 11 September 2001, she can be seen looking at the camera, having just given a talk at a conference aimed at tackling the problems faced by women in Africa. Entitled, *Focus on Women*, the conference brought together HIV+ women, journalists, NGOs, medics, policy makers and international activists to come up with concrete proposals to address the HIV crisis. Sandra had just presented her life history with the aim of bringing to life the challenges people experience but are rarely captured in official statistics and reports. The telling of one's life history is an effective and necessary means of communicating the issues beyond mere numbers. As someone who was public about her status from a young age, Sandra had retold her life history many times in many different contexts. Life histories involve a complex temporality in which the past is reshaped from the vantage point of the future, including a recasting of critical events whose causality, consequences and outcomes are understood retrospectively. As with other kinds of narrative account, life histories can also coalesce and become reified into established or static forms. Each of us creates a life story for ourselves and for others, which can become almost canonical versions of events that may or may not bear a close relation to the truth and, like all autobiographical narratives, involves a construction of the self that might not correspond to other people's interpretations and understandings.

Consequently, in order to open up the narrative process, Sandra and myself engaged in a research method that built on fieldwork techniques I had previously developed (Irving 2007, 2011a, 2016) and which can be termed the Life Journeys Method. The Life Journeys Method is very simple and involves physically retracing the journey of someone's life chronologically. The first stage is to plot the shape of someone's life journey from past to future onto a map, then the second stage is to physically travel that route in chronological order, stopping at key locations. The process involves the person narrating out loud their spontaneous thoughts, ideas and memories as they emerge, and responding to questions as they travel around the shape and contours of their life. As a basis for Sandra's life journey, we used the story she had presented at the conference; the idea being that physically moving around and tracing the trajectory of her life would open up new possibilities for memory and expression. As such the following photo essay, which Sandra entitled 'Existence is Curved', is an attempt to plot Sandra's Life Journey, beginning with the house in which she was raised.

Existence is curved

This building (Figure 3.3) is a staff house on the premises of the Nile Hotel, a five-star hotel located in central Kampala where Sandra's father worked. Although owned by the hotel, this was the family home and Sandra spent most of her childhood and teens living at the house. Her father's steady employment meant she had a comfortable existence and worked hard towards her education. When Sandra was seventeen years old, she fell in love with one of the receptionists at the hotel. They did not sleep together but would hold hands, have long conversations, spend their free time together and eventually became boyfriend and girlfriend. People, places and things are not always what they appear to be and it turned out that Sandra's boyfriend was not a receptionist but a soldier and spy. In countries where the state is less extensive than in western contexts, it often relies upon a network of persons to maintain control, surveillance and security, and many hotels have people placed in various roles to keep a check on the movements and actions of outsiders. Even the activities of lowly anthropologists such as myself are tracked during times of instability or on the eve of a high profile visit, such as on one occasion when Muammar Gaddafi visited and I received a knock on my door late in the evening to check I was at home.

This meant that when Sandra left home to live with her boyfriend – 'informally' as opposed being accompanied by the usual formal blessings and ceremonies of her culture – she moved from her modern family home to a rundown military building shared with three or four other families. This building (Figure 3.4) was the place in which their relationship was consummated, and is almost certainly the place where Sandra caught HIV.

Sandra loved her boyfriend but was unhappy living under such cramped conditions with other families, so they found a small two-roomed place in a local slum. Although her place did not have water or electricity and she had to cook on an open fire in the street outside, they were both very happy and started a family.

FIGURE 3.3 *Sandra's childhood home. Photo by Andrew Irving*

FIGURE 3.4 *The building where Sandra most likely caught HIV. Photo by Andrew Irving*

FIGURE 3.5 *Life in the Slum. Photo by Andrew Irving*

Sandra had a young daughter, Zam, and her life and the family's future seemed settled. One day Sandra was at home cooking outside on the street when her boyfriend rushed past without saying a word to her. Sandra followed him into the house and asked what was wrong. He told her that he had just been diagnosed with AIDS. Sandra stayed with him and outside the food was left to burn.

Sandra's boyfriend had been selected for a routine HIV test as part of standard military policy to ensure that all personnel have regular check-ups. Eight weeks after finding out he was HIV+, Sandra's boyfriend was dead.[1]

Bed nine

This is bed nine (Figure 3.6) where Sandra's boyfriend passed away. Following his death, Sandra was left alone, living in the slum with no income or money and a young child to feed, clothe, educate and support. It was possible that she was also HIV+ and might die soon. Sandra went for an HIV test and found out that she too had the virus. Her boyfriend's family came and took

FIGURE 3.6 *Bed Nine. Photo by Andrew Irving*

FIGURE 3.7 *The Testing Clinic. Photo by Andrew Irving*

Sandra's daughter away against her will on the grounds that she had no money or means of raising her child alone, and that she might fall sick and die soon. As her boyfriend's family lived in the far west of the country, a long and expensive journey away, it was unlikely that she would be able to see her child many times before she too succumbed to AIDS. The loss of her child was extraordinarily traumatic for Sandra. Although looking back at the actions of her boyfriend's family, she can now understand their rationale as to why they took her child away, this did not not make the loss of her child any easier to bear. Instead it left her bereft, and unable to perform her role as a mother to nurture, care for and raise her child (see Irving 2011b). On discovering that she had HIV and then losing her child, Sandra recounted how she also lost the feeling that she was a human being and had little to look forward to on earth. Life became meaningless and 'I locked myself in a dark room and the only thing I thought of was death.'

It was the voice of another soldier on the radio, Major Rubaramira Ruranga that changed Sandra's life. The Major was worried about his HIV status and went for a test in the late 1980s. For the test, blood is drawn and examined for anti-bodies indicating the presence of HIV and it commonly takes a couple of weeks for the test to be processed and the results to be disclosed. In Major Ruranga's case it took thirty days. The time between taking the test

FIGURE 3.8 *Sandra 11 September 2001. Photo by Andrew Irving*

and receiving the results is a period of liminality and uncertainty that Major Ruranga described as 'a very strange and complicated month' in which he encountered the world as someone who may or may not have a terminal illness and found himself imagining two possible futures, which in the late 1980s, was one of life or one of death. After a month of waiting, the Major went to pick up his results and the man behind the desk said: 'there are two numbers: 1 and 2. If you are 1 it means that you don't have AIDS. If you are number 2, then it means that you have AIDS. You are number 2.'

The major was preoccupied by images of the Ugandan singer Philly Lutaaya, who had gone public about his HIV status and whose demise was tracked through the national media. One particular photograph of Lutaaya on the verge of death haunted Major Ruranga who saw: 'a diseased flesh that could still speak and think', and in anticipating his own future, he thought: 'Am I to become that?' Soon after, the major publicly declared his status and set up The National Guidance and Empowerment Network of People Living with HIV/AIDS, giving up his military career to fight AIDS. Nowadays he is on the other side of the testing desk and often sees people who have just been diagnosed. 'I am one of you' he says and then takes off his shirt to show his herpes zoster scars. 'You are not alone. We are in this together, and together we can fight it.' It was in this guise that Sandra heard the major talking about his experience on the radio and giving out his phone number for anyone who was listening. Sandra scribbled it down and called him. The next day they arranged to meet. She looked at him across the desk and burst out crying. Over the next few weeks, talking with the major began to dismantle her fear. Her humanity was restored and her faith in life was renewed. Soon after, Sandra went public about her status and became a peer counsellor, educator and activist alongside the major.

Sandra: 11 September 2001

By the time Sandra gave her life testimony to the *Focus on Women* conference on 11 September 2001, she had not seen her daughter in the five years since her boyfriend's family had taken her away. She recounted the story of the loss of her daughter as part of the life history told to the assembled activists, journalists, medics and policy-makers attending the conference. At the end of her testimony she thanked them for listening and then the conference stopped for a break. On leaving the room, Sandra walked outside onto the hotel grounds, composing herself and getting ready for lunch, and she turned left. As she did so, a young woman who had been listening – a journalist from New York called Emily Bass who was one of the conference organizers – came out of the other door and turned right and they bumped into each other. Emily said to Sandra, 'Thanks so much for that very moving testimony of your life. I really hope you can get your daughter back. When I come back next year, I hope we can meet and let's see if we can do anything.' In response, Sandra said: 'Thank you very much, I really appreciate it but this is probably the last time we'll meet or you'll see me'. Emily asked why and Sandra said, 'I've had some very bad news. My CD4 cell count is down to 12. I've lost 30kg. The doctor thinks that I probably won't have much longer.'

CD4, blood and radical contingency

To put Sandra's future expectation of death into perspective: her CD4 count of 12 cells per mm^3 of blood was life-threateningly low. HIV/AIDS is an immune deficiency syndrome that makes the body susceptible to infections, tumours and virally induced cancers. Consequently, a person does not die from AIDS, but from various opportunistic infections and diseases that the immune-compromised body cannot stave off. CD4 cells are vital to the immune system insofar as they are key to coordinating the body's responses. A healthy adult may have a CD4 count of up to 1200 cells per mm^3 of blood compared to Sandra's count of just 12 cells per mm^3, placing her at substantial risk and giving her the expectation of imminent death.

The advent of antiretroviral medications in 1996/97 had radically changed the future for people living with HIV/AIDS in Western countries. Antiretroviral medications boost the CD4 count and have the potential to massively reduce the effects of the HIV virus in the body. In Western countries antiretrovirals have restored health and re-opened time, space and the future for many hundreds of thousands of people, triggering a massive shift of in consciousness, body and emotion away from death and back toward life. Having anticipated an impending death, hundreds of thousands of people with HIV/AIDS had to learn how to 'live' again. Many found it impossible to return to their previous lives and are now living in a future they never imagined they would see, often having made irreversible decisions and life choices when they thought they were going to die (Irving 2016). In tragic contrast to those living in Western countries, the vast majority of people throughout many parts of the world, including Africa, were denied access to antiretrovirals, and as a result millions of people continued to die from treatable opportunistic infections, experiencing sickness and anticipating their future death in the knowledge of life-saving medications, freely available in the West, but effectively disallowed to them as a consequence of their nationality and economic status.

Antiretroviral medications are cheap to make but expensive to buy. In 2001, a year's supply of triple combination antiretrovirals cost around $300 to manufacture, but driven by the profit to be made from the US insurance system, the market price in the USA and elsewhere in the world averaged US$10,000 per person per year, or US$835 per month. To put this in the Ugandan context, at the time medication would cost around ten times the entire monthly income of a qualified professional, such as a teacher or nurse. Although Indian pharmaceutical companies offered to manufacture and distribute the medication to Uganda at cost price – which at around US$1 a day would have made them affordable – Western multi-national drug companies, lawyers, copyright specialists and the judicial system combined to repeatedly block such attempts through sanctions, bullying and law courts. In doing so they attempted to determine levels of suffering for African people that would not be tolerated for European and North American populations. Consequently, the medications were set at a global market price, ensuring that Sandra and other Africans with HIV/AIDS were unable to access life-saving medication that would have relieved their suffering, opened their futures and prevented the deaths of millions.

Accordingly, the advent of antiretrovirals in 1996/97 fundamentally altered and exacerbated the differences between different parts of the world, illustrating how experiences of living with HIV/AIDS cannot be understood unless placed in a global comparative context (Irving 2011b). Sandra had to confront a future of illness and death in the knowledge that a 'cure' was freely available elsewhere in the world but was denied to her due to her land of birth, national identity and economic circumstances. This reveals an unequal definition of the person that was enforced through a nexus of legal, economic and political powers, and emphasizes the relative status and value of human life. Sandra could imagine a future of health but was unable to live that life given her body was designated as expendable and of lesser importance than profit and ultimately not worthy of saving as determined by individuals, institutions and companies in distant places.

The conversation between Sandra and Emily in which Sandra anticipated her death happened around 11.30 a.m. on 11 September 2001, which meant it was still only 3.30 a.m. in New York. Little could anyone imagine that a few hours later, at 8.46 a.m. a high-jacked plane would strike the first of the Twin Towers, nor that a second plane would strike at 9.03 a.m. At 9.59 a.m. the South Tower collapsed and the North Tower soon followed at 10.28 a.m.

As news of the World Trade Center disaster came through to Uganda, Emily became distraught, not just because her home city had been attacked but because her father worked in the North Tower. Just a few hours earlier, life seemed much more stable and certain for Emily, her parents and the people of New York. Death for the majority of the American population was based on a specific cultural expectation of what constitutes a natural life trajectory and was associated with old age. An early death was seen as unnatural and the contingency of life – whereby a person could die at any moment – was rarely prominent in most people's daily concerns. The news coming from New York thus disrupted the established order of life and expectations of the future, and opened a process of critical reappraisal and reconsideration. By contrast, in Uganda, it is widely understood that one is old enough to die as soon as one is born. Children tend to be present to most things that life offers and will have seen numerous dead persons before they become adults. Around one in seven births end in death for either the mother or the baby, and in 2001 14.1 per cent of children did not live to see five years old. Life and one's future are widely understood as uncertain and contingent, and death is seen as something that can strike at any time.

On learning that the North Tower had been hit, Emily found herself caught in a liminal space between life and death alongside Sandra. In 2001 it was difficult to make a routine phone call in Kampala, given that Uganda has one of the lowest number of landlines of any country in the world. Often it was impossible to even call across the city, let alone make an international phone call to New York on 11 September 2001 when America's phone network was inundated. Emily was confronted by a range of possible futures in which her father was alive, missing, critically injured, dead or rescued, the outcome of which was unknown. As news of Emily's situation spread, Sandra and her fellow Ugandan women who were at the conference began chanting and praying for Emily's parents. The next morning, word came through that Emily's father was alive and unhurt. He had not been at his desk – perhaps he had gone to the gym, perhaps he had stopped to buy a newspaper, perhaps his train was delayed, perhaps he ironed his shirt or stopped off to buy a bagel – Emily did not know, but word had come though that he was alive. He had not been at the World Trade Center.

Sandra recounted to me how Emily then came to find her and shared the news of her father's survival. Sandra was overjoyed and Emily's next words, as Sandra remembers them, were: 'God has spared the life of my parents. Because their lives have been spared, they now have a duty to save someone else's life. And so, even though they don't know this yet, they are going to pay for your medications.' Soon after, Sandra started on antiretroviral medications and slowly began to regain her health. Her wellbeing restored, the following year she was able to start working steadily and married her colleague, John Bosco, who was also HIV+. Together they moved into a small bungalow in Kitende and soon after, Sandra's daughter joined them. Then with the advent of the global fund initiative in 2004, Sandra was able to access free medications.

The future is not written but neither is the present

Had Sandra finished her life story and on coming out of the door had turned right rather than left, she would most likely be dead. If Emily had come out of the other door and turned left rather than right, Sandra would most likely be dead. If the World Trade Center had not been hit or if Emily's father had been at his desk, Sandra would most likely be dead. This illustrates how the simple act of turning left or right can open up radically different futures, in this case of life and death, and how these are embedded within the complex inter-relations of persons, actions and events in a world shaped by contiguity, contingency and the global political economy.

The relationship between action and the indeterminacy of the future that emerges in Sandra's story reinforces William James's observations that truth and reality do not inhere within the present or belong definitively to the moment of perception, but necessarily exist 'further on' through the unfolding of experiences that 'continually gives us new material to digest' (James 2000: 150). In other words, the meaning of an experience or event is only revealed over time through an unfolding of future events and experiences. The crucial meeting that took place when Sandra turned left and Emily turned right, proved not to foreshadow Sandra's impending demise, but to open up a different life trajectory in which the events of 9/11 changed Sandra's future, alongside hundreds of thousands of other people's.

On one hand, this reveals how the present consists of multiple possible presents, whose character remains undetermined and is subject to revision in light of future events that have not happened. On the other hand, it reinforces that there is always some form of practical, contiguous connection – as opposed to merely conceptual or conjectured association – between present and future events. Elaborating on this, I suggest there are at least three modes of action that shape our practical engagement with the future. The first of these is when we try to impose a structure on the indeterminacy and contingency of the future so as to make the future knowable in a particular kind of way. On a mundane level, this might simply be planning what to cook or how to spend the evening, while a less mundane example would be an HIV+ person planning for their children's future well-being in the event of prolonged sickness or their death. In each instance there is a process of planning and decision-making involved in which specific futures are imagined, narrativized and made possible, and in which there is an attempt to impose a structure on the contingency of the future, albeit in the knowledge of potential failure. This process has a specific cultural and pragmatic character, an example of which is when one of Sandra's friends was diagnosed with HIV/

AIDS and another friend asked her whether she decided to buy a motorbike or a cow when she had found out. It was a question that did not make sense to me, but revealed a particular way of engaging with the future insofar as to other Ugandan women the rationale was clear: both the motorbike and cow could provide ongoing income in the event of prolonged illness or death – the cow by producing milk every day and the motorbike by being hired out as a boda-boda taxi – thereby providing income for children's future education and school fees in one's absence.

A second mode of action, which is equally prevalent, is where we act in the world without necessarily consciously thinking about or rationalizing it. It is only retrospectively that we engage in a process of narrative reconstruction whereby a structure is imposed on the world from a position of hindsight, as per Kierkegaard's decree that 'life is lived forwards but understood backwards'. Or perhaps, following Lawler, it is a mode of action that can be seen as 'being both lived and understood forwards *and* backwards in a spiral movement of constant interpretation and reinterpretation. People constantly produce and reproduce life stories on the basis of memories, interpreting the past through the lens of social information and using this information to formulate present and future life stories' (2014: 32).

There is at least one further mode of action of the kind that we perform on an ongoing basis that sometimes possesses radical consequences for our whole existence, such as turning right or turning left. A person turns left and bumps into an old friend and gets offered a new job or turns right and gets knocked over by a car. As such the act of turning left or right stands as a metonym for all the other actions we perform multiple times a day and which expose us to the radical contingency of the future, including futures that we do not and will never know about. In Sandra's case it shows how the future is continuously shaped, sometimes minimally and sometimes radically, by the actions of others on an intensity and scale that takes us beyond the limits of scientific understanding.

Coda

On 22 March 2010 I arranged to meet Emily in Dizzy's Diner on 9th St and 8th Ave in Brooklyn. I had never met Emily before and she arrived having just had her first baby. I recounted Sandra's Life Journey to Emily, as given the inherent mutability of memory and narrative, I was interested in Emily's interpretation and version of events. One of Emily's first responses was: 'Well, I don't even believe in God, so why has Sandra said that?' My own response was 'perhaps the contingency of those events means that it is necessary to ascribe a kind of fate, divine intervention or of religiosity. I wonder if she is trying to impose some kind of meaning on contingency by appealing to God? Don't all of us impose structure and meaning on contingent events?' Emily responded: 'Although I don't believe in God, you know what's interesting, and I've never told anybody this, but the African women who were singing and chanting, I think they did something. I think their chanting worked'. Then Emily surprised me again when she said, 'I don't think that we met on that piece of grass either. I think we had the conversation when Sandra ended up sitting next to me at the dining table.' When I returned home after seeing Emily, I wrote down a summary of the conversation in my field-notes whereby I tried to understand the different events and interpretations.

I wonder if Emily, Sandra and myself are all seeking some kind of explanation to make the contingency not contingent, to make the turn of future events somehow necessary, to provide contingency with cause, an effect and an explanation. It is almost as if the mind cannot help but work along contiguous lines and form some kind of connection, whether that is religious, scientific or in my case anthropological. Or perhaps we have entered the realm of the mythical: a realm where past, present and future events take on the character of myth and/or certain dream-states and the imagination becomes intertwined with the materials of the world. Not so much Hume's golden mountains but Lévi-Strauss's Asdiwal, where there is a free play of time and place, where signs and symbols can be interchanged at the level of speech and storytelling, but at the level of deep structure, the structure remains. Consequently, whether one bumps into each other on the grass or at the dining table, or appeals to the high power of god or science, it does not matter, as the structure remains the same.

The different interpretations reinforce how memory is unstable, right down to the proteins and molecules in the brain, and how memory pertains as much to the future as it does to the past. Every time a memory is accessed it becomes labile and becomes re-patterned into the brain within a new emotional context, be that tragedy, humour, relief or whatever. As such, the future continually provides new contexts for the expression and articulation of memory through storytelling and narrative that becomes physically patterned into brain and body so as to reshape and reconstruct the past. With the addition of my own narrative in the form of this chapter, there are now three versions of the events of 9/11, none of which are settled. As such, the accounts of 9/11 that are contained in this chapter do not reveal immutable truths, but ones that are subject to revision by future modes of being within in a continuous process of disillusion wherein:

"The destruction of the first appearance does not authorize me to define henceforth the 'real' as a simple probable, since *they are only another name for the new apparition*, which must therefore figure in our analysis of the *dis-illusion*. The dis-illusion is the loss of one evidence only because it is the acquisition of *another evidence*" (Merleau-Ponty 1968: 40; emphasis in original).

Note

1 When Yoweri Museveni, the current leader of Uganda, led a five-year guerrilla war (1981–6) against Milton Obote's violent regime, Museveni's rebellion was backed by Cuba and Libya. When Museveni eventually seized power in 1986, he faced the problem of how to hold onto a post-revolution nation and a number of high-ranking military personnel were selected to go to Cuba and Libya to undergo advanced military training. Sixty officers were sent to Cuba and received medical check-ups on their arrival. Shortly after, when Castro and Museveni met in Zimbabwe in September 1986 at a meeting of Non-Aligned Heads of State, Castro pulled Museveni aside and informed him that out of the sixty soldiers he sent, eighteen had been found to have HIV/AIDS. Both men were concerned that this might reflect the level of prevalence among the general population. Museveni responded quickly, spoke about the problem in the media and implemented a series of measures that are credited with reducing the scale and spread of HIV/AIDS. As a consequence, Ugandan soldiers and military personnel have regular check-ups and are frequently tested for the HIV virus, and it was via one of these routine tests that Sandra's boyfriend found out he was HIV+.

References

Aristotle. *On the Soul; Parva Naturalia; On Breath.* W. S. Hett (trans. 1936). Cambridge, MA: Harvard University Press.

Hume, David, 1739. *A Treatise of Human Nature.* London: John Noon. Available online: https://www.gutenberg.org/files/4705/4705-h/4705-h.htm (accessed 20 October 2016).

Irving A. 2005. 'Life Made Strange: An Essay on the Reinhabitation of Bodies and Landscapes'. In W. James and D. Mills (eds), *Qualities of Time: ASA Monograph 41.* Oxford and New York: Berg.

Irving A., 2011a. 'Strange Distance: Towards an Anthropology of Interior Dialogue'. *Medical Anthropology Quarterly* 25 (1): 22–44.

Irving A., 2011b. 'I Gave My Child Life but I Also Gave Her Death'. *The Australian Journal of Anthropology* 22: 332–50.

Irving A., 2016. *The Art of Life and Death: Radical Aesthetics and Ethnographic Practice:* HAU Malinowski Monograph Series. Chicago: University of Chicago Press.

James, William, 2000. *Pragmatism and Other Writings.* London: Penguin.

Lawler, Steph, 2014. *Identity: Sociological Perspectives,* 2nd edn. Cambridge: Polity.

Merleau-Ponty, Maurice, 1968. The *Visible and the Invisible.* Evanston, IL: Northwestern University Press.

4

Cripping the future: Making disability count

Faye Ginsburg and Rayna Rapp

Introduction

> If one considers people who now have disabilities, people who are likely to develop disabilities in the future, and people who are or who will be affected by the disabilities of those close to them, then disability affects today or will affect tomorrow the lives of most Americans. The future of disability in America is not a minority issue. Current statistics suggest that the number of people with disabilities living in the community or in institutional settings now totals more than 54 million. (Institute of Medicine 2007: 16)

Disabled people have more than a dream of accessible futures: we continue to define and demand our place in political discourses, political visions and political practice, even as we challenge those very questions and demands. More accessible futures depend on it (Kafer 2013: 169).

How are we as a society to successfully incorporate, support, and care for the increasing numbers of Americans with disabilities, a future that ultimately includes all of us? As the quotation from *The Future of Disability in America* (FoD) indicates with stark clarity, the number of people with disabilities has grown dramatically in the twenty-first century. This chapter places the perspectives of demography and disability studies in conversation with our anthropological research to ask what is the relationship between 'counting disability' and 'making disability count'? As feminist scholar Alison Kafer persuasively argues from a disability studies perspective, the political and existential stakes for recognition of disability are high, especially in imagining and creating what she calls 'accessible futures'.

Written in the language familiar to policy analysts and demographers, *The Future of Disability* (FoD) shares many of the concerns that Kafer's quote articulates. This volume by the Institute of Medicine is one of the very few policy-oriented publications that bring focused attention to this increase in numbers and its implications for the future.

As disability scholars and activists frequently point out, the fifty-seven million people now classified as disabled, along with their allies, are rarely considered as a significant political constituency with sufficient power to draw attention in local, state or federal elections, let alone the American political imaginary. And, despite dramatic predictions suggesting that people with disabilities across the life span will constitute an expanding proportion of the US population for the foreseeable future, we are struck by the remarkable absence of almost any discussion of the policy implications of these demographic projections, outside of specialized research centres. With rare exceptions, policy debates – which increasingly focus on trimming programmes for social support in an increasingly neoliberal public sphere – largely ignore the rights and needs of the diverse and growing numbers of Americans with disabilities.

How might we imagine the future of disability in the US that takes into account the demographic social facts along with the concerns of disability scholars? How do these intersect with the presence and absence of disability in everyday life and popular culture? For example, Emily Kingsley, a scriptwriter for television programme Sesame Street and longstanding indefatigable advocate for the inclusion of disabilities on children's television and other forms of public culture for nearly half a century, speaks compellingly about the impact of this lack of political recognition as a fact of the 'habitus' of daily life, even in the most mundane aspects of consumer capitalism.

Every day I go through catalogues I get in the mail to see if there is a model with a wheelchair. I do a disability check. Why aren't we in advertising? I have a form letter on my computer that I use every week:

To Whom it May Concern:

I will not be ordering anything from your catalogue. People with disabilities are America's largest minority. No one realizes we have pocketbooks.

We have not yet gotten our voice, yet we are 57 million people strong. We have not yet found our Martin Luther King. (Emily Kingsley March 22 2012, NYU presentation)

The advertising circulars are one more instantiation in everyday life of the erasure of disabled citizens in so many arenas, creating the illusion of able-bodied normalcy as the hegemonic condition. Despite legislation that mandates inclusion of people with disabilities in public life, such everyday realities are diagnostic of an ongoing lack of recognition for them, not only in the present but also as part of an anticipated future. This point is underscored by Alison Kafer, who argues persuasively that as a social category, disability is continually rendered invisible and undesirable.

> [...] the value of a future that includes disabled people goes unrecognized, while the value of a disability-free future is seen as self-evident ... casting disability as a monolithic fact of the body, as beyond the realm of the political and therefore beyond the realm of debate or dissent, makes it impossible to imagine disability and disability futures differently ... I argue that decisions about the future of disability and disabled people are political decisions and should be recognized and treated as such. Rather than assume that a 'good future' naturally and obviously depends upon the eradication of disability, we must recognize this perspective as colored by histories of ableism and disability oppression. (Kafer 2013: 3)

Many other disability scholars have underscored this erasure of disability – past, present, and future – as a social fact in the US (McRuer 2006; Sandahl 2003; Schweik 2009). Their efforts are given additional political heft by putting them in conversation with demographers, who are forecasting the growing presence of disability in the American body politic.

Who and what counts? The Epistemology of numbers

What is not normal? What needs to be fixed? What needs to be prevented?

The act of forecasting is useful not for the predictions, but rather in forcing awareness of futures not necessarily bound by what is familiar (Fujiura and Parish 2007: 192).

Many important historical trends are fuelling the anticipated growth in the numbers of people with disabilities. These include deinstitutionalization, improvements in medical care, and the on-going impact of the Americans with Disabilities Act. Before the 1970s, efforts to provide alternatives to the dehumanizing world of custodial institutions, many people lived, languished and died behind locked doors, segregated from their families and communities (National Council on Disability 2012). Medical advances have saved and often improved the quality of life of those diagnosed with life threatening conditions and chronic illness across the life span (Anderson and Horvath 2004). These include (among others) low birth weight infants who are NICU beneficiaries but who statistically are at higher risk for cognitive disabilities (Stephens and Vohr 2009); military veterans returning from Afghanistan, the longest war in US history, often with PTSD, TBI, amputations and a range of other issues (Hoge et al. 2004); and people living into extreme old age with all the frailties and caregiving that entails (Poo 2015). Thus, many people are surviving and living with disabilities who might not have in the past. They are living independently, sometimes with assistants, with families or friends, or in supported environments integrated into community life, or often in less than desirable circumstances.

While these social transformations wrought by political change and medical care collectively represent a huge step forward, obtaining services and support has not been easy. People with disabilities continue to experience economic and political precarity as well as barriers to community integration (National Council on Disability 2014). Based on data from the last census, they are nearly twice as likely as those considered able-bodied to have an annual household income of $15,000 or less. The unemployment rate for adults is ten times greater than the national rate: 65 per cent are unemployed. Nearly one third of those who work earn an income below the poverty level, and racial and ethnic minorities are at greater risk (ibid). These social facts raise difficult questions regarding the inequalities shaping the experience of disability in the United States and what the actual shape of accessible futures might be.

The rising numbers of people with disabilities encompass a broad and extremely heterogeneous array of circumstances that have profoundly different implications for accommodations that might be required at different points in the life cycle. Clearly, the support systems are different for a dyslexic child entering school, a post-polio adult navigating family life or a wheelchair user negotiating the workforce. Additionally, new categories are constantly emerging. These social facts are evident to us, emerging from the research we have been carrying out since 2007 in 'disability worlds' that are marked by both stigma and cultural innovation using longstanding ethnographic methods: participant observation fieldwork in schools, labs, with families, at film festivals, in adaptive cultural programmes at museums and theatres; long-form qualitative interviews with activists and innovators, life histories with parents, and analyses of media and secondary documents, especially the proliferating memoirs reflecting on 'cripping the new normal' in personal, familial, and community life. A reflexive approach enabled us to study and theorize our own experiences as parents of children with disabilities along with those of our research subjects as we all navigated the complex medical and educational bureaucracies that shape the world of 'special education'.

Along with our interlocutors and allies, we struggled with the difficulties of less than adequate transition programmes for young adults that made clear the diminished futurity imagined for disabled citizens. Additionally, we often found ourselves productively caught up in the projects we were studying, at times taking an active role in enabling the very activities we were examining, working with local schools for students with learning disabilities, helping design and incubate a model alternative transition programme at our university. Such projects and the broader place (or lack of it) of disability in cultural imaginaries that addressed futurities, resonated with the work of disability scholars we were encountering such as Kafer and her compelling writing on accessible futures, along with the demographic realities noted above that bespeak a rapidly changing future that is hidden in plain sight.

In this section, we explore two particular conditions that have grown enormously in numbers and public recognition in the twenty-first century: Alzheimer's disease and Autism Spectrum Disorder. We focus on them because they raise important questions about escalating needs for specific accommodations and caretaking now and in the projected future of the body politic, and these are conditions that are neither predictable, preventable nor curable, but whose numbers are increasing exponentially. The realities of living with these conditions reverberate through the experiences of so many people in the US (and elsewhere), changing the landscape of normalcy that characterizes contemporary life. While each condition brings with it an exquisitely particular set of empirical realities, these two raise particularly compelling questions as well as future-making projects that have spurred widespread discussion across many fields, from medicine to the arts. In these cases, we see how the seemingly distinct fields of numbers and narratives each bespeak a changing futurity in which disability will increasingly be incorporated into a 'new normal'.

The demographic data we have been exploring raise important questions about the future of caretaking for those who cannot fend for themselves, including many intimate allies and loved ones, along with the service providers and paid caretakers who are part of their lives (Poo 2015). The projected need for caregiving, both paid and unpaid, is predicted to explode as the population ages. Age-related dementias are especially prominent as conditions that require considerable support; many more of our elderly live well into their nineties, often – although not always – with considerable frailty, including cognitive losses. A recent report projects that the number of people over sixty-five diagnosed with dementia will double by 2040, 'skyrocketing at a rate that rarely occurs with a chronic disease' (Belluck 2013). Such demographic projections can mask the fact that increased life span is dramatically stratified in the US: the national life expectancy (with regional variation) for African-American men is around sixty-seven years old, a full eight years less than their white counterparts. Ageing, of course, involves far more than simple chronological time: various adverse events (medical neglect, racism, poverty) might actually create age-related disability (diabetes-related amputations; arthritis, congestive heart failure with consequence of decreased mobility) in a chronologically 'younger' population (Cook 2015).

The familial and psychological impact of ageing and accompanying dementia is always profound. As Donald Moulds, acting assistant secretary for planning and evaluation at the federal Department of Health and Human Services, commented, 'The long-term care costs associated with people with dementia are particularly high because of the nature of the disease. People eventually become incapable of caring for themselves, and then in the vast majority of cases, their loved ones become incapable of caring for them'. Dr. Michael Hurd, an economist and lead author of the study, speaking to the implications of this research, made clear that the costs go beyond the numbers, which, he explained 'could not capture the full toll of the disease'. In a refreshingly candid if sobering moment on the limits of disciplinary knowledge, Hurd offered an existential reflection on the implications of this study: 'One thing we haven't talked about, and it's not in the paper, is the tremendous emotional cost,' he said. 'Economists are coldhearted, but they're not that coldhearted' (Belluck 2013: A1).

Alzheimer and dementia are not the only diagnoses with ballooning numbers that implicate different kinds of caregiving. Autism Spectrum Disorder (ASD), for example, is a diagnosis that generally requires consid-erable support (Hoffman 2013). And while the methodologies by which they are collected are contested, the numbers have almost doubled in less than a decade. The implications for social support are clear. As autism expert Deborah A. Fein explained with eloquent simplicity in response to the latter study: 'We need to find ways of funding and providing help to these children' (quoted in Hoffman 2013: A17).

Indeed, unpaid family caregiver services – provided by family, friends and neighbours – were valued at $450 billion per year in 2009, a steep increase from $375 billion in year 2007; these relationships will likely continue to be the largest source of long-term care services in the US (Family Caregiver Alliance 2012). At the same time, 'the need for professional caretakers is skyrocketing ... Yet the 3 million people currently in the home care workforce cannot meet even the current need, let alone the demand for care that will accompany the elder boom ... By 2018, demand for homecare workers will increase by more than 90 percent' (Poo 2015: 3–4; Boris and Klein 2012).

Avalanches, looping and futurity

These rapidly escalating figures for the exemplary cases of Alzheimer and ASD, have had an impact on more than caregiving. The growing public awareness around them illustrates a contemporary instance of philosopher of science Ian Hacking's 'avalanche of numbers'. He used this phrase to highlight the rise of probabilistic and statistical reasoning that shaped regimes of knowledge in early modern Europe. The gathering of numbers became central to modern governmentality. These statistics are marshalled as evidence of the need for regulation and social policy, a practice that in the eighteenth-century was initially deemed 'political arithmetic'. But, of course, as the phrase itself suggests, numbers are never simply objective facts; the categories under which they are collected are subject to cultural perceptions and relations of power. And with the dramatic expansion of certain diagnoses, we are in part seeing what Hacking calls 'a looping effect' in which the very existence of the classification itself increases the likelihood of people accepting and enacting it on an individual as well as group level (Hacking 2002). Such processes undergird the way the body politic is governed in the present and imagined in the future.

In his book, *The Future as Cultural Fact,* Arjun Appadurai builds on Hacking's ideas, juxtaposing two ways of constructing ideas about the future that are relevant to our discussion of demography, disability and biopolitics (Appadurai 2013). Appadurai names these (1) the ethics of possibility, embracing a horizon of hope, and (2) the ethics of probability, emerging from regimes of quantification. As he explains:

> By the ethics of possibility, I mean those ways of thinking, feeling, and acting that increase the horizons of hope, that expand the field of the imagination, that produce greater equity in what I have called the capacity to aspire, and that widen the field of informed, creative, and critical citizenship. [This ethics is part and parcel of transnational civil society movements, progressive democratic organizations, and in general the politics of hope.] By the ethics of probability, I mean those ways of thinking, feeling, and acting that flow out of what Ian Hacking calls 'the avalanche of numbers,' or what Michel Foucault saw as the capillary dangers of modern regimes of diagnosis, counting, and accounting. (Appadurai 2013: 295)

We find Appadurai's formulation generative as we bring together the discursive fields of demography – an ethics of probability – and an ethics of possibility spelled out in critical disability studies. How do we engage with the apparent explosion in the numbers of people with disabilities that demographic data track and forecast through Appadurai's framework for an ethics of possibility? Can we use this knowledge to produce not only awareness but also 'critical sites for negotiating paths to dignity, recognition, and politically feasible maps for the future'? (Appadurai 2013: 288).

Appadurai's work is resonant with other contemporary anthropologists in focusing on how future imaginaries open up or foreclose cultural practices in the present (Miyazaki 2015; Rabinow 2011; Tsing 2015). Indeed, they/we are intellectually aligned with a range of critical scholarship under disparate terms – such as potentialities, anticipation, futurity, and hope – that has emerged in the twenty-first century, spurred by the rapid transformations wrought by globalization, climate change, social precarity, long-term warfare, new digital technologies, migration, chronic illness, biomedicine/global pharmaceutical markets, increasing economic inequalities and more (Adams et al. 2009; Taussig et al. 2013). Disability lurks in all of the aforementioned problems and possibilities. Disability is rarely directly addressed in these works, or more broadly in the anthropological literature that considers futurity, such as Appadurai or Miyazaki, whether in the US or the developing world, despite the fact of its perennial, ubiquitous and increasing presence, with only a few exceptions (cf. Mattingly 2014; Rouse 2009). This omission is consequential. As Kafer reminds us, disability is almost always accompanied by discrimination and erasure in the present, which virtually guarantees its absence from 'the future as cultural fact.' As she remarks:

> To put it bluntly, I, *we*, need to imagine crip futures because disabled people are continually being written out of the future, rendered as the sign of the future no one wants. This erasure is not mere metaphor. Disabled people – particularly those with developmental and psychiatric impairments, those who are poor, gender-deviant, and/or people of color, those who need atypical forms of assistance to survive – have faced sterilization, segregation, and institutionalization; denial of equitable education, health care and social services; violence and segregation, and institutionalization; and the withholding of the rights of citizenship. Too many of these practices continue, and each of them has greatly limited, and often literally shortened, the futures of disabled people … . We must begin to anticipate presents and to imagine futures that include all of us. (Kafer 2013: 46)

Cripping the American imaginary

Kafer is not alone. She is part of an important expanding conversation among critical disability scholars deeply influenced by feminism, queer theory, critical race theory, affect theory, biopolitics and animal and environmental studies, who identify themselves as 'crip' theorists (Chen 2012; Crenshaw 2015; Erevelles 2011; Linton 1998; McRuer 2006; Puar 2017; Sandahl 2003; Garland-Thomson 2013). These disability scholars have appropriated the once-pejorative term 'crip', used to stigmatize those with atypical movements ('cripples'). They have resignified it as a verb indicating a radical repositioning of the concerns of disabled subjects from the margins to the centre, much as the word 'queer' has been similarly reclaimed. Most importantly, the term 'crip' highlights the significance of coalitional movements for collective transformation of the actually existing world. As Rob McRuer explains:

> Many consider the defiant reclaiming and reinvention of *crip* is linked to the critical reinvention – by activists, artists, and scholars – of *queer*. Most important, queer and crip activisms share a will to remake the world, given the ways in which injustice, oppression, and hierarchy are built (sometimes quite literally) into the structures of contemporary society. (McRuer 2012: 1)

The concerns raised by crip theorists are more than academic. They are erupting across a wide swath of public culture; the affective and experiential depth of the lived demographic realities sketched above are catalyzing lively creative work reaching diverse audiences. We argue that these are creating 'disability publics', a term we use to call attention to how people with disabilities and their allies are interpellated and materialized through a range of media, across widely distributed networks of people with shared experiences of disability. These constitute an emergent form of recognition as well as locations for alternative engagements on the part of both producers and audiences.

The cultural works discussed here reflect a widespread desire to communicate about the existential reality of living with a particular disability across the life course. They are the instantiations in other registers of the rising numbers and increasing awareness that the expansive future of disability can create. In our prior writing, we have attributed this emergence to what we call 'narrative urgency a creative response to the experiential pressures that give shape to an alternative understanding of everyday life lived against the grain of 'normalcy' (Rapp and Ginsburg 2001, 2011). We think of these creative works – books, movies, blogs, poetry, and more – as inscribing 'unnatural histories' that reflect the diversity of disability that is still too rarely part of public discourse, despite a generative genealogy of counter-discursive texts. This sort of 'public storytelling' has worked its way into media of all sorts and in many parts of the world, ranging from personal memoirs and television shows to scholarly works that offer compelling perspectives on the 'new normal' established by living life with a difference (Bérubé 1996; Frank 2000; Grinker 2007; Rapp and Ginsburg 2001).

The innovative projects we describe below push back against a hegemonic representational economy in which children are easily launched, adults are continuously in the work force, soldiers return seamlessly to viable lives, elders decline gracefully, cognitive differences are inconsequential, and unruly emotional states and sexual desires are invisible outside normate categories, to mention only a few of the vast cascade of tropes in which daily life in the US is typically rendered. The disjuncture between such dominant narratives and the quotidian experiences of the rapidly increasing numbers of those living in disability worlds fuels a robust and growing field of counter-public cultural production. As cultural studies scholar Michael Warner argues, a counter-public is often mobilized against its '... subordinate status. The cultural horizon against which it marks itself off is not just a general or a wider public but a dominant one' (Warner 2002: 119).

Of course, resignifying a hegemonic frame is in itself a project of futurity, even when those who count disability demonstrate that numbers increasingly are on 'our side'. We remain far from the broadly inclusive imaginary envisioned by the activists who long struggled for the legislation, that led to the ADA, as well as those who have come of age since its passage. Nonetheless, the utopian future the ADA bureaucracy potentially represents continues to spur action aimed at remedying sites of neglect, from curb cuts to classrooms to cinemas. In other words, these historical contingencies – when the increasing presence of disability as part of everyday life meets the uneven landscape of inclusive legislation – give rise to the sense of narrative urgency that catalyzes counter-public production. The more popular works discussed below, we suggest, are 'cripping' the American imaginary in ways that are establishing 'disability publics', materialized through a variety of media. Across a variety of genres, they constitute an emergent, future-oriented form of recognition produced by mediated relations on the part of both producers and audiences with investments in embracing particular understandings of disability. The capacity of these works to reach widely distributed networks of people with shared experiences of disability is fundamental to their efficacy in expanding relevant discursive fields.

Consider how 'disability publics' are evolving in the twenty-first century for our two cases of Alzheimer and Autism Spectrum Disorder, whose recent exploding demographic impact we discuss above. As recently as three decades ago, the categories of senility and dementia covered a range of degenerative cognitive diseases associated with ageing. Now, Alzheimer is routinely part of public discussion as part of the overall demographic escalation that activist authors have dubbed 'the elder boom' (Poo 2015) (Tarach-Ritchey 2012). As Ai-Jen Poo, co-author of *The Age of Dignity: Preparing for the Elder Boom in a Changing America* (2015), writes: 'I think there's a sense of urgency that people are experiencing at a very personal, familial level. Our task is to really take that into the public arena and start a different kind of public conversation about it.'

In the arts and letters, that conversation has already started. The dilemmas of 'the new old age', for example, have been everywhere evident. In 2014, Julianne Moore received an Oscar for Best Actress in *Still Alice* for her moving portrayal of a professor coping with early onset Alzheimer and its profound effect on her family (Glatzer and Westmoreland 2014). Other feature films on Alzheimer preceded *Still Alice*, laying the groundwork for its increasing presence in public culture, while giving shape to the widespread anxieties stirred by increasing clinical diagnosis, intensive caregiving and their 'looping effects' discussed below. The critically acclaimed 2006 Canadian film *Away From Her* (Director: Sarah Polley), was adapted from *The Bear Came Over the Mountain*, a short story by Nobel prize-winning author Alice Munro.

Close to home, we have followed the popular weekly *NY Times* blog, 'the new old age', which coined that name in 2008. Weaving together existential, medical and practical perspectives from both journalist/authors and reader/ commentators, this blog explores 'aging and caregiving covering topics such as medical decision-making, housing and long-term care, government policies, end-of-life choices, the personal rewards and headaches of caring for aging loved ones, becoming a kind of online support group' (http://newoldage. blogs.nytimes.com/2015/01/09/a-new-direction/). The robust responses to every topic signal how widespread the issues surrounding caregiving and extreme old age have become, quickly constituting a present and future platform for this particular rapidly growing disability public.

We also note the remarkable popularity of the aptly named graphic memoir *Can't We Talk About Something More Pleasant?* (2014). Cultural commentator and New Yorker staff cartoonist Ros Chast takes her title from her Jewish mother's words, expressing the elder Chasts' reluctance to speak about their declining circumstances. The title itself also suggests a broader social denial of the unaddressed needs of a frail elderly population. Chast's bestselling bittersweet book chronicles her efforts as an adult and only child to care for her ageing, eccentric, and once-fiercely-independent Brooklyn parents; as they lived into their mid-nineties, their lives were changed by dementia and deterioration. While Chast's work always sells well, this particular book received far more widespread recognition than her prior ones. Review after review made clear that the book's popularity tapped into pervasive concerns and shared dilemmas of eldercare among her readers who constitute yet another instance of an increasingly self-aware disability public – in this case emerging around ageing – as articulated in the copious commentary that follows online reviews of the memoir.

Other forms of cultural production move beyond narratives 'about' to genres drawing on modalities that can be inclusive of those with Alzheimers, such as music and improvisational drama. *The Unforgettables* is illustrative; this unusual chorus is made up of individuals with dementia and their caregivers. Established in 2011 by Dr Mary Mittelman, director of the Center for Psychosocial Research and Support Programs at the Comprehensive Center on Brain Aging at NYU Langone Medical Center, her intention is 'to give families and people with Alzheimers a respite from the disease—a sense of normalcy, a moment of happiness and ease'. Inspired by the innovative and very successful Alzheimer's Art Program at the Museum of Modern Art entitled Meet Me at MoMA. *The Unforgettables* 'rehearse weekly, select their own songs, learn standard breathing and performance techniques' and offer public performances twice a year, building a very particular disability public, that incorporates those with Alzheimers, their caregivers, and other allies. We argue that taken together these kind of creative efforts, exemplary of a much larger social field (Bourdieu), now comprise an Alzheimer's future imaginary.

No judgements

Of course, the eruption of narratives and other forms of cultural production addressing the existential realities and futurities of this changing demographic landscape is not confined to works on ageing and mortality. The ever-expanding category of Autism Spectrum Disorder (ASD) has catalyzed its own forms of significant cultural activism. A myriad books, websites, blogs, You Tube videos, TED talks, documentaries, feature films and television shows provides venues for the creation of disability publics around ASD. For example, the British writer Mark Haddon's 2003, prize-winning book *The Curious Incident of the Dog in the Night-Time,* based in part on his experiences working with children with disabilities, has been particularly influential. This fictional mystery is told and solved in the voice of an adolescent mathematical prodigy with characteristics resembling Asperger's syndrome (although the term is never used in the book). The story has been adapted to great acclaim for the London and New York stages in 2012 and 2014 respectively.

In New York City, shortly after the theatrical debut of *Curious*, an 'autism friendly' matinee was organized by the Autism Theater Initiative (ATI). Formed in 2011, the ATI is dedicated to making Broadway theatre accessible to ASD audiences, their families and other allies, with the support of the Theater Development Fund, a longstanding non-profit organization that encourages diverse audiences to attend live theatre and dance productions. This was the fifth Broadway play adapted for audiences on the spectrum for whom lights and volume are adjusted, 'fidget toys' and earplugs are provided, and people are free to move around and make noise during the performance, part of ATI's 'no judgement' motto. To be sure all feel welcome at ATI events, the theatre sells out to this particular demographic; a brigade of red-shirted volunteers are trained to assist audiences on the street as they approach the theatre. At the training we attended, we received unexpected and revelatory instructions that drew on ATI's experience of a prior performance of the *Curious Incident*, demonstrating how moved many people were by the opportunity to participate, unjudged, in Broadway theatre.

Parental memoirs are a staple of the disability publics formed around autism, exemplified in Ron Suskind's bestseller *Life Animated: A Story of Sidekicks, Heroes and Autism*. In this moving story of his family's journey with Owen, his autistic son, Pulitzer prize-winning journalist Suskind recounts how they all learned to 'express love and loss, kinship, brotherhood' through the language of Disney movies whose scripts Owen had memorized. Over time, these formed his primary communication system, one that the family learned to embrace, opening up an alternative pathway to shared futures.

Beyond compelling perennial parental narratives, first-person accounts of people with autism have had a huge impact, on opening up a sense of autistic futures, initially emerging with the notable autobiographical works of American autistic activist and professor of animal science Temple Grandin's 1996 book *Thinking in Pictures*, and Australian writer, artist and singer-songwriter Donna Williams' 1992 memoir *Nobody Nowhere* (Grandin 2010; Williams 1998). Both women have gone on to author many more books; their writings have been adapted as television dramas, and most importantly, have inspired countless others who identify as having ASD to tell their own stories across a range of platforms. More recently, in 2010, for example, Jesse Saperstein, an Asperger's self-advocate, wrote *Atypical: A Life in 20 and 1/3 Chapters*, a memoir from childhood through his early twenties in which he chronicles his outsider status, overcoming bullying and rejection, and finding a path toward self-acceptance and the making of a young adult life (Saperstein 2010). Two years later, David Finch published his account of his late discovery of his own Asperger's from a different point in the life cycle, well described in his title: *The Journal of Best Practices: A Memoir of Marriage, Asperger Syndrome, and One Man's Quest to Be a Better Husband* (Finch 2012). In 2014, 'Aspie mentors' provide advice on coping with the daily stressors that they themselves have identified as being the most significant, in a collection entitled *Been There. Done that. Try This! An Aspie's Guide to Life on Earth* (Attwood 2014). These articulate self-advocates are doing more than illuminating their lives as part of the arc of human difference. Beyond reaching and building a disability public, they have designs on the future, throwing a lifeline to others who share their experiences and are struggling to find their place.

One of the most notable locations is found in the work of the Autistic Self Advocacy Network (ASAN), notably their self-published work, *Loud Hands:*

Autistic People, Speaking, described on their website as 'a collection of essays written by and for Autistic people … from the dawn of the Neurodiversity movement' to contemporary blog posts of today, 'preserving the community's foundational documents' in the interest of creating accessible futures (Bascom 2012). The title *Loud Hands* has an important and profoundly instructive genealogy. As the editor Julia Bascom explains in the foreword:

> Abuse and silencing is a constant, pervasive theme in the lives of autistic people, and for many people it is best expressed by that old familiar phrase from special education: *Quiet hands! Loud Hands* means resisting. *Loud Hands* means speaking however we do, *anyway* – and doing so in a way that can be very obviously Autistic. It means finding ways to talk and think about ourselves on our own terms …. It starts with the basic foundational idea that *there is nothing wrong with us.* We are fine. We are complete, complex, human beings leading rich and meaningful existences and deserving dignity, respect, human rights, and the primary voice in the conversation about us. We can have loud hands. To say that flapping can be communication, that autistic people have voices regardless of whether or not we speak orally, and that our obviously autistic communication and thoughts have intrinsic worth is an inherently revolutionary thing. This anthology, and The Loud Hands Project as a whole, serves to document and explore that. Bit by bit, piece by piece, we're rewriting the world into one where our voices are heard. (Bascom 2012: 8, 10)

Like so many of the projects we have been describing, Loud Hands is clearly propelled by a combined sense of social justice and narrative urgency to creatively construct a more radically inclusive future. Numbers are on their side. As is the case with all media, a dedicated and expanding audience of ASD people and their allies is fundamental to survival, success, and the creation of an accessible future.

Thinking forward

The emerging works we have described here are only a small sample of a continually expanding set of future-making projects across a range of experiences and genres. They are, we argue, beginning to fill a vacuum left by an absence of public recognition in other idioms, forging a counter-public world reflective of what we see as the present and coming demographic explosion in disability. In this chapter, we make the case that the seemingly distinct fields of numbers and narratives each bespeak a changing futurity in which disability will increasingly be incorporated into 'the new normal', whether through demographic imperatives, narrative expression, and/or the force of political mobilization. In order to comprehend the impact of the upturn in numbers of Americans with disabilities throughout the life cycle, we have tacked back and forth between the abstractions of population trends and a range of media forms that express distinctive experiential realities. We have used the cases of Alzheimer's and autism, chosen as twenty-first century exemplars of recent and proliferating diagnoses, rapidly expanding demographics as well as disability publics in formation. Given the inevitable increase in disability across the life cycle sketched in our discussion of demography, and the expanding expectations of inclusion, we suggest that the intersection of disabilities and futurities will be under constant negotiation. We hope that our work as anthropologists can play a key critical and practical role to play in contemporary debates about futures in general and accessible futures in particular.

Acknowledgements

We thank the editors of this collection, and Juan Salazar in particular, for their helpful conversations in thinking through our material in relationship to the book's project. We are grateful to all our interlocutors and allies who have helped us develop our thinking for this project, and the funding agencies that have supported it including The Spencer Foundation, The Guggenheim Foundation, The National Endowment for the Humanities, and the Humanities Initiative (now The Center for Humanities) at NYU. An earlier version of this chapter was published in the online journal *Somatosphere* (Ginsburg and Rapp 2015).

References

Adams, V., M. Murphy and A. E. Clarke, 2009. 'Anticipation: Technoscience, life, affect, temporality'. *Subjectivity* 28 (1): 246–65.

Anderson, G. and J. Horvath, 2004. 'The growing burden of chronic disease in America'. *Public Health Reports* 119 (3): 263–70.

Appadurai, A., 2013. *The Future as Cultural Fact: Essays on the Global Condition*, 1st edn. London: Verso.

Attwood, T., 2014. *Been There. Done That. Try This!: An Aspie's Guide to Life on Earth*, 1st edn. C. R. Evans and A. Lesko (eds). London and Philadelphia: Jessica Kingsley.

Bascom, J., 2012. *Loud Hands: Autistic People, Speaking.* Washington, DC: Autistic Self Advocacy Network.

Belluck, P., 2013. 'Dementia Care Costs Are Soaring, Study Finds'. *New York Times*. A1. Available online: http://www.nytimes.com/2013/04/04/health/dementia-care-costs-are-soaring-study-finds.html (accessed 30 March 2015).

Bérubé, M., 1996. *Life As We Know It: A Father, a Family, and an Exceptional Child*. New York: Pantheon Books.

Boris, E and J. Klein (eds), 2012. *Caring for America: Home Health Workers in the Shadow of the Welfare State*. New York: Oxford University Press.

Chast, R., 2014. *Can't We Talk about Something More Pleasant? A Memoir*. New York: Bloomsbury.

Chen, M., 2012. *Animacies: Biopolitics, Racial Mattering, and Queer Affect*. Durham, NC: Duke University Press Books.

Cook, L., 2015. 'Black Americans Have Fewer Years to Live – Here's Why – US News'. *US News & World Report*. Available online: http://www.usnews.com/news/blogs/data-mine/2015/01/05/black-americans-have-fewer-years-to-live-heres-why (accessed March 30, 2015).

Crenshaw, K., 2015. *On Intersectionality: The Essential Writings of Kimberle Crenshaw*. New York: The New Press.

Erevelles, N., 2011. *Disability and Difference in Global Contexts: Enabling a Transformative Body Politic*. New York: Palgrave Macmillan.

Family Caregiver Alliance, 2012. '*Selected Caregiver Statistics*, Family Caregiver Alliance'. Available online: https://www.caregiver.org/print/44 (accessed March 19, 2015).

Finch, D., 2012. *The Journal of Best Practices: A Memoir of Marriage, Asperger Syndrome, and One Man's Quest to Be a Better Husband,* repr. edn. New York: Scribner.

Frank, G., 2000. *Venus on Wheels: Two Decades of Dialogue on Disability, Biography, and Being Female in America*. Berkeley, CA: University of California Press.

Fujiura, G. T. and L. S. Parish, 2007. 'Emerging policy challenges in intellectual disabilities'. *Mental Retardation and Developmental Disabilities Research Reviews* 13 (2): 188–94.

Garland-Thomson, R., 2013. 'Disability Studies: A Field Emerged'. *American Quarterly* 65 (4): 915–26.

Ginsburg, F. and Rayna Rapp, 2015. 'Making Disability Count: Demography, Futurity and the Making of Disability Publics'. *Somatosphere*. May 11, Inhabitable Worlds Series. Available online: http://somatosphere.net/2015/05/making-disability-count-demography-futurity-and-the-making-of-disability-publics.html (accessed 16 April 2016).

Glatzer, R. and W. Westmoreland, 2014. *Still Alice*. Los Angeles: Sony Pictures Classics.

Grandin, T., 2010. *Thinking in Pictures. Expanded Edition: My Life with Autism,* 2nd edn. New York: Vintage.

Grinker, R. R., 2007. *Unstrange Minds: Remapping the World of Autism*. New York: Basic Books.

Hacking, I., 2002. 'Inaugural lecture: Chair of Philosophy and History of Scientific Concepts at the Collège de France, 16 January 2001'. *Economy and Society*, 31 (1): 1–14.

Haddon, M., 2003. *The Curious Incident of the Dog in the Night-Time*. London: Jonathan Cape.

Hoffman, J., 2013. 'Parental Study Shows Rise in Autism Spectrum Cases', *New York Times*. A17. Available online: http://www.nytimes.com/2013/03/21/health/parental-study-shows-rise-in-autism-spectrum-cases.html (accessed 20 June 2013).

Hoge, C. W., C. A. Castro, S. C. Messer, D. McGurk, D. I. Cotting and R. L. Koffman, 2004. 'Combat Duty in Iraq and Afghanistan, Mental Health Problems, and Barriers to Care'. *New England Journal of Medicine* 351 (1): 13–22.

Institute of Medicine, 2007. 'The Future of Disability in America'. Available online: http://www.nap.edu/catalog/11898/the-future-of-disability-in-america (accessed 18 March 2015).

Kafer, A., 2013. *Feminist, Queer, Crip,* 1st edn. Bloomington, IN: Indiana University Press.

Linton, S., 1998. *Claiming Disability: Knowledge and Identity.* New York: New York University Press.

Mattingly, C., 2014. *Moral Laboratories: Family Peril and the Struggle for a Good Life,* 1st edn. Oakland, CA: University of California Press.

McRuer, R., 2012. 'Cripping Queer Politics, or the Dangers of Neoliberalism'. *S&F Online* 1–2. Available online: http://sfonline.barnard.edu/a-new-queer-agenda/cripping-queer-politics-or-the-dangers-of-neoliberalism/ (accessed 19 March 2015).

McRuer, R. (with a foreword by Michael Bérubé), 2006. *Crip Theory: Cultural Signs of Queerness and Disability.* New York: New York University Press.

Miyazaki, Hirokazau, 2015. 'Hope in the Gift—Hope in Sleep'. In S. Liisberg, E. O. Pedersen and A. L. Dalsgård (eds), *Trust and Hope: Negotiating the Future: Dialogues between Anthropologists and Philosophers*, 209–18. Oxford: Berghahn.

National Council on Disability, 2012. 'Deinstituionalization: Unfinished Business'. Available online: http://www.ncd.gov/publications/2012/Sept192012/ (accessed 17 October 2016).

National Council on Disability, 2014. *National Disability Policy: A Progress Report.* Washington, DC: National Council on Disability.

Poo, A., 2015. *The Age of Dignity: Preparing for the Elder Boom in a Changing America.* New York: New Press.

Puar, J. K., 2017. *Affective Politics: States of Debility and Capacity.* Durham, NC: Duke University Press.

Rabinow, Paul. 2011. *The Accompaniment: Assembling the Contemporary.* Chicago: University of Chicago Press.

Rapp, R. and F. D. Ginsburg, 2001. 'Enabling Disability: Rewriting Kinship, Reimagining Citizenship'. *Public Culture* 13 (3): 533–56.

Rapp, R. and F. Ginsburg, 2011. 'Reverberations: Disability and the New Kinship Imaginary'. *Anthropological Quarterly* 84 (2): 379–410.

Rouse, C., 2009. *Uncertain Suffering: Racial Health Care Disparities and Sickle Cell Disease,* 1st edn. Berkeley: University of California Press.

Sandahl, C., 2003. 'Queering the Crip or Cripping the Queer?: Intersections of Queer and Crip Identities in Solo Autobiographical Performance'. *GLQ: A Journal of Lesbian and Gay Studies* 9 (1): 25–56.

Saperstein, J. A., 2010. *Atypical: Life with Asperger's in 20 1/3 Chapters,* 1st edn. New York: Perigee Books.

Schweik, S. M., 2009. *The Ugly Laws: Disability in Public*. New York: New York University.

Stephens, B. E. and B. R. Vohr, 2009. 'Neurodevelopmental Outcome of the Premature Infant'. *Pediatric Clinics of North America* 56 (3): 631–46.

Tarach-Ritchey, A., 2012. *Behind the Old Face: Aging in America and the Coming Elder Boom*. CreateSpace Independent Publishing Platform.

Taussig, K.-S., K. Hoeyer and S. Helmreich, 2013. 'The Anthropology of Potentiality in Biomedicine: An Introduction to Supplement 7'. *Current Anthropology* 54 (S7): S3–S14.

Tsing, Anna. 2015. *The Mushroom at the End of the World: On the Possibility of Life in Capitalist Ruins*. Princeton, NJ: Princeton University Press.

Warner, M., 2002. 'Publics and Counterpublics'. *Public Culture* 14 (1): 49–90.

Williams, D., 1998. *Nobody Nowhere: The Remarkable Autobiography of an Autistic Girl*. London: Jessica Kingsley Publishing.

5

Contemporary obsessions with time and the promise of the future

Simone Abram

Contemporary obsessions?

This chapter considers the notions of future that are embedded in the notion of land-use planning, sometimes known as Urban Planning or Town and Country Planning. Since planning as it is practiced in Western Europe would appear to be inherently future-oriented, it offers insights into future-methodologies both as ethnographic objects (planning's futures) and for ethnographic methods themselves (studying planning's futures). Through a discussion of forward planning and planning for housing in England, the chapter highlights the different temporal horizons of the future, the varying notions of human agency in achieving particular futures, whether dangerous or mundane, and the very different means of conceptualizing both a static future of the imagination, and a dynamic trajectory between now and then. While planning futures are sometimes conceptualized as Utopian, the reality of governmental planning is far more mundane and instrumental, with only quite occasional appearances of overblown scenarios or imagined worlds. More commonly, future planning is reduced to a process of applying governmental method- ologies based on quite abstract policy imperatives. This chapter shows how Utopian or Dystopian futures bounce in and out of the mundane practice of governmental planning to show how bureaucratic processes work to reduce broader future concepts to manageable mechanisms.

Land-use planning is an example of future-thinking to have emerged strongly in the twentieth century, in contrast to conventional religious or enlightenment temporalities and most certainly with different temporal horizons. Foucault noted a shift in the concern of governments once the development of statistical techniques enabled them to manage their populations (or at least to imagine that they did), but this can be complemented by the observation that the concern to govern changed in form again from the nineteenth century to the twentieth century. The most notable shift was the increasing attention paid not just to managing the population now, but in controlling its future. The field of town planning thus emerged in its contemporary form in the UK early in the twentieth century on the back of new sciences of hygiene, for example, as well as through the domestication of colonial development practices (Reade, 1987; Porter 2010; cf. Peattie 1970). The social movements that were to become institutionalized through the Town and Country Planning Association and then formalized in various parliamentary Acts, for example, aimed to improve the conditions of the poor, in the name of progress and humanity, ultimately aiming to replace Christian charity with comprehensive Welfare by means of rights related to land and property. In brief, they were concerned with what Reade refers to as 'the land question' (1987: 36), essentially a question of class. Land-use planning gradually evolved into a concern with the 'balanced' distribution of economic activity, followed by attempts to promote material equality after World War II, before it morphed into a primarily technical bureaucratic operation to maximize resource use, presaging a bouncing back and forth between government-directed social improvement versus investor/market-led development. Gradually, through the twentieth century, a stronger imperative to instigate increasingly comprehensive state forward-planning emerged (Murdoch and Abram 2002).

Despite a declared political adherence among many Western governments to 'free' markets, the practice of demanding long-term future plans from regional and local government bodies continues. At the central governmental level, the motivation for planning is often rhetorically linked to grand, global or existential issues: the need to tackle issues that cannot be accommodated in the market, by individuals or isolated groups such as climate change, environmental pollution, or civilizational aims. The motivation to plan thus relies on both apocalyptic and utopian ambitions, but as it moves into practice, the invocation of threatening or inspiring scenarios becomes more marginal, appearing more often as a framing comment or reference.

Materially planned futures

In the UK, the state requires all local authorities (municipalities) to produce regular forward plans that are used as guidelines for decisions on particular development applications made by external parties in the planning period.

This reflects a split in planning practice between future-oriented policies and the detailed regulation of particular acts of development. The scope of forward plans has varied over time, but such plans generally set out directions of future development, from the broad brush (an aim to be sustainable) to the specific (x number of units of development in y location). The four to five year planning period is usually considered in relation to a future-horizon of up to two decades, so a more distant future is the premise for more concrete near-future policies. Each plan is ostensibly public, and is put in the public domain for comments and objections before it is authorized. This is pragmatic, in the sense that planning is about externalities – ensuring that development does not impinge on neighbouring property (or the rights of its owner), but also hard won through post-war campaigns for citizen-participation. Although the planning system does categorize development actors into proposers and objectors of specific policies, in practice objectors often have alternative suggestions as well as different approaches to articulating priorities for the future. Anthropologists have long taken for granted that the objects of their interest are the subjects of regimes, and it makes sense to see that governmental urban or land-use planning are means by which the state attempts to govern populations, and through which contests over who controls land and resources are played out. I use the term 'played out', since 'resistance' and its corollary, 'force' offer a crude dualistic model for the multi-party struggles over loosely specified aims in varying contexts. While the focus in studies of resistance is largely on the issues at stake and how various actors organize to attempt to control them (or resist their control), anthropologists are now paying more attention to the subtle ways by which the future is presented materially in the everyday (Pink and Lewis offer a discussion in terms of resilience: 2014). The future is not only invoked in the grand debates about future plans noted above, but future urban plans have quiet ways of making themselves present.

Since the post-war period, British planning has also required local authorities to make public announcements of all applications by landowners for permission to embark on development activities (known as 'planning permission'). Questions over particular, concrete futures have found their way into material forms in largely obfuscatory, if public, ways. Lists of current applications usually appear in small print in the adverts section of the local press (which in Britain is largely the vehicle for reporting local crime and planning issues). Sheets of formally coded, tightly printed A4 text also appear in the location of a site that is the subject of planning permission, often nailed to nearby lamp-posts, or sometimes taped to trees. The use of visual methods to observe the materialization of the future in the present reveals broader, if equally taken for granted, visual indications of future plans. Hoardings are often a precursor to the transformation of a building site, for example, either anonymously shielding secret activities, or flamboyantly advertising a future utopia, complete with the name of its sponsor.[1] Thus the signs of future construction activities are displayed in the present through various visual means other than the actual activities of building (see Figure 5.1). Our ability to interpret these signs depends on our familiarity with contextual information about building regulations, planning permission, tax exemptions or other institutional conditions. All is not always as it seems, however, since the promise of completion may be elusive. For example, for years Spain was rife with half-finished buildings where one floor was left unfinished, since tax was only liable on completed buildings. Ireland was left with arrays of half-built villas and ranches when the financial crisis led to an abrupt cessation in the flow of capital for building projects. And as Baxstrom reports, residents in some areas of Kuala Lumpur might find buildings suddenly demolished or constructed without notice as they leave their houses in the morning, or return at night (2013).

Such observations might suggest that futures have only a rhetorical (including visual) role in planning practice. But planning practice refers to a broad range of activities, from urban design to abstract policy development. While one might imagine that a plan is a kind of 'blueprint', a detailed site-specific design for something to be constructed, British plans are more like policy papers including general principles and some general site-identification. In this they are quite different from the development plans found in other European countries. Norwegian plans, for example, often contain detailed holistic mapped-guides to development, tying in provision of schools, medical centres, sports grounds, shops and other facilities related to new housing development. Swedish housing development plans include design principles and rules on the number of metres between housing and children's play areas. British plans contain no design guidance, outside broad designations such as conservation areas or areas of 'outstanding natural beauty'.

These forward policy plans, while interesting documents in themselves, are only a small part of the planning process. Rather like the dry minimal minutes of long, crowded, contentious meeting, they reflect little of on-going practices of revision, negotiation, political competition and public contest. The many, differently conceptualized futures that are elaborated and debated during the process of planning are often quite invisible in the plan document itself, and the plan is later invoked rarely, perhaps only referred to as one factor to be considered when applications to develop a particular site are debated in council planning committees. Even so, the plan – either the document or the idea of a plan existing – operates as a kind of promise that requires validation, and promises, as Austin recognized, may live for a long while without being fulfilled, as long as their fulfilment can be imagined (Abram and Weszkalnys 2013). Even a municipal housing plan promises something. Whether it is hope

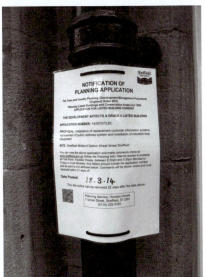
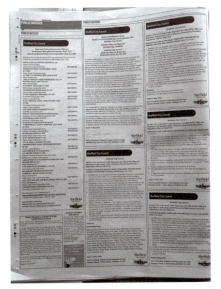

FIGURE 5.1 *Banalized urban futures materialized. Images from the city of Sheffield. Photos by Simone Abram.*

or fear, it is a statement about the future that must have some credible chance of becoming, if it is to maintain its status as a policy. Whether promises made into the plan then begin to become apparent in the hoardings and notices on boards by building sites becomes a measure of felicity that could (although it very rarely is) become a measure of governmental credibility once its imagined future becomes the present or past.

Planning for the future

Studies of the future note that futures are not merely visions of possible worlds, but that they generate action in the present to effect or avoid those visions (see Wallman 1992). Nowhere is this clearer than in state and local practices of planning, since planning, by definition, is a means to try to stabilize the very uncertainty of the future. Planning proceeds by ascertaining predictabilities and attempting to secure them by design, or, as Abram and Weszkalnys suggest, by conceptualizing the possibilities that time offers space (2013).

One means by which this is attempted is through the adoption of statistical and demographic procedures. Population trends, house-building records and economic forecasts circulate in a hierarchical flow from central government to local government and then back to central government, in an example of what Rose and Miller call the state's own system (1990). Until 2013, the system worked by first gathering information locally, aggregated to a centralized planning level, then disaggregated down again to distribute the additional capacity required. There are 'statutory consultees' at each step of the planning process, including service providers, national interest groups and NGOs, including RSPB (Royal Society for the Protection of Birds: a major UK landowner), TCPA (Town and Country Planning Association), CLA (Country Landowners Association), HBF (House Builders Federation), utilities, health services, education services, Friends of the Earth, National Trust, etc. (Murdoch and Abram 2002).

Since 2013, when the English regional tier of government was abolished, each district has to produce a Local Plan with a fifteen-year horizon, taking account of 'longer-term requirements' and being kept up to date. Each local authority has to prepare a 'Strategic Housing Market Assessment' (note the introduction of markets), to identify the likely need for housing in their area to meet demographic projections. They must also prepare a 'Strategic Housing Land Availability Assessment,' ostensibly to identify land that could satisfy the identified market demand for different scales and mixes of housing (DCLG 2012). While apparently delegating planning to the most local level, in fact these local plans must now be in accordance with a series of national plans for major infrastructure, housing, gypsy sites, waste management, and so forth.

This is all well and good in theory, but what does it mean in practice? In a series of publications throughout the late 1990s and early 2000s, Jonathan Murdoch and I outlined the workings of this system in practice, and in 1997, I spent six months doing fieldwork on a local plan in Aylesbury Vale to examine the process of local planning 'on the ground'. We used a combination of methods, including analysing the planning texts and reviewing all of the objections made to the proposed plans, taking guided tours of the districts with different people, in-depth interviews with a cross-section of these objectors (from citizens to landowners and statutory authorities) and with officials, attendance at public examinations of the policies, council meetings, protest actions, and participant observation in one designated development site over six months. Taking the plan as the focus of the ethnographic enquiry, rather than a particular location, our research was more non-sited rather than multi-sited (Abram 2001a), although we also pursued a kind of nested geographical focusing. So while our research activities took us all over the southeast of England, we focused in first on the county of Buckinghamshire (north west of London), within that the district of Aylesbury Vale, and within that, the settlement of Haddenham. By 'following the plan' and its various policies, we were able to use principles from ANT to trace the links and relations between actors and actants, and to use ethnographic methods to dig below the policies and institutions and understand how each element was interpreted by the actors involved. Since planning disputes are often about the broader implications of policy and the significance for different participants of the plans proposed (including elements of landscape-nationalism), each party often adopts stereotyping language about their opponents. To get beyond the performative conflictual language of 'nimbyism' or 'selfish capitalists', and the manipulative PR strategies of the professional participants, we needed to understand the human actors are rounded social beings. In-depth extensive ethnographic methods were the means to achieve these aims.

It was swiftly clear that little of the planning perspective from the district council planning office was shared by local residents, while house builders approached the planning system through game-playing with the ultimate and over-riding concern of maximizing profit and 'shareholder value'. Much of the debate around the plan concerned housing numbers (see Abram 2001b). In the large village where I did most of my participant-observation, many residents recognized that houses in the village were far too expensive for young or lower-earning people, but that additional housing numbers identified in the plan would not ensure that smaller, cheaper housing would be constructed. The village's history is documented back to Saxon times; it was a key location in the English civil war, and one of the first English villages

FIGURE 5.2 *The village idealized from the inside. Photos by Simone Abram.*

to buy itself out of servitude to the church. A village of land-owning farmers (or 'yeomen'), it had held an annual market for centuries, and had declined only during the general urbanization of the twentieth century, particularly post-World War II. A new estate of 400 houses built in the 1970s in a village of then around 2,000 people had been a great upheaval, and villagers described how it had taken many years before the 'old' village had adapted to the new arrivals. Expanding village activities and traditions to accommodate new residents was demanding and was felt to have endangered village social life for some time. Continued expansion changed the nature of the village, from an intensely social location to a commuter dormitory. Escalating prices also meant that 'our children' were forced to move away, a doubly difficult problem for low-earning young families who were forced to move away from the free childcare and support that grandparents provide. Most villagers were keen that smaller and cheaper homes should be made available for village families, but as illustrated above, this is not catered for in the planning system. So, while villagers would say that they welcomed affordable homes, they could not see any justification for more highly priced 'executive housing', and objected most strongly to the proposed plans.

At the same time, villagers had concerns about broader social and environmental issues, relating to the capacity of village services to accommodate a growing population (a medical centre, library, two primary schools), the potential increase in car traffic and associated pollution (including noise pollution and road danger to children), loss of landscape, including views from existing buildings, and so forth. The future vision of villagers was thus heavily influenced by the idiom of village life, the risk of overwhelming the social relations imagined as a small rural community, and the generalized issue of 'over-development' and loss of biodiversity, alongside inter-generational justice. Some villagers were also concerned that the value of their property might diminish if the village became a town, which could make it difficult to move elsewhere, to some other village more fitting to their ideal of village life if the current one were to be 'ruined' through 'excessive development'. Groups of villagers met in each others' comfortable living rooms to plan demonstrations outside planning meetings; actions to raise money to employ barristers to fight their case against the plans; and general village awareness-raising. On another day, one might meet them helping out at a coffee morning for elderly people, at Morris-dancing training sessions in preparation for Mayday, or practicing handbell-ringing for the village fête. This description does not do justice to the variety and distinctions of village life, of course. There were also newer residents who campaigned to stop lorries visiting the poultry farm in the middle of the village (much to the farmer's distress); a distinctive working-class community within the village; a generation of professionals who had downsized in the 1970s; a range of Christian fellowships and churches (Anglican, Methodist, Unitarian); as well as various commercial organizations, including the national headquarters of a charity founded in the village, manufacturing and other business. Even so, during the 1990s, the village had lost its local bank branches, most of its shops and several pubs, although quite a few remained. Many villagers I interviewed, however, described their 'discovery' of the village through the approach to the church and village green, and seeing the vision of the idyllic English village, 'knew' that they would move here and perpetuate that ideal.

In contrast, the future-vision of the planners, shared at least partly by members of the planning committees at regional and to some extent local level centred on the question of where to house future generations. These imagined future generations were not imagined as kin or offspring of current actual residents, but as a general demographic proportion of the national

Haddenham Inset

FIGURE 5.3 *The village seen in planning documents (Aylesbury Vale District Local Plan Proposals Map 2004)*

future population who deserved good housing as well as anyone. Their future vision was also framed around an environmental concern with climate change and a need to reduce pollution and energy consumption. This concern was channelled through criteria-based evaluations such as national policies on ideal features of sustainable settlements, including the magical 10,000 population figure of government guidance, and the possibility of reducing people's 'need to travel' by providing housing and employment sites in the same settlement, and expanding those settlements with connections to public transport.

For the planning authorities, this history of increased housing – the building of several large housing estates around the original village – became not a reason for some other village to take its turn to increase its housing stock, but a trend that justified further expansion. In DCLG's terms, sustainable housing should be located where there was access to work and transport, and a population of 10,000 was considered sufficient to justify investment in public transport infrastructure. Based on its proximity to railway connections (a commuter service taking around an hour to London) and the presence of manufacturing industry (paper products, garden equipment and later spice processing – see Abram 2004), the village was identified even at the regional level as a likely location for further housing development that would be considered 'sustainable'. In other words, from the planners' perspective this village could expand 'sustainably'.

Amongst these diverse formulations of the future, planning arguments about the appropriate number of new houses, derived from the rather arcane and abstract statistical techniques of the ministry were perceived as an extremely blunt instrument, but dominated (and continue to dominate) both planning and media discussions about housing. Debates in the media about housing in Britain, or at least in England, revolve around all sorts of arguments about a shortage of housing. But as Danny Dorling has pointed out, there are more than enough dwellings in all English cities to accommodate the people who require housing. The so-called housing shortage in the UK is more accurately understood as a problem of unequal access to housing finance and relates to the location of available housing. Through the forum of their Federation, house builders adopted an approach of discussing construction numbers, and have largely co-opted government departments into thinking in terms of annual housing completions as the key measure for housing policy evaluation. By comparing household formation and housing construction, government and lobbyists succeeded in reducing land-use planning to more or less the allocation of housing construction figures and business land availability. They became a system for producing profitable planning permissions. Even governments convulsed by housing numbers have retained a system of housing numbers, despite apparently seeking to delegate housing decisions to local councils. One reason it works so well is that resistance is nicely

FIGURE 5.4 *Village houses. Photos by Simone Abram.*

contained and directed towards local disputes, which can be characterized as petty or self-interested, while numbers are attributed with a sense of disinterested detachment, remaining mostly unassailable above the fray. Housing numbers are not invincible, and arguments over allocations of numbers are routinely held in the relatively rarefied context of regional inter-authority negotiations. What is of interest here is the contrast between the lively, localized and relational visions of the future discussed among tenants, villagers, urban residents or other social groups, and the narrow bureaucratic cipher of housing numbers as future-orientation.

This discussion about housing futures illustrates important aspects of forward planning. Forward planning is like consulting oracles in that it is less about desired and feared future than about commenting on the world as it is today, and how we would prefer that it was. It is unlike consulting oracles in the manner of its practice, being embedded in statistical methodologies, demography and cartography, the inaccuracies of the data quietly under-stated. Increased attempts to involve citizens in planning debates since the 1990s have stumbled at exactly this point, since house builders urging the need for new housing have been largely out of step with local concerns about how the world should be. While house builders and government have been obsessing over housing numbers – just as James Scott indicates – local actors have systematically understood that local decisions are largely predetermined in a hierarchical system. As they learned in practice, objections to a local plan weighed little when the identification of a location for housing had been already secured in a regional plan. To challenge the local decision, they must have challenged the regional decision and been involved in making objections and representations to the regional planning enquiry for the strategic plan. And so on up the system and down again. In other words, to challenge a local plan effectively, you must have already been engaged in challenging plans for around five years at least, to secure the conditions for your local challenge to be successful. In other words, you require a vision of future potential plans many years in advance if you are to be in a position to amend plans for local futures.[2]

What is planning about?

Futures in planning practice take varied forms. Visions of the future becomes figures around which to articulate hopes and fears for collective life, for ideals about nature and culture, about spiritual beliefs and moral standpoints. In the village mentioned above, a great deal of energy was expended by villagers on the reconstruction of the village pond, complete with pumps and water filters, to ensure that it matched the chocolate-box image that made it such an ideal location for filming popular TV series, and gave the village the veneer of being 'archaic' and timeless. The village green was constantly in the process of being perfected to match an idealized image of Englishness that it had probably never previously inhabited. This archaic timelessness was thus the object of future concern, a concern that the future should maintain continuity, that the village should, if anything, be allowed to fulfil the romantic ideal of the English village, while accommodating wealthy commuter demands for luxury living and ease of transport. The future, just as the present, thus encompassed the juxtaposition of contradictory desires and fantasies. Planning futures need to remain sufficiently distant in the future or distant enough in space so as to pose as little threat as possible to the imagined sociable tranquillity of village life.

State or investor-led planning proposals thus emerged into the village as threats to an ongoing project of creating a certain kind of English middle-class home, with the inclusion of housing for subsequent generations of village families. At least for some, that future should include the possibility of sharing current goods with future generations of kin. At the same time, a consistent criticism of planning futures is that they are inadequately informed by the past. Villagers who were not familiar with planning process were aghast at the lack of prior research before proposals were circulated. No concept of the vernacular history of the village was present in the plan's policies, with the village's entire, contested, radical and archaic history obscured by projected trends in house-building completions. As mentioned above, while villagers saw the previous housing expansions as a trial they had survived, planners saw them as a precedent (an argument that was rehearsed throughout the planning process). From the village perspective, planning's future had no history, invalidating its imagination of the future. So now the future of planning looks rather different: less an open debate about future ideals – be they utopian (ambivalent) or rationalistic – and more a battle over the here and now, and between different continuities. Through proposed plans, a distant and potentially disruptive future came crashing into the lives of villagers, dedicated as so many of them were, to the continuity of the present.

What does anthropology tell us about planning?

Anthropological analysis of the future offers a means to disaggregate the ways that the future is of concern to different people at different times, in different ways, and enables us to see how particular futures may become dominant for shorter or longer moments, or how particular futures appeal in certain contexts. In much the same way that anthropology of history was less concerned with 'what happened in the past' than how histories were discussed, interpreted and reproduced in the present, Wallman's 1992 volume distinguished between writing about how things would be in the future, and considering visions of the future today. She noted different kinds of futures that featured in traditional ethnographies – futures related to specific activities or points in time (harvest, initiation, ceremonies or desired arrivals, such as cargo) but little discussion of future in the abstract. Wallman herself wondered whether the absence of discussion of the future in anthropological research demonstrate an absence of the concept in non-industrial cultures, in which case it might not be a concept with comparative force, or whether these ethnographers did not ask informants about non-specific future time? (Wallman 1992: 3).

Rosenberg and Harding (2005) are among those who point out that the supposedly linear futures of the West have never been exclusive, even in that most Western of societies, the USA. Unilinear progress towards an abstract future exists in parallel to the event-focused and circular or ritual futures that Wallman outlines. The future, rather like the past, appears in different guises (cf. Zonabend 1984). The future has different scales – natural, global, social or personal – that are not congruent, and just as in the non-Western societies of an earlier Anthropology, modern people imagine futures associated with ritual or ceremonial cycles (Christmas is always coming), futures in our own biochronology, and varied as well as conflicting visions of futures predicted or desired. We are now well aware that people can hold multiple senses of temporality, just as there are different scales and senses of the past, so it follows that we can hold multiple futures. Planned futures are similarly scaled and contested, filled with competing notions of idealism and pragmatism. As Rosenberg and Harding insist, the future in the modern West 'is not the empty category that it is supposed to be' (2005: 8). On the contrary, they argue that the conflict of futures past and present is central to modern temporality, and that this is a paradox of modern dispositions toward the future: 'while we are taught to believe in the emptiness of the future, we live in a world saturated by future-consciousness as rich and full as our consciousness of the past' (p. 9). What fascinates Rosenberg and Harding about the future is its infinite potential, as it opens up to a myriad possibilities, in contrast to a past that is finite: finished, closed and determined.[3] If the modern period rejected prophecy, it welcomed new techniques of foreseeing the future, projecting fictions and fantasies onto open-ended time. One means of imagining these futures was by fixating on future-dates, dates that were destined eventually to become the past, but remained far enough ahead to allow for wildly fictive visions of personal flying machines, or technological totalitarianism.

These futures veer between the fantastic and the threatening, both of which can be equally realizable or unimaginable. While town planning is conventionally oriented to a time-horizon that is rarely more than generational, modern industrial society's material impacts will be felt for multi-generational timespans. The lack of fit between the management techniques of contemporary states and the problems to be managed offers a striking insight into the limitations of states and their bureaucracies.

The limitations of conventional planning are clear in Masco's discussion of Desert Modernism, which considers a future threat that is both real, concealed, and continuous, as well as self-perpetuating: the on-going future danger scenario that is nuclear waste storage in Nevada (2005). Here, confident political promises about safe 10,000-year storage facilities are belied by on-site engineers' discussions of the difficulty of securing 100 years of safe storage in a site that is subject to geological faults and variable rock types. Whether or not the storage is technically secure for 100, 1,000 or 10,000 years, what kind of state is it, Masco asks, that a 10,000-year storage facility could envisage? Can we imagine a nation-state that lasts for ten thousand years, or even a hundred thousand years?[4] A narrative of 'absolute technical mastery and control of nature' (p. 36) gives legitimacy to the state's attempts to manage nuclear waste, but has little techno-scientific basis. There are thus two rather different narratives of the future, one envisioning an eternal nation-state that will manage radioactive waste over thousands of years, and one in which the technology of storage might be guaranteed for a hundred years, but after which a new technology must be sought to solve the ongoing problem. Both narratives could be thought of as modern in different ways, but the contradiction between political visions of a techno-state and the reality of the state of technology are smoothed over by naïve beliefs in technological futures that will secure not only material, but also political continuity.

Conclusions

The future is not going away. On the contrary, anthropologists are becoming increasingly focused on understanding how imagining the future, planning for the future, and acting on the future can tell us about life today. As this analysis of the way that futures are manifested in planning demonstrates, there are many kinds of future – abstract or fantasy, concrete or eventful, domestic or familial, public or political and so on. There are as many ways, if not more, of negotiating this future, of seeking to secure the passage from now to then, of securing action today that ensures desired futures or avoids undesired futures. And exhortations about possible futures can act as signposts for contemporary action, as well as to legitimize current choices.

A central paradox of statutory planning in Britain is that it often appears not to accomplish this action of envisioning a desired future and facilitating the move towards it. On the contrary, it appears to be a means to perpetuate existing capitalist relations of investment and return, to stabilize property values and protect the interests of financial investors and commercial actors.[5] Yet participants in planning processes understand that such plans will hinder or facilitate their preferred future from coming into being. During the planning process, multiple futures co-exist, as Wallman and Rosenberg and Harding also note.

These contested futures far from the kinds of imaginative future that fuels the hope that has captivated some anthropologists (Crapanzano 2004; Miyazaki 2004; Josephides 2014), although its corollary, despair, is never far away. Such work begs the question of how we can account for the work of imagination that the future demands. Josephides argues that the sense of possibility in hopes about the future are existential, with hope oriented towards a future that is different from the past, and anthropological interest being in the ways in which people desire that future and act on their desires. In other words, to hope is to imagine a future, while to imagine is to think in the present, whether that is about the future or the past. To imagine is thus existential in that it is an act of being human and eliciting meaning. Imagining the future can thus be conceptualized as a way of thinking out what it is to be oneself, by expanding one's horizon beyond oneself. Planning futures, on the other hand, are supposed not to be about the self, but must be about the grounded and socio-political imagination of the progression from now to a bounded reality to come, yet its means of imagination corresponds to Josephides' existential practice. It is worth noting that such existential imagination is also neither linear nor consistent: changes can be traced in the concepts of future that emerge in planning over time. In the Norwegian context, for example, Vike finds striking changes in the character of the future since World War II (2013). In the post-war period, the welfare state was a future object, for which sacrifices could be made now in the journey towards a utopian future. But in the current welfare state, citizens expect satisfaction now – the welfare state is understood to be in a contemporary future, in which its imperfections are understood as fatal flaws in the present, not obstacles on the way to an ideal future.

If thinking about the future – or imagining a future – is a means of thinking through existence, then Guyer's critique of the changing horizon of the future can be understood as a broad critique of contemporary life. Guyer describes an unease with contemporary present in what she calls 'a strange evacuation of the temporal frame of the "near future" ... of the process of implicating oneself in the ongoing life of the social and material world that used to be encompassed under an expansively inclusive concept of "reasoning"' (2007:

409). Her argument is directed towards changing economic policy, and in particular the combination in monetarist and neo-liberal economics of a prophetic vision of a distant future in which market values work themselves out to perfection, with an immediate future of action in which money supply is regulated in order to achieve that distant goal of prices determined by supply and demand. For Guyer, this long-term (the long-term in which Keynes noted that 'we are all dead') has a parallel in messianic prophecy of evangelical Christianity. Life is divided between the present and the end-times; the present as a hiatus between two eternities, thus removing history and reason and evacuating the space of medium-term action. Her concept of temporal horizons is particularly useful in contrasting the scales of future that are argued through planning, with its immediate, near, medium and distant timescales.

In summarizing where the analysis of planning futures takes us, we may usefully add to the list of statements that Wallman compiled, which offer a valuable starting point for conceptualizing the significance of the future in contemporary rhetoric and practice:[6]

- That the future can be used to justify present action – a forward-looking version of mythical charter.
- Scenarios of the future function to illuminate the present and/or to offer at-a-distance and so politically (and emotionally?) safe ways of criticising it.
- Belief in the future underpins the sense of self and its survival.
- Changes in those beliefs, however generated, can work radically to alter the way individuals and groups relate to each other, to the natural environment, and to culture itself. (Wallman 1992: 16)

To these we might add that the future can be put to work in the service of a promise, in the context of a correct set of ritual and social circumstances such that the future does not merely hold out promise, but is implicated in the act of promising. Such promises may be politically effective or infelicitous. We do not necessarily know that the promise is infelicitous until the promised outcome is not fulfilled, by which time the promise may have served its purpose.

One further capacity that the future has is thus to defer dilemmas that are irreconcilable, to structure difficulties and to respond to dissonance. We know that our lives today are initiating consequences that can be catastrophic in the future. We know that driving cars or burning gas contributes to climate change, yet for most people it is impossible to continue with their established life without these things happening. The collective – and certainly the political – response, not surprisingly, is to shunt them forward, to make promises about how we may act in the future; promises that may or may not be infelicitous, or more or less convincing.

State planning is also imagined as a mechanism to compensate for the inability of citizens otherwise to address large, overarching or structural challenges of the kind generated by state modernism itself (hence the resort to idealized settlement sizes for sustainability). The archetypal Western Modernist abstract notion of 'The Future' is dependent on a unilinear view of time and optimism, with an underlying sense of progression toward something better. Enlightenment visions of progress required an optimistic future to counter a puritan day of doom in which earth and humanity would inevitably be destroyed. Ironically, astronomy tells us that this will come, but given that the timescale of its coming is on such a different plane to our own sense of lifetime and time passing, it remains possible to remove it in some way from everyday consciousness (cf. Guyer 2007). It is another form of the death that we all know is coming, that is part of life, and that largely fails to dampen human enthusiasm for that life. The future offers life *and* death, and this is one of its paradoxes: not resolved but suspended because of the incompatibility of the ideas and the uncertainty of their timings. As Guyer has pointed out, the horizons of the future are shifting, but they still provide a guide to the present through the imaginative work of linking different futures with present possibilities and moral imperatives. This chapter has thus considered the fantasy of planned futures that enable a life in the present.

Notes

1 The European Commission has long employed a persistent tactic of public awareness-raising by insisting that its emblem be displayed on any development project in receipt of European Union funding.

2 The same effectively applies to political engagement, since alliances and compromises over local planning decisions happen within the council over a long period, and each local politician is in a minority position in relation to specific housing locations.

3 Rosenberg and Harding consider the Y2K bug as a contemporary reproduction of apocalyptic dread, one that, of course, was a huge anti-climax.

4 See http://www.intoeternitythemovie.com/ (accessed 20 October 2016) on the Finnish 100,000 year repository for nuclear waste. See also Salazar, J. F. (2015) analysis of this film as a case of futuring in documentary film.

5 In contrast to Scandinavian plans, with their glowing slogans about idealized common social futures, British plans offer little to the casual reader.

6 Within Wallman's collection there are essays that challenge the very deterministic notion of future that is implicit in the statements, such as the

framing of 'the natural environment'. In countering accusations that Inuit are accused of not being 'future-oriented', Jean Briggs emphasized the investment in equipping children to become competent adults, in contrast to the rejection of material accumulation that is sometimes seen by colonial critics as an inability to think ahead. On the contrary, the nomadic life requires a shrewd form of investment in adaptable objects that remove the need for accumulated objects, and the long-term is practiced in the sustaining of relations over time (Briggs 1992).

References

Abram, S., 2001a. 'Amongst Professionals: Working with Pressure Groups and Local Authorities'. In D. Gellner and E. Hirsch (eds), *Inside Organisations: Anthropologists at Work*, 183–203. Oxford: Berg.

Abram, S., 2001b. 'All that Fuss Over 100 Houses: Identities and Moralities of Building on Land'. In M. Saltman (ed.), *Identity, Ethnicity and Territoriality*, 71–92. Oxford: Berg.

Abram, S., 2011. *Culture and Planning*. Aldershot: Ashgate.

Abram, S. and G. Weszkalnys, 2013a. 'Elusive Promises: Planning in the Contemporary World: An Introduction'. In S. Abram and G. Weszkalnys (eds), *Elusive Promises: Planning in the Contemporary World*, 1–33. Oxford: Berghahn.

Abram, S. and G. Weszkalnys (eds), 2013b. *Elusive Promises: Planning in the Contemporary World*. Oxford: Berg.

Atiyah, P. S., 1981. *Promises, Morals, and Law*. Oxford: Oxford University Press.

Austin, J. L., 1962. *How to do Things with Words*. Oxford: Oxford University Press.

Baxstrom, R., 2013. 'Even Governmentality Begins as an Image. Institutional Planning in Kuala Lumpur'. In S. Abram and G. Weszkalnys (eds), *Elusive Promises: Planning in the Contemporary World*, 137–53. Oxford: Berg.

Bear, L., 2014. 'Doubt, Conflict, Mediation: The anthropology of modern time'. *Journal of the Royal Anthropological Institute*, Special Issue 20 (S1).

Briggs J. L., 1992. 'Lines, Cycles and Transformations: Temporal Perspectives on Inuit Action'. In S. Wallman, *Contemporary Futures. Perspectives from Social Anthropology*, 83–108. London and New York: Routledge.

Crapanzano, V., 2004. *Imaginative Horizons*. Chicago: Chicago University Press.

Department for Communities and Local Government (DCLG), 2012. *National Planning Policy Framework March 2012* (ISBN: 978-1-4098-3413-7).

Dorling, D., 2015. *All that is Solid: How the Great Housing Disaster Defines Our Times, and What We Can Do About It*. Harmondsworth: Penguin.

Guyer, J., 2007. 'Prophecy and the near future: Thoughts on macroeconomic, evangelical, and punctuated time'. *American Ethnologist* 34 (3) 409–21.

Josephides, L., 2014. 'Imagining the Future: An Existential and Practical Activity'. In W. Rollason (ed.), *Pacific Futures: Projects, Politics and Interests*, 28–47. Oxford: Berg.

Masco, Joseph, 2005. 'A Notebook on Desert Modernism: From the Nevada Test site to Liberace's Two-hundred-pound Suit'. In D. Rosenberg and S. Harding (eds), *Histories of the Future*, 23–49. Durham and London: Duke University Press.

Miller, P. and N. Rose, 1990. 'Governing Economic Life'. *Economy and Society* 19: 1–31.

Miyazaki, H., 2004. *The Method of Hope*. Stanford: Stanford University Press.

Murdoch, J. and S. Abram, 2002. *Rationalities of Planning*. Aldershot: Ashgate.

Nader, Laura, 1972. 'Up the Anthropologist – Perspectives Gained from Studying Up'. In D. H. Hymes (ed.), *Reinventing Anthropology*, 284–311. New York: Pantheon Books.

Peattie, L. R., 1970. *The View from the Barrio*. Ann Arbor: University of Michigan Press.

Peattie, L. R., 1987. *Planning: Rethinking Ciudad Guayana*. Ann Arbor: University of Michigan Press.

Pink, S. and T. Lewis, 2014. 'Making resilience: everyday affect and global affiliation in Australian Slow Cities'. *Cultural Geographies* 21 (4): 695–710.

Porter, L., 2010. *Unlearning the Colonial Cultures of Planning*. Aldershot: Ashgate.

Reade, E., 1987. *British Town and Country Planning*. Milton Keynes: Open University Press.

Rosenberg, D. and S. Harding, 2005. *Histories of the Future*. Durham and London: Duke University Press.

Salazar, J. F., 2015. *Science/Fiction: Documentary Film and Anticipatory Modes of Futuring Planetary Change. In Companion to Contemporary Documentary Studies*. A. Lebow and A. Juhasz (eds), 43–60. Malden, MA and Oxford: Wiley-Blackwel

Scott, J. C., 1998. *Seeing like a State: How Certain Schemes to Improve the Human Condition have Failed*. New Haven: Yale University Press.

Searle, J. R., 1969. *Speech Acts: An Essay in the Philosophy of Language*. Cambridge: Cambridge University Press.

Vike, H., 2013. 'Utopian Time and Contemporary Time: Temporal Dimensions of Planning and Reform in the Norwegian Welfare State'. In S. Abram and G. Weszkalnys (eds), *Elusive Promises: Planning in the Contemporary World*, 35–55. Oxford: Berg.

Wallman, Sandra, 1992. *Contemporary Futures. Perspectives from Social Anthropology*. ASA Monographs 30. London and New York: Routledge.

Zonabend, F., 1984. *The Enduring Memory: Time and History in a French Village*. Manchester: Manchester University Press.

6

Pyrenean rewilding and ontological landscapes: A future(s) dwelt-in ethnographic approach

Tony Knight

Anthropology and the future shadow of potential catastrophe

Human civilization expanded and flourished during the Holocene, the clement period beginning 11,700 years ago following the Late Glacial Maximum. This period has now ended (Waters et al. 2016); many scientists believe that we are in a new geological age, the Anthropocene, in which human activities rival 'the great forces of Nature' (Steffen et al. 2007: 614). Indeed, our impacts on the biogeochemistry of the oceans, rivers, topsoil, and atmosphere, are causing global climate change (ibid.) and the sixth mass extinction (McCallum 2015): the Earth is entering a 'planetary terra incognita' (Steffen et al. 2007: 614). The hegemonic socio-political systems and their immanent fossil-fuel-based agro-industrial processes that have driven this massive global change have created a geologically, biologically and socially turbulent present (Lewis and Maslin 2015). With its unevenly distributed Anthropogenic causes and influences at the global level and dramatically diverse local implications, the anthropocene is characterized by a deep sense of inequality, injustice and uncertainty. Frequently imagined in apocalyptic terms (Ginn 2015; Swyngedouw 2010), the Anthropocene clearly situates humans within the penumbra of a future shadow of potential catastrophe.

Indeed, given the degree of uncertainty surrounding the social, cultural and environmental fields of our ethnographic gaze, it is increasingly critical that anthropology ceases limiting itself to being a reflexive witness to the ethnographic present. Partnering with local field subjects and state institutions, we must co-embrace the future to help communities better understand and traverse the challenges of the Anthropocene. My objective in this chapter, then, is to develop an anthropological argument and approach to exploring 'future worlding' and 'dwelling in the future', to critically engage with these uncertain imbricated futures. Ulf Hannerz (2003: 174) similarly calls for anthropologists to publicly embrace what he calls the 'macro-scenarios' widely contemplated as (negatively) defining complex 'present and future worlds'; he suggests that we can use ethnography to 'give a human face – better yet, a number of human faces, and voices – to large-scale, too easily anonymous processes' (ibid.: 176).

I will draw on my fieldwork in the French Pyrenees, where I studied conflict between 'traditional' pastoralists and conservationists resulting from the reintroduction of bears and wolves, to demonstrate that an empirically and theoretically sound engagement with such macro-scenarios and their uncertain futures is quite realizable within our core ethnographic methodological framework. Indeed, Robert Textor (1995) has long propounded using targeted ethnographic questioning to elicit informants' views of their future(s). To minimize the pressure of direct questioning, my approach is less structured, so informants can project themselves informally into their future *worlding*, an ongoing, generative process imagining a future *being-in-the-world* (Heidegger 1962). Building on Heidegger's work, Ingold (1993) argued that people dwell-in the world, experiencing it synaesthetically and in an embodied manner: the landscape becomes a part of us and yet we are a part of it. By rejecting the nature-is-real / nature-is-constructed dualism, this 'dwelling perspective' becomes one

> according to which the landscape is constituted as an enduring record of – and testimony to – the lives and works of past generations who have dwelt within it, and in doing so have left something of themselves there. (Ingold 1993: 152)

My theoretical framework develops this *future(s) dwelt-in ethnographic approach*, using the point-of-view of *being* there with my informants, in their *dwelt-in* future reality, to contextualize different future local worlds situated within potential grander socio-geopolitical ecologies. As I explore this deceptively simplistic localized situation, I reveal that it can potentially be seen as a microcosm of the broader conflictual relationships between humans and nature that lie at the heart of the Anthropocene. This will show how

ethnographic research can help reinstall anthropology as an important facilitator in future policy-making and planning. Of course, given its epistemological
conditioning to focus on the ethnographic present with an implied causality in
historicity (Persoon and van Est 2000: 10), this might also represent an(other)
existential challenge for anthropology.

Nevertheless, we must acknowledge that futures have not been totally
ignored within anthropology, and this helps greatly in framing a theoretically
sound futures-centric methodology. Luminary Margaret Mead, for example,
was an anticipatory anthropologist, politically engaged in creating more
desirable future possibilities. As Mead (2005 [1977]: 329) understood them,
such futures were not 'pre-determined' or 'predictable', but 'open-ended ...
something that lies within our hands, to be shaped and molded (*sic*) by the
choices we make in the present time'. Thus the future should not be viewed
as something that somehow passively happens, for this clearly cannot be the
case; there is a plurality of possible futures, not one single 'future' extended
from the past through the present. Indeed, Rainer Maria Rilke mused in his
Letters to a Young Poet, 'the future is entering into us ... in order to transform
itself in us long before it happens' (1903: 30). The future, then, is a reality
shaped by the present while simultaneously *shaping* the present.

Indeed, anthropology's role in contemplating such future ontologies was
tentatively interrogated over a quarter of a century ago by the Association of
Social Anthropologists in its 1990 'Anthropology of the Future' conference.
Boissevain (1992: 78) was encouraged by his (unsuccessful) engagement
with the 'emerging present', acknowledging that he should have situated
his work within a more thorough historical understanding encompassing the
longue durée and not just the immediate past as he had done. Strathern
(1992: 185) argued that human-nature relationships were already being
challenged by rapidly changing technological progress that would give
humans increasing control over ordinarily 'natural' processes. Therefore, she
argued, anthropological ideas should intend to 'make a radical impression
on the future – provided ... some kind of continuous link can be maintained
with the present that will be its past' (ibid.: 176). Finally, Peter Harries-Jones
(1992: 157ff.) presciently argued that anthropologists should be more implicated in holistic biocultural ecosystems thinking combining present and
future imaginaries of the biosphere with local and global human cultural
systems. Thus if anthropologists were to participate meaningfully in discussions about ecological and cultural survival, then a future-visioning approach
was essential.

Nevertheless, despite these promising beginnings, Milton (1990: 22)
observed that the conference failed to 'make a coherent package'. Indeed,
anthropologists still rarely consider future imaginaries in their research
(Persoon and van Est 2000: 14). Yet, they increasingly consider their cultural

subjects within the context of their 'natural' environment and thus should be well qualified and situated to ethnographically ground futures research to evoke the hopes, fears, and other imaginaries of the peoples they study. As an environmental anthropologist working with conserving biocultural landscapes (Knight 2016), this seems self-evident to me; conservation is intrinsically future-oriented (Persoon and van Est 2000: 19). Conservationists (and many quantitative scientists) use lessons-learned from past initiatives to model future scenarios to predict the most likely outcomes based on the methods being considered. In effect, scientists are trying to constrain the range of possible futures within models of probability and preferability based on different ways of conducting the present (Adam 2006; Bell 2010).

Public anthropologists who wish to co-produce knowledge with their ethnographic communities (Pink and Abram 2015) in order to help make potentially better future worlds can draw on such scientific frameworks to develop more robust futures methodologies.

Pyrenean pastoralism

Pastoralism has been central to Pyrenean culture for millennia and is still important today, although facing unprecedented pressure from globalization, politically-conditioned European subsidies, and neoliberal requirements for lowest-cost and maximum productivity. Pastoralism is (simplistically) the traditional extensive grazing of herd animals. Pyrenean transhumant pastoralism is defined by the vertical translocation each summer of almost 600,000 sheep from the plains and low-mountain farms to the high mountain *estives* (pastures) at elevations between 1,500 and 3,000 metres. Small-scale farming exploitations typically own from sixty to 500 or so animals, and join forces to create *groupements pastoraux*, pastoral collectives, that employ seasonal shepherds responsible for maintaining the *estives* while caring for combined flocks of 800 to over 3,000 sheep.

My fieldwork was conducted in the Couserans, a small, topographically challenging territory in the southwest of the French department of Ariège in the Central Pyrenees. The approximately 35,000 hectares of Couserans *estives*, smaller and more fragmented than in the rest of the department, are notoriously treacherous due to their relief and loose, rocky surface (see Figure 6.1). About 15,000 sheep as well as a few thousand cattle and horses (about a third of the department's meat production) use the *estives*.

I chose the Couserans for my research, as it is 'ground zero' for the presence of reintroduced bears, and is now expecting the imminent arrival of wolves making their way naturally from the southern Alps. Extensive pastoral farming and large predators are a socially explosive combination, and

FIGURE 6.1 *Berestet* estive: *steep and rocky, but reasonably accessible. Photo by Tony Knight.*

in Europe, the two coexist nowhere without incurring unsupportable depredations (Kaczensky 1999: 68). Conflict between pastoralism and predator conservation in such areas is inevitable, and probably the best way to visualize this is through ethnography.

A winter walk in the Couserans

'Merde!' Nathalie[1] stopped suddenly, and jabbed her *bâton* into the hard ground sending a small stone flying over the edge of the path on which we were walking. The narrow trail rose steeply, cutting through the dense forest that towered like a wall above us, falling sharply away on our right. There was no protection barrier. Marie-Claire and I stopped and turned to face Nathalie; tears were forming in her eyes. 'Damned écolos [collective description for citizen environmentalists, conservationists, and ecologists],' she said quietly.

These were the first words spoken in the fifteen minutes since we had left the village of Cominac, some 900m up in the Couserans, still visible in the valley below us (see Figure 6.2). Despite it being early March, the weather was abnormally warm and it felt bizarre to be below the snow line; at this time of year, snowshoes were usually essential equipment.

In the bright mountain sunshine and the light westerly breeze, none of us wore coats; the two women accompanying me were dressed in jeans and *polaires* (simple fleece jackets). The only things that distinguished them from 'ordinary' hikers and tourists were their hands and faces, grained by years of working outdoors in the mountains, and their *bâtons*, not the standard-equipment tourists' telescopic aluminium hiking poles, but time-polished traditional wooden canes used by Pyrenean *bergers* (shepherds). This had been suggestive enough to provoke an interested reaction from some young people hovering next to the community bulletin board as we entered the village.

Two members of the group, women, wore identical t-shirts, emblazoned with the green, half-moon shaped logo of FERUS, enclosing the unmistakable silhouettes of a bear, a wolf, and a lynx. They were attaching a poster to the board inviting people to an upcoming discussion in Massat, a nearby village and haven for hippies, *baba-cools,* and other refugees from civilization. FERUS, from the Latin word for wild or savage, is a major predator conservation association in France. Quickly assessing the *bâtons* and faces of my companions, one of the FERUS militants asked if we might join the meeting to discuss the importance of pastoral-predator cohabitation for biodiversity and development, adding that the participation of *bergères* (shepherdesses) would be very welcome.

Marie-Claire fleetingly touched Nathalie's arm, imploring her not to engage, although my ethnographic self was quietly wishing for precisely such an engagement. I was not disappointed. 'You FERUS people are always so presumptuous!' Nathalie's voice was sharp, angry.

> I sell my cheese at local markets, and when you see me there, it's always the same. You see an organic-dairy shepherdess and just assume that I must be *pro-ours* [pro-bear] and ask me to take your flyers to give to my customers. Well, I'm not. I've nothing against bears, and I tell your colleagues that. Our bears – our Pyrenean bears – died out decades ago. I don't transhume my cattle, so I don't risk any predation, but I can't support this reintroduction of bears, or God forbid, wolves, in our mountains. They don't belong here. I support my fellow *éleveurs* (livestock farmers) ... not the bears. If we have to live with large predators, we'll be forced to abandon the *estives*, perhaps permanently abandon pastoralism. I, I ... (Field notes, 03/2014)

Marie-Claire jumped in, to help out her friend:

> The mountains can survive without the bear. Ariège can survive. But without the *éleveurs* and their *brebis* [ewes or sheep] and *vaches* [cows], it would be catastrophic. Just look at this [gesturing with her arm at the mountain vista beyond the village]. It's beautiful. The *estives*; the forests;

FIGURE 6.2 *View from Cominac. The high* estives *are still covered with snow. Photo by Tony Knight.*

the peaks … It's just so … It makes you want to be here. That's what people come to the Pyrenees for. Not bears or wolves. Not wilderness. Without pastoralism, these mountains will become totally overrun. And that wouldn't be good for biodiversity, it would be terrible! Who'd want to visit a mountain where all that beautiful verdure [pointing with her arm] is gone, *réensauvagé* [rewilded] by thorns and brush; where all the *sentiers* (mountain paths created by pasturing sheep) are impassable? (Field notes, 03/2014).

Friction: An ecomodernist divide

The above ethnographic vignette reveals many ecological and social issues that cloud large predator conservation in the Pyrenees, particularly the core disagreements between the *pro-* and *anti-ours* groups. The *pro-ours écolos* believe they have a moral and legal duty to reintroduce brown bears in order to restore some 'balance' to local ecosystems, without which, making a viable future world becomes an undesirable probability. This forms part of a broader argument to combat the sixth mass extinction of life on the Earth, which is claimed to be occurring many thousands of times faster than during the Cretaceous terminal extinction, 65 million years ago (McCallum 2015: 2498). Humanity is the metaphorical asteroid for this sixth mass extinction and, therefore, we must urgently intensify our efforts to reverse the loss of biodiversity which otherwise will be catastrophic for human survival (Ceballos et al. 2015: 4).

The *écolos* argue that pastoralists and predators have 'always' coexisted in the Pyrenees, and they imagine a future in which continued cohabitation will be beneficial for biodiversity while creating opportunities for development income based on ecotourism's desires to spend time in an idealized 'pristine' nature.

The brown bear (*Ursus arctos*) and the wolf (*Canis lupus*) are keynote species, nonhuman 'spokespersons' for biodiversity whose state of wellbeing indicates the current and future resilience of the broader ecosystem. By the end of the nineteenth century, wolves were extinct in the French Pyrenees, and bears numbered fewer than 150; the ecosystem was not doing well. Indeed, by the 1980s, fewer than twenty bears remained.

Following the 1984 Bern Convention and the 1992 Rio Convention on Biological Diversity, France reintroduced three Slovenian brown bears in the Western Pyrenees during 1996/97 and five more in 2006. Such rewilding imagines apex predators as nonhuman engineers who will (re)engineer the present ecosystem to resemble an implicit 'wilder' past state, to enable a preferred future 'wild' ecology adapted to the uncertainties of the Anthropocene. Such ecologies predict 'better' ecosystem services and more resilient biodiversity; reintroducing top predators creates a trophic cascade where effects trickle down through lower trophic levels. For example, reintroduced wolves in Yellowstone National Park reduced elk numbers and dramatically improved damaged riparian ecosystems (Beschta and Ripple 2009).

The *écolos* are guided by such 'rational' conservation science, but also by much harder to define emotions; they frequently perceive bears and wolves as among the most iconic symbols of 'wild' and wilderness, animals who perfectly define their culturally constructed authenticity of this preferred future landscape. There are, however, important epistemological differences between the various *écolos*. Ecologists and conservationists are working together scientifically to understand the past and present ecosystem, and the multiple species upon which it is depends. Conservationists, though, have a specific additional agenda to *conserve* certain of these species for future posterity. Thus, in the present, they are worldmaking with a view to improving the chances of these species' future survival; in the case of the brown bears, they determined that a planned reintroduction was necessary. In doing so, they are following a Weberian logic of science, which, as Adam (2005) notes, 'is grounded in a mode of enquiry that was established for objects in motion'. In this way, these scientists can define a probable outcome for their project based on a causal chain whose goal is to minimize any divergence from their desired objectives as the chain moves forward. The resulting worldmaking will inevitably overlap or be different than those of other actors.

Citizen environmentalists, such as the group we met in Cominac, make up the most publicly vocal segment of the *écolos*, and their ways of thinking are often quite different. They emotionally insert themselves into a preferred, imagined future-present and see a world that meets their own ideals. They then look backwards in time to visualize what the past-present would look like in order for the future-present to be realized. In this way, they are using a reversed causality, a 'teleological explanation' (Adam 2011: 10), commencing in this imagined future that affects their actual present.

For precisely this reasoning, the environmentalist *écolos* see themselves as agents of change; they have taken ownership of their imagined future. It should be no surprise, then, that they have also totally embraced 'natural' rewilding. In 1992, *Canis lupus italicus* travelled from northern Italy to the southern French Alps; today, there are around 300 wolves in France, mostly throughout the southeast. The wolves' success is largely due to anthropogenic interventions, specifically the initial concealment of their presence and their protected-species status. Italian wolves first arrived in the Pyrenees in 1999, but today, there are still only a few 'lone' wolves in the massif; they have been unable to form a reproductive pack. This ecologically improbable situation is most likely due to illegal 'precautionary' poaching by hunters (field notes, 2013/14). Nevertheless, it is only a matter of time before wolves repopulate the Pyrenees as they have the southern Alps.

However, the future ontological wild ecology chosen by the environmentalists imagines a very specific role for pastoralists: either they will have continued to cohabit 'harmoniously' with wild nature (as implied by the FERUS militant's comment on the benefit of pastoral-predator cohabitation), or they will have ceased to exist. Such a dichotomous pre-condition is unfortunately reinforced by the scientific and political discourse which holds that Pyrenean pastoralists have 'always' cohabited with large predators (MEDD 2006: 31), a meme frequently reiterated by environmental militants. Again, then, the future-cause can be traced back to its historical effect, in this case, throughout the *longue durée*.

Another present implication of this *écolo* future worlding, is that pastoralism-predator cohabitation is actually feasible. The argument is that fewer than 150 of the 600,000 sheep that use the *estives*, less than 0.025 per cent, are killed by predators each year. Furthermore, these 'negligible' predations could 'easily' be reduced if the *bergers* were to 'do their jobs properly. You know, like, actually work, and protect their sheep. Enclose them in pens at night. Use patous [livestock guardian dogs (LGD)]' (field notes, Joelle, 06/2014). Immanent in this argument is that present and future pastoralists should conduct their work as they used to in the past, when flocks were indeed guarded at all times by shepherds and LGDs, and penned overnight. Multi-generational pastoralists accept this history, but refute its usefulness for the present because their practices have changed dramatically over the last few centuries, in particular, shifting production from dairy to meat. Dairy farming demanded much smaller flocks enclosed at night so the shepherds could milk the animals. However, this practice disappeared several generations ago, as there was no longer any such need for sheep being raised for meat.

Pastoralists also deride the environmentalists' statistics while proclaiming adamantly that no predations are ever acceptable. Today, reflecting Nathalie's claim that the original Pyrenean brown bear is extinct, the thirty bears who still survive in the Pyrenees are from the reintroduced Slovenian stock, a different sub-species. These bears are not trans-Pyrenean, but spend most of their time in the Couserans. A truer rate of predation calculated against 15,000 sheep, is 1 per cent (forty times greater). Furthermore, the predations mostly occur in just five *estives*, and individual *éleveurs* frequently lose 10 per cent or more of their flock in a single bear attack, when sheep panic on loose scree and fall to their deaths. As Nathalie implored, for most *éleveurs*, predators and predations are simply unsupportable, and have no place in the Pyrenees. Her comment that a forced cohabitation will cause pastoralism to be abandoned visualizes a probable, but undesirable future, in which the number of bears will be exponentially greater than today; all parties accept that several hundred bears are needed for a sustainable population. Thus while today, predations are very high in just a few localized zones, the future imagines these zones expanding across the entire massif. Furthermore, the future also promises a significant wolf population mirroring the issues in the southern Alps, where predations are several thousand per year. In this type of scenario imagining, then, pastoralists also project themselves into the future – a world imbricated with the others I have discussed – only to find that they no longer exist, that they became 'extinct' in the past-present (see Figure 6.3). Moreover, this past-present confirms Marie-Claire's concern that the pastures will become naturally rewilded by impassable pre-forest, and ultimately new forest. While she sees this as a threat to tourism development, many environmentalists see it as a return to a more 'pristine' wilderness, and therefore something to be desired. Ultimately, then, the pastoralists have everything to lose, whereas environmentalists' worldmaking efforts succeed in both of their imagined futures, with or without pastoralists.

The conservation programme is therefore condemned as a deliberate attempt to replace a past landscape where pastoralists have had no predations for generations, with a future landscape where predations will ultimately force the abandonment of pastoral activities, simply to appease environmentalists' desires for a 'wilder' future world. Any appeal for a synergistic, symbiotic cohabitation between pastoralism and large predators is dismissed as political rhetoric obfuscating its real motives. Indeed, Rewilding Europe,

FIGURE 6.3 Eleveurs *demonstrate fear of their own extinction. Photo by Tony Knight.*

the leading association promoting European rewilding, is actively appro-priating abandoned, or imagined-abandoned, land for their projects, and has this to say about pastoralism:

> It is not economically sustainable in the long term. So we want to develop a new, parallel approach, that we call rewilding, which will work much better for many of these areas and give space to develop new, modern ways of combining income, jobs and business with biodiversity conser-vation … [Domestic grazing animals] do an *almost as good grazing job as the wild herbivores*, to keep our lands open. (Rewilding Europe 2015, my emphasis).

Rewilding Europe reveals its desire for a wilder Europe based on the premise that 'wild' is better than 'domestic', and therefore human interactions should ideally be removed from this future wilder landscape. Paradoxically, this is justified by a modernist rhetoric of continued economic development, especially increased 'sustainable' ecotourism (Rewilding Europe 2015). Along with much conservation thinking, then, rewilding becomes one component of what is becoming known as ecomodernism.

An Ecomodernist Manifesto promotes using global 'social, economic, and technological powers' to develop a 'good Anthropocene' that 'stabilize[s] the climate, and protect[s] the natural world' (Asafu-Adjaye et al. 2015); science and technology will integrate synergistically with 'free markets' to develop conservation and geoengineering solutions, and further intensify/productivize human activities (especially farming) to free up enough land to assure the ecosystem services required by these markets. In other words, this is a vision for 'land sparing' (rewilding), not 'land sharing' (Phalan et al. 2011).

Ecomodernism, then, is future worlding characterized by an increas-ingly technological modernity and its inevitable, but apparently necessary, ecological ruination (Collard et al. 2015). Such a world is potentially yet another imbrication, but nevertheless appeals to many ordinary people who see it as a continuously enhanced life-as-usual. Furthermore, scientific and economic communities believe themselves the most qualified makers of such a world, justified by future-cost/benefit analyses and continuing rhetoric predicting decreased global poverty and hunger (Asafu-Adjaye et al. 2015). This is clearly a worlding imaginary that demands critical deconstruction by anthropologists, sociologists, political ecologists, and environmental humanitarians concerned with improving rights for humans and the natural world.

In the preceding discussion, I have used ethnographic research into the historiographic *longue durée*, the present, and the future. I have attempted to insert myself into the various actors' dwelt-in future worlds so that I can join them in being-in their ontological realities. Clearly, I would have liked to have done much more of this co-worlding, but that will have to wait for future research. Nevertheless, anthropologists can also facilitate such a dwelling-in-the-future understanding by drawing on existing ethnographic research that provides insights into, for example, (de)colonial and post-colonial research (see Collard et al. 2015) that reveals the effects of intensely industrializing farming processes. However, ethnography, alone, might be inadequate. Almost certainly, to challenge such ecomodernist future worlding imaginaries, these disciplines will need to adapt some of the statistical modelling techniques common to more quantitative sciences. Anthropology, in particular, might benefit from exploring other innovative futures-visioning methods. The key issue to confront is the generally superficial considerations given to social implications (Sharpe 1998).

Not surprisingly, ecomodernism is already vociferously contested (Crist 2015; Hamilton 2015), notably because it prioritizes the preservation of neoliberalism rather than nature, while obfuscating past, present, and future roles of politics; its thesis, according to Clive Hamilton (2015: np), is 'not merely untrue. It is irresponsible'. Neoliberalism is, indeed, the underlying socio-economic paradigm within which both Pyrenean 'traditional' pasto-ralism and conservation operate. It is a 'governing rationality', beyond capitalism, through which everything is economized (Brown 2015: 30); 'every field of activity' is a market (ibid.: 33) requiring all human beings to become market actors 'rendered as capitals' (ibid.: 65), with the sacrifice of 'all other hopes and dreams' (Graeber 2013: 203). The future itself, then, is a market actor and future identity/value is determined by continuous unbridled specu-lation at the expense of the present. Thus worlds are 'made and lived in the name of preempting, preparing for, or preventing threats to' neoliberalism (Anderson 2010: 777). Therefore, as I have shown above, the often narrowly focused goals of modern conservation and environmentalism can lead to worlding that presumes a particular desired future – ignoring the imbrication of many possible alternate futures – that might conflict with those hoped for by the people most implicated (Sharpe 1998).

Colliding ontological landscapes

The friction between pastoralists and conservationists, as I have expounded, is an inevitable outcome of neoliberal development ideologies (Tsing 2005). Yet, while this might be a useful construct to try to understand what is happening in the present and past I feel that it is inadequate in addressing the future for it assumes that common sense will reveal common ground with which to resolve such friction. To the contrary, I believe this friction comes not from ideological differences in the neoliberal uses of a shared single 'nature', but from the collision of ontologically different 'natures' that form a more challenging pluriverse with an imbricated spatiality and temporality.

The dominant discourses represented in my ethnographic data are culturally constructed and fused with authority and power, but founded more in collective memory than historicity. The popular discourse of many residents, tourists, and environmentalists reveals that for them, the Pyrenees are a needed antithesis of modern, urban civilization, a shared beautiful and 'wild' nature in which pastoralism has always more or less peacefully coexisted with large predators (field notes, Laurent, 10/2013). The mountains in which the pastoralists dwell – 'our mountains', as Nathalie called them – are also beautiful but have never been 'wild': 'We've architected the Pyrenees for four thousand years. It's always been a "humanized nature", and it'll always be a "humanized nature"' (field notes, Dominique, 12/2013). When the 'wild' – bears and wolves – transgressed this pastoral landscape, increasing use of technology (traps and weapons) and habitat destruction caused by modernity all but extirpated them (Knight 2016).

Despite the semiotic and symbolic epistemologies of these differing relationships with nature, they are not alternative perceptions or representations of a single shared environment. Rather, they depend on profound meanings that have developed between humans and nonhumans being-in the specific landscapes over the *longue durée*. Each human group dwells in its own specific reality in which landscape, activities, ideologies, imaginaries, and realized/realizable temporalities intertwine in ways that occlude any understanding of how the other group cannot dwell in the same reality. Thus the two realities become ontological landscapes that constantly collide (Knight and Montesi forthcoming).

Ultimately, as revealed by the future(s) dwelt-in ethnographical approach I have highlighted (which might not have surfaced in traditional ethnographic study), the friction between the two worlds is not situated in the past and present, but reflects contested futures, each an ontological reality incapable of accepting any alternatives as things stand today. If a mutually desirable future world is to be made, then my analysis shows that the only possible way to achieve this would be to work with both *écolos* and pastoralists and encourage them, perhaps in an experimental laboratory-like setting, to project themselves into a future-present in which cohabitation is actually functioning. By co-interpreting this future-present, we might collectively determine what the eco-social structures look like (with or without a neoliberal operating framework, for example), and then use this data as causal requirements with which to move backwards in time to the past-present, highlighting the various changes that occur.

Conclusion

In this chapter, I have presented an approach to researching futures using current ethnographic and anthropological interpretation. This approach has helped me immensely in my understanding of the pastoral/conservation conflict in the French Pyrenees. However, to take this research to the next level would require implementing a worldmaking laboratory which would allow pastoralists, conservationists and other implicated stakeholders to conduct co-worlding experiments to visualize a future-present that success-fully sustains each of their distinctly different ontologies. This would allow stakeholders to then travel back through time observing the worlding changes that occur as milestones towards achieving the future-present. These milestone changes would certainly require transdisciplinary (minimally anthro-pological, sociological, cosmopolitical, economic, ecological and geographical) analysis drawing on qualitative and quantitative modelling approaches to develop a most-probable implementation plan that can then be effected in the past-present.

Would such an approach work in other scenarios? I have worked with colleagues on various human-nature and 'green' neoliberal interventions across the world, and we agree that each case study reveals ontological collisions (Knight and Montesi 2017). While these studies do not overtly contemplate futures, they do encourage me as to the value of using the approach I have outlined here.

More importantly, I believe that the need to collaborate and develop effective futures approaches is imperative. When I reflect on the extreme friction occurring between Pyrenean environmentalism and pastoralism I see this ontological collision as a microcosm of the massively more complex global human-nature challenge presented by the Anthropocene. This challenge requires overcoming the seemingly irrational resistance of the majority of the privileged hegemonic minority – a group sometimes referred to as the 'west' or the 'global north' – to the necessary scale of change required to avert an anthropocenic catastrophe. This, too, is an ontological collision. 'We' (this group, with whom I identify) are increasingly aware that if human civilization is to survive, then we must make a world in which humanity successfully coexists with an atmosphere, oceans, and landscapes all conducive to a thriving biodiversity. Yet, this future-present cannot be conserved without destabilizing our past-present ontological identity with its complicit inter-relationship with the neoliberal hegemony that is actively destroying it (see Moore 2014).

Worse, global future imaginaries (including ecomodernist) invariably point to geoengineering 'solutions' to 'save the world'; 86 per cent of the

Intergovernmental Panel on Climate Change scenarios predicting a better than 50 per cent chance of maintaining global warming within 2°C are predicated on global-scale geoengineering (Anderson 2015: 899). The essence of the Anthropocene, then, is entangled in global neoliberal power relations revealed through the complex political ecologies of an emerging anthropocenic/scientific governance. This raises serious questions as to whether or not democracy is even compatible with such governance: who will control the technologies and their implementations, and who will be responsible for their unforeseeable consequences at unimaginable local levels?

At the intersection of the local and global, anthropology has an incredible opportunity to facilitate imaginaries that address the pessimistic uncertainties of the Anthropocene and help open pathways to realizable, optimistic futures. I imagine a worldwide public anthropology that profoundly examines its multitude of field sites in order to expand our temporal assessments of local dwelt- and dwelling-in experiences, explicitly considering multispecies and human-nature entanglements. This will require a rapid epistemological shift in our methods to truly embrace contemplating our ethnographic futures within transdisciplinary research. Together, these myriad informed biogeo-cultural vignettes from public anthropology might begin to meld together a global vision for future imaginaries that are more desirable for human and nonhuman wellbeing.

Note

1 All names are changed to assure anonymity.

References

Adam, B., 2005. 'Briefing 5: Max Weber on futurity'. Available online: http://www.cardiff.ac.uk/socsi/futures/briefing5.pdf (accessed 20 October 2016).

Adam, B., 2006. 'Futures Told'. Available online: http://www.cardiff.ac.uk/socsi/futures/wp_ba_futurestold160306.pdf (accessed 20 October 2016).

Adam, B., 2011. 'Towards a twenty-first-century sociological engagement with the future'. *Insights* 4 (11): 1–18.

Anderson, B., 2010. 'Preemption, precaution, preparedness: Anticipatory action and future geographies'. *Progress in Human Geography* 34 (6): 777–98.

Anderson, K., 2015. 'Duality in climate science'. *Nature Geoscience* 8 (12): 898–900.

Asafu-Adjaye, J., L. Blomqvist, S. Brand, B. Brook, R. Defries, E. Ellis, C. Foreman, D. Keith, M. Lewis, M. Lynas, T. Nordhaus, R. Pielke Jr, R. Pritzker, J. Roy, M. Sagoff, M. Shellenberger, R. Stone and P. Teague, 2015. 'An ecomodernist manifesto'. Available online: http://www.ecomodernism.org (accessed 10 October 2016).

Bell, W., 2010. 'Public Sociology and the Future: The Possible, the Probable, and the Preferable'. In V. Jeffries (ed.), *Handbook of Public Sociology*, 89–106. Plymouth: Rowman and Littlefield.

Beschta, R. L. and W. J. Ripple, 2009. 'Large predators and trophic cascades in terrestrial ecosystems of the western United States'. *Biological Conservation* 142 (110): 2401–14.

Boissevain, J., 1992. 'On Predicting the Future: Parish Rituals and Patronage in Malta'. In S. Wallman (ed.), *Contemporary Futures. Perspectives from Social Anthropology*, 68–80. London: Routledge.

Brown, W., 2015. *Undoing the Demos: Neoliberalism's Stealth Revolution*. New York: Zone books.

Ceballos, G., P. R. Ehrlich, A. D. Barnosky, A. Garcia, R. M. Pringle, T. M. Palmer, 2015. 'Accelerated modern human-induced species losses: Entering the sixth mass extinction'. *Science Advances* 1 (5): 1-5.

Collard, R-C, J. Dempsey and J. Sundberg, 2015. 'A manifesto for abundant futures'. *Annals of the Association of American Geographers* 105 (2): 322–30.

Crist, E., 2015. 'The reaches of freedom: A response to *An Ecomodernist Manifesto*'. *Environmental Humanities* 7: 245–54.

Ginn, F., 2015. 'When horses won't eat: Apocalypse and the anthropocene'. *Annals of the Association of American Geographers* 105 (2): 351–9.

Graeber, D., 2013. *The Democracy Project: A History, a Crisis, a Movement*. London: Penguin Books.

Hamilton, C., 2015. 'The technofix is in'. Available online: http://clivehamilton. com/the-technofix-is-in-a-critique-of-an-ecomodernist-manifesto/ (accessed 28 April 2015).

Hannerz, U., 2003. 'Macro-scenarios. Anthropology and the debate over contemporary and future worlds'. *Social Anthropology* 11 (2): 169–87.

Harries-Jones, P., 1992. 'Sustainable Anthropology: Ecology and Anthropology in the Future'. In S. Wallman (ed.), *Contemporary Futures. Perspectives from Social Anthropology*, 157–71. London: Routledge.

Heidegger, M., 1962. *Being and Time*. J. Macquarrie and E. Robinson (trans.). Malden, MA and Oxford: Blackwell Publishing.

Ingold, Tim, 1993. 'The temporality of the landscape'. *World Archaeology* 25 (2): 152–74.

Kaczensky, P. M., 1999. 'Large Carnivore Depredation On Livestock In Europe'. *Ursus* 11: 59–72.

Knight, T., 2016. 'Rewilding the French Pyrenean Landscape: Can Cultural and Biological Diversity Successfully Coexist?' In M. Agnoletti and F. Emanueli (eds), *Biocultural Diversity in Europe*, 193–209. Basel, Switzerland: Springer.

Knight, T. and L. Montesi (eds), forthcoming. 'Landscape ontologies in collision: food, politics, and (non)human transformations in the neoliberal era'. *Journal of Political Ecology*, Special Section.

Lewis, S. L. and M. A. Maslin, 2015. 'Defining the Anthropocene'. *Nature* 519 (7542): 171–80.

McCallum, M. L., 2015. 'Vertebrate biodiversity losses point to a sixth mass extinction'. *Biodiversity and Conservation* 24 (10): 2497–519.

Mead, M., 2005 [1977]. 'Our Open-ended Future'. In R. B. Textor (ed.), *The World Ahead: An Anthropologist Anticipates the Future*, 329–38. New York: Berg.

Ministre de l'écologie et du développement durable (MEDD), 2006. 'Plan de Restauration et de Conservation de l'Ours Brun Dans les Pyrénées Françaises 2006 – 2009'. Available online: http://www.developpement-durable.gouv.fr/Plan-de-restauration-et-de.html (accessed 20 January 2016).

Milton, K., 1990. 'Anthropology of the future: The 1990 ASA Conference'. *Anthropology Today* 6 (4): 22–3.

Moore, J., 2014. 'The Capitalocene, Parts 1 and 2'. Available online: http://www.jasonwmoore.com/Essays.html (accessed 20 January 2016).

Persoon, G. A. and D. M. E. van Est, 2000. 'The study of the future in anthropology in relation to the sustainability debate'. *Focaal* 35: 7–28.

Phalan, B., M. Onial, A. Balmford and R. E. Green, 2011. 'Reconciling food production and biodiversity conservation: Land sharing and land sparing compared'. *Science* 333: 1289–91.

Pink, S. and S. Abram (eds), 2015. *Media, Anthropology and Public Engagement*. New York and Oxford: Berg.

Rewilding Europe, 2015. 'Frequently asked questions'. Available online: https://www.rewildingeurope.com/frequently-asked-questions/ (accessed 5 February 2016).

Rilke, R. M., 2012 [1903]. *Letters to a Young Poet*. Snowball Publishing.

Sharpe, B., 1998. 'First the forest: conservation, "community" and "participation" in Cameroon'. *Africa* 68 (1): 25–45.

Steffen, W., P. J. Crutzen and J. R. McNeill, 2007. 'The Anthropocene: Are Humans Now Overwhelming the Great Forces of Nature?' *Ambio* 36 (8): 614–21.

Strathern, M., 1992. 'Reproducing Anthropology'. In S. Wallman (ed.), *Contemporary Futures. Perspectives from Social Anthropology,* 172–89. London: Routledge.

Swyngedouw, E., 2010. 'Apocalypse Forever? Post-political populism and the spectre of climate change'. *Theory, Culture and Society* 27 (203): 213–32.

Textor, R. B., 1995. 'The ethnographic futures research method: An application to Thailand'. *Futures* 27 (4): 461–71.

Tsing, A. L., 2005. *Friction: An Ethnography of Global Connection*. Princeton, NJ: Princeton University Press.

Waters, C. N., J. Zalasiewicz, C. Summerhayes, A. D. Barnosky, C. Poirier, A. Gałuszka, A. Cearreta, M. Edgeworth, E. C. Ellis, M. Ellis, C. Jeandel, R. Leinfelder, J. R. McNeill, D. Richter, W. Steffen, J. Syvitski, D. Vidas, M. Wagreich, M. Williams, A. Zhisheng, E. Grinevald, E. Odada, N. Oreskes and A. P. Wolfe, 2016. 'The Anthropocene is functionally and stratigraphically distinct from the Holocene'. *Science* 351 (6269): 137–47.

7

Digital technologies, dreams and disconcertment in anthropological worldmaking

Karen Waltorp

My doctoral fieldwork (February 2014–August 2015)[1] focused on the affordances of smartphones for young Muslim women, second-generation immigrants with transnational networks living in a social housing estate in Nørrebro, Copenhagen. The research inevitably entwined with current political debates in the Danish context, where I grew up as part of the majority population in the small nation of 5.5 million citizens. The women I worked with are part of a Muslim minority of approximately 230,000 (Jacobsen 2012: 112).

Since 9/11 the place of Islam in Denmark has been heavily debated both in the media and in politics, with new laws and regulations continually introduced since the early 2000s (Rytter and Pedersen 2014: 2304). In Denmark what came to be known as the 'cartoon crisis' in 2005–6 saw drawings of the Prophet Mohammad moving from the pages of Danish newspaper *Jyllands Posten* to the entire world, deeply offending many Muslims (Mahmood 2009). Many ethnic Danes on their part felt deeply offended that Muslims who had been welcomed in Denmark would disregard one of the principles held highest in the country: freedom of speech.

The Danish state became actively involved in the US-led 'war on terror' in Iraq and Afghanistan. The securitization policy inwards and outwards intensified with religiously motivated attacks on European ground, and on the local level visitation zones (*visitationszoner*) were introduced in 2004 in the parts of Copenhagen where I do fieldwork. Various other pre-emptive measures in a 'security/integration response' cast the Muslim population as the 'usual suspects', affecting the everyday lives of ordinary Danish Muslims (Rytter and Pedersen 2014). As the symbolically potent 'Migrant Bill' (L87) was recently approved by parliament (as of 26 January 2016) implementing measures against letting refugees and other immigrants into Denmark (and bringing families) it added to a growing feeling among some of my Muslim inter-locutors of being unwanted in the country where they were born and grew up. In short, debates about integration, citizenship, belonging and shared futures formed a politically charged climate as the backdrop of my fieldwork.

Widespread future scenarios, images built around 'the clash of civil-izations' between Islam and the West (Huntington 1993), circulate and inform people in their passages through public life in intricate ways. Such scenarios purport to be early warnings, attempts at consciousness-raising, but arguably work as self-fulfilling prophecies and global mythologies (Hannerz 2015: 803; Werbner 2004: 462–3). In Denmark, a number of political commentators embraced the scenarios of clashing civilizations or a subtle Muslim takeover as realistic scenarios (Rytter and Pedersen 2014: 2310). Anthropology offers no clear-cut counter-prophecies in the face of such future scenarios, but it unfixes and unsettles them through being 'more thoroughly grounded in the rich materials of world ethnography and in anthropological thought' (Hannerz 2015: 804). Due to this unfixing nature, it may be a much less effective tool in capturing the popular imagination. Yet I argue that it is an important move, to insist on an open-ended worldmaking through our writings and encounters.

This chapter is a response to the increasing calls for an engaged anthro-pology, part of this edited volume's larger prospect of a future-oriented anthropology. I work from one of the most disconcerting encounters in my fieldwork: the kidnapping of Isra, the daughter of Amal, a young woman of Palestinian-Jordanian origin whom I befriended while carrying out fieldwork in the Copenhagen social housing estate. At first, I found it nearly impossible to make sense of Amal's reactions to her daughter being taken away, and only gradually did I come to understand it as meaningful *and* paradoxical: without severing family ties, she behaved in a manner that kept the future open – and continues to do so. I focus here on Amal's Muslim/Danish tactics and on *sabr,* the religiously informed attitude of patience. I describe dreams and digital technologies as an infrastructure of the flow of images of the future – an infrastructure that has a tendency to disappear from focus and blend into the background in much research, but will be made the explicit focus here.

In the following passages, I move from a particularly dark Friday afternoon in October 2014 where Amal's eight-year-old daughter was taken/saved/ kidnapped (depending on who's perspective is taken as the departure point) to the responses and future orientations that I discerned in Amal's actions and attitudes over time. In this move, I insist on the difficult task of researching futures anthropologically as they emerge and are experienced by interlocutors and the anthropologist, striving to espouse 'prospective' or even hopeful orientations, regardless that these will always be of a 'provisional, indeterminate and open-ended nature' (Miyazaki 2004: 137): what Hirokazu Miyazaki calls hopeful reflections on knowledge, rather than mere disclosure.

I suggest that being faithful to our ethnographic encounters, and to living with difficult differences, disconcertments and paradoxes – on all scales from within the individual person, within groups and within societies – demands that we stay with the trouble and disconcertments. To reiterate, while not necessarily producing counter-narratives to future-scenarios, a future-oriented anthropology works towards subtly unfixing and unsettling them. In Miyazaki's work, he seeks to illustrate the idea of ethnography as an art of reception and response. In his book *The Method of Hope* (2004), the Suvavou people, disenfranchised by the Japanese government, have kept their claims to the(ir) land open by repeatedly reorienting their knowledge toward the future, and incessantly re-phrasing their demand (Miyazaki 2004; 2014: 520). Miyazaki seeks to replicate this hopeful stance in his analysis and writing. In the specific ethnographic case at hand in this article, the attitude of *sabr* (patience) was a religiously motivated, hopeful stance on the part of Amal that I struggled to understand. A stance that was present simultaneously with other strategies, more easily recognizable within the modern concept of the individual as striving to gain agency over his or her own life and future (see Mahmood 2012). I seek to describe the workings of *sabr* without losing sight of the tactics that Amal simultaneously applied that contradicted this very stance.

My attention to future-making is through a focus on digital technologies and dreams as particular techniques for researching the future anthropologically, and as co-generating imagination and futures in underdetermined ways. The way that dreams in my fieldwork was understood as relating to the future is connected to the concept of the imaginal realm (*alam al-mithâl*) (see Chittick 1994; Corbin 1976; Marks 2016), and offers a way to engage with what lies beyond and between the intelligible and sensible/corporeal realm. Contemporary relationships across the world are constituted and play out through practices such as co-presence in and through digital media and technologies (Pink et al. 2016: 16).

Throughout my research the smartphone and social media platforms both configured centres of attention, and worked as fieldwork devices to interrogate imaginings of futures in its emergent forms. These imaginings were often manifested in glimpses: a quote or picture posted in a social media platform, or a private message presenting a 'hoped for future self' rather than a 'factual' present state. The focus on *sabr*, tactics, digital technologies and dreams as future-producing is a response to and replication of my encounters in the field. This is inspired by Miyazaki's (2014: 526) call for a 'shared commitment to achieving analytical openness and the various divergent forms in which such openness may materialize in any specific ethnographic situation': an open-endedness that is a patient, responsive stance and direction, rather than a means to an end.

The incident

Twenty-six-year-old Amal came to her daughter's school to pick her up on a Friday afternoon, but she was not there. When Amal returned home, she found suitcases and the passports of her daughter and her now ex-husband to be missing. She kept the possibility open that he did not intend to stay away with their daughter, simultaneously acting as if a kidnapping was in fact happening, and alerting the police that very same day. Amal had been married to her paternal cousin, her father's brother's son (FBS) and Isra was now staying with her grandparents in Jordan. On the following Monday, they contacted Amal's father to let him know what had happened. They contended that Denmark was not a good place for Isra to grow up.

I met with Amal in Copenhagen, a week after the incident had taken place: we smiled at each other, kissed each other on the cheeks, and hugged. Longer than usual. Amal lit a cigarette and updated me on the events following immediately after the kidnapping. Amal had no direct contact with her ex-husband after he left Denmark with their daughter. She talked to her daughter regularly on Viber,[2] able to see her face 'live' on the pink iPad that Isra had brought with her from Denmark. Amal was unsure whether she could believe her daughter when she insisted that she was happy.

> We'll speak our language, I told Isra when we Facetimed the first time. I didn't say the word Danish, just called it 'our language' … and she told me in Danish, that she knew they would be leaving, but her father made her not say anything about it to me or to anyone else. When we talked, Isra repeated, 'I'm fine, mama, I'm with my cousins and having a fun time, you don't need to call all the time, I'm on vacation …

Was Isra 'just on vacation', after all, as she said? Was this a kidnapping, or could it be re-negotiated? Amal was in suspense. She had overheard her uncle and former father-in-law tell Isra to sit down next to him, while she talked to her on Viber. Amal would pose Isra a question in Danish, and she would watch Isra on-screen look up behind the iPad, and the answers to Amal's questions would come hesitantly. Soon Isra said she was not allowed to speak Danish anymore and preferred to only speak in Arabic.

One night, some months after the incident, during one of the many sleepovers at Bita's place in Nørrebro, Bita (Amal's friend of twenty-five years' standing), and another close interlocutor analysed the situation. Bita viewed it in light of her own experience as a child in Denmark. She identified with Isra trying to do the right thing towards both her mother and father. She spoke in rather clear-cut sentences:

> I feel sorry for Isra. You have to have been through something like that to really understand it. I fucking hope, by God, that Amal's ex will be punished for what he's done. I tried the same thing with my mom and dad. To get your dad to leave your mom alone, and not end in 'argument-argument', you do everything you can to make your dad happy. But I should have just let them divorce, that would've been better … The father loves his daughter – and he doesn't know what he's doing to her …

We went back to discussing the legal aspects of the situation. Amal and Bita disagreed on whether it was national legislation in Jordan or *sharia* (Islamic law) that would guide how the family there would solve the situation. Amal spoke:

> I looked more into it, and according to *sharia*, the child belongs with the mother until the age of twelve, or until a girl starts menstruating. After that, the child belongs (equally) with both parents … I was told that this is what it's like in Jordan too. Still I don't want Isra to worry. I just take away her worries and say: 'Have a nice time, I've told the school that you are on vacation' – because she worried about school – but I can feel that she isn't happy … she isn't happy. I feel it.

Amal worked with a number of intermittent, tentative future scenarios that she did not concretize when I pressured her on the matter. She sometimes struggled with the feeling of seeing no horizon at all, not feeling like getting up in the morning and carrying on, seemingly oscillating between different states of mind, through which the world was disclosed to her. An imaginative horizon of multiple plans and possibilities is in no way straightforward or 'singular', as the person is 'engaging in a retrospective/ prospective process and drawing on previously collected knowledge and possible paths of actions, focusing 'rays of attention' on a plurality of possible states' (Mische 2009: 696). Interpreting actions is invariably predicated on the time that passes, and in light of other events, past and future that re-signify the 'original' event. Different temporal moments (both futures and pasts) co-existed in the present as guiding tendencies for Amal. In the days, weeks and months following the kidnapping, the uncles in Amman discussed the matter over the telephone with Amal's father in Copenhagen, Amal eavesdropping by the door.

My questions to Amal, infused with impatience and a wish to know concretely the likelihood of one scenario over another and what to do next were met by Amal with unfinished sentences, silences, diversions, or simply: 'I don't know Karen, I hope *Insh'Allah* (God willing).' I sensed these shifts in Amal's mood in both telephone conversations, text messages and face-to-face. Instead of a profile picture on her WhatsApp-profile,[3] a short text was displayed:

> **Crying** is the only way your **eyes** speak when
> your **mouth** can't explain how things
> made your heart **broken**.

Through digital technologies Amal sent out tentative, hopeful and despairing images and into the world; open-ended requests that might do unforeseen work. Amal sent these digital images out into the world, and lobbied intensely with family members and others in the local community, exploring both the possibilities within the legislations of the Danish nation state as well as *sharia*. I will go into these various responses and attitudes in more detail below, starting with the simultaneous lobbying-tactics and *sabr*.

Constant lobbying and *sabr*

Sometimes I had trouble understanding that Amal's inaction was an action: how could she let time pass and not *do* more, freak out? While in fact Amal was doing something: practicing patience for her family in Jordan and everyone else to witness, both directly and mediated through gossip and by sharing pictures on various social media platforms. As Saba Mahmood reminds us, drawing on her fieldwork with women of the piety movement (*da'wa*) in Egypt, the subject's exteriority and interiority can be in a relationship where a bodily act (and in my reading, a 'selfie' taken in various situations) is both an expression of, and a means to, the realization of the subject. As 'many dimensions of practice – linguistic and nonlinguistic – cannot be grasped in terms of a theory of representation alone' (Mahmood 2012: xi), we need to depart from the idea of performing/form as not sincere (see also Hirschkind 2006: 15, 94–5).

Ultimately, Amal needed her family's support whatever she chose to do. They are her network, her world and her future. And she needed God to bear the trials he himself put on her. *Sabr*, living according to the knowledge that God ultimately knows best, is not to be confused with inaction. It is a virtue highly valued that helps a person bear the tests that God presents in *dunya* (this world) before the Day of Judgement. Within this framework, the way to get Isra back was not for Amal to go to Jordan and fetch her by force – which in any case she could not do – as the Danish police had made it clear that they could do nothing to help her unless her ex-husband was within the EU-borders. Instead Amal travelled to Mecca and Medina with her father, praying, drawing closer to God. As she herself pointed to, though, this stance was applied after having 'tried everything': she had gone to the police, the Foreign Ministry, the Social Services, the free Legal Aid, lawyers specializing in kidnapped children, trying every official route she could think of. 'This is Denmark – how come no one can help me, my child has been kidnapped, hello!' The last hello seems a metaphor for the non-response to her call for help that Amal experienced from the Danish state.

She did succeed in having lawyers from Legal Aid contact the Swedish and Norwegian embassies, but to no avail. She convinced her father to meet with a lawyer specializing in cases with kidnapped children. A simultaneous tactics of lobbying with various family members seemed to work better. After Amal and her father had visited Isra and the family in Jordan, and many subsequent talks back and forth between the senior men in the family had ensued, it was agreed that Isra would be returned to Amal and the family in Denmark before the beginning of the new school year August 2015.

As this promise of Isra's return was ultimately not kept, Amal again contacted the police. At the station, she was told 'There's nothing we can do,' the officer adding, 'You can try to kidnap her back yourself, that's what I would do, I guess.' The only tangible result of the police interview recounted above was Isra being 're-categorized' as having been out of the Danish system since the Friday afternoon in October 2014, where Amal had called the police to alert them. Amal was told to pay back child support and housing subsidy for the months that had passed since.

If Amal was to act on her own single-handedly, without the consent and support of her family, she would possibly get her daughter back, but the everyday life they had lived before the kidnapping and their social network and support structure would be lost in the process. Her family would be deeply disconcerted should she disregard the way her parents and her father's family in Jordan would seek to solve the situation. Thinking through future relationships is an important part of considering the consequences of action and it implies differing models of causality, agency and influence. In the case at hand, for example, divine intervention seems one of the underlying frames at play in relating to the future. Contemplating one's own death, *dhikr al-mawt*, is a fundamental reminder of behaving ethically in this life (Hirschkind 2006). The final test is when one is faced with God, naked, to be judged.

What is important, Christian Suhr writes, drawing on his work with Danish Salafi's is 'the cultivation of certain virtues, so that one may embrace what is being given with thankfulness (*shukr*), perseverance and patience (*sabr*) … Emphasis is not so much on agency in the sense of the ability to act outwardly, as on the ability to receive what is being given with an ethically correct sensitivity … the relevant part of the self that needs to be freed is not so much the mind–brain "ego", but rather the "heart" (*qalb*) and its ability to respond emotionally and ethically in accordance with its circumstances' (Suhr 2013: 167). According to my Muslim interlocutors, the return for *sabr* is blessings, mercy and guidance of Allah. Yet these blessings might be very concrete. In Amal's case she was consciously hoping and praying to God to grant her support and to make her ex-husband and their relatives change their minds and return her daughter. Her hardships facilitated her becoming more religious, and displaying, or rather enacting, religiosity became a strategy – perhaps the only viable strategy for getting her daughter back.

Amal lived through the trials put on her. She attempted to show in her actions over the year following the kidnapping, that she was patient, pious, a good person – a good mother. She was hoping and constantly lobbying for the short-term return of her daughter, whilst aligning with God and the ultimate long-term perspective. Through this practice, she was given strength to carry on in this tragic situation of impasse, showing 'radical open-endedness entailed in the exchange with God'. (Miyazaki 2014: 521). As she commented: 'Where would I end up if I didn't focus on patience? In the psychiatric ward? This is my child – it is a piece of me.'

According to my interlocutors, the help from God can be asked and received via prayer and via dreams. In what follows, I turn to dreams as infrastructure for the flow of images of the future, and afterwards to digital technologies as an infrastructure for images impacting the future.

Dreams as infrastructure for images and technique for researching futures

Amal's former marriage was arranged, her ex-husband came from Jordan to Denmark in his late twenties, and Amal, a young school-girl at the time, was born and grew up in Copenhagen. The couple were very differently situated in terms of belonging in and to Denmark, and in ways of envisioning their future, and that of their daughter, accordingly. In one of my first conversations with Amal's ex-husband, he asked me what my husband thought about my spending so much time with Muslims. To my surprised reply that he did not mind, he then asked without a trace of irony in his voice, 'Is he not racist at all?' The media and political discourses concerning migrants and refugees in the last decades in Denmark, as alluded to in the introduction, arguably contribute to what positions and futures are seen as possible.

Prior to the kidnapping, Amal had asked God for help in her endeavour to improve the marriage by making a *du'a* (prayer) before going to sleep. She woke up bathed in sweat from horrible nightmares several times during the night. She told me about this the following day over the phone, very affected by what she saw as a bad sign for the future. Among my interlocutors, it is very common to operate with *isthikara*: When unsure as to the correct action to take in life choices, such as marriage, people frequently ask God to send them a sign concerning the outcome. They then pray and go to sleep (see also Edgar and Henig 2010: 254). With the Islamic belief of God as all-seeing, all-knowing and unbound by time and place, the proposition that a dream can be a realm in which the future is present and not ahead of us in a linear sense, is both sensible, imaginable and intelligible.

A close friend of Amal's had experienced bad dreams about Amal during the period leading up to the kidnapping. I knew this both from text messages, which Amal had shown me, and from one friend in particular, who was very upset about it: she saw Isra in her dreams being caught under something and crying out for help. Then the kidnapping happened. Over a year later I was visiting Nørrebro, driving around Copenhagen with Amal and another friend during a cold night in December 2015. Amal recounted a recent dream: she was at the zoo or circus, a mix of the two, and there were people all around. Amal could see the little train that takes people around the zoo approaching Isra at very low-speed. Amal, removed from Isra who was happy in the dream because they were together in this fun place, could see that Isra was not aware that the train was headed directly towards her. She called out to Isra, who could not hear her, and she did not reach her because of all the people gathered whom she had to move through. Isra fell and Amal hurried to help her on her feet again. People were laughing in the dream, and Isra was embarrassed. In the dream she had said to her mother, 'You're not helping me, why didn't you help me?' In the dim light in the car I could see tears on Amal's cheeks, and I lightly touched her arm. She asked us to change the subject. 'I can't …' she said, the sentence dying out.

William Chittick, building on the work of Sufi mystic and philosopher Muhyî al-Dîn Muhammad ibn 'Alî ibn al 'Arabî, argues that 'a dream image needs to be described in terms of both subjective experience and objective content … an isthmus or interworld—standing between two other realities or worlds and needing to be defined in terms of both' (1994: 70). The imaginal realm (*alam al-mithâl*) 'far from being an individual fantasy, accounts for the way people's collective wishes bring the unthought into the thinkable, beginning with dreams, myth and metaphor' (Marks 2016: 8). Gregory Bateson (2000 [1972]:

38–58) from a different line of argument ends up also pointing to dreams as being like myths or fables. He writes about dreams that 'they don't predict the future. Dreams are sort of suspended in time. They don't have any tenses … if dreams have not tenses and are somehow suspended in time, then it would be forcing the wrong sort of objectivity to say that a dream 'predicts' something. And equally wrong to say that it is a statement about the past, it's not history …' (ibid: 51). In this understanding, the moral is not stated in the dream, but the whole dream *is* the moral. It is then up to the psychoanalyst within the Freudian tradition to get the patient to find the moral, Bateson writes (ibid: 52).

Amira Mittermaier, drawing on her fieldwork in Egypt, turns our attention in a different direction, namely how 'certain dreams come to the dreamer as opposed to being produced by her or him' (2012: 248). In this sense, the dreamer is 'never in charge' (ibid.: 254) because dreams come from Elsewhere, troubling the notion of 'a unified subject' and pointing towards 'the imaginal realm' (ibid.: 249, 260). In my material the dreams encountered emerge as an amalgam of divine or spiritual intervention, the practices of *du'a* (prayer), the nightly dreaming, and the negotiating with oneself and others about what meaning the dream holds. Paying attention to dreams can be a technique of ethnographically researching the future, as Iain Edgars proposes; the images of ourselves and images that we portray to the world when rehearsing future action explores imaginative resources and reveals implicit knowledge and emotional states (Edgar 2004: 1).

Researching uncertain futures through digital technologies

I received snaps[4] from Amal as she visited her daughter in Amman, accompanied by her father, the second time. Almost a year had passed since the incident. There were 'selfies' of Amal looking worried with accompanying texts that underlined that she was nervous and excited. While in Jordan, her 'Snapchat MyStory' (a compilation of snaps which all one's contacts can view) was updated every day with pictures and videos of Isra, Amal and her father having fun; at the pool, at fun fairs, and out and about on excursions in Jordan. There are snaps with mother and daughter posing together in identical pyjamas and looking happy. There are pictures from restaurants and at home in a garden, sharing food with family members; uncles, aunts, and cousins. I (and her other friends, sisters and sister-in-law) snapped back, adding heart emoticons to the picture and 'liked' her posts in the Instagram social media platform.

I received a snap of Amal's sad face and a text stating that she did not want to 'leave the apple of her eye', her 'one and only love, forever', her beloved Isra. Then later a snap of a plane in the airport at night, and an accompanying text: 'Goodbye Isra' with a sad smiley-emoticon with a tear down the cheek. I was on the telephone with Amal a few days later. It was only 2.00 p.m., but I could hear her and her mother already preparing dinner in the background, the noise of chopping vegetables and scrambling with pots and pans. Several of Amal's sisters and their husbands were coming for dinner, so there would be a lot of people.

It was hard visiting Isra in Jordan, Amal confided over the telephone. But she pulled herself together, and made sure that they made the most of their time together. I was curious as to what happened before she left her daughter again. What was said, or agreed on, concerning the future.

Amal: I told her 'You know you just call me, and if you want to come to me, you know where I am.' 'Yes, mama, I know,' she said. She can call me and tell me to come anytime, and I will find a way, but I do not want to put more stress on her. She is very concerned with not upsetting her father, and says that she is happy there.

Karen: I'm beginning to understand … You remember when I told you that time at the café that I think I would be standing in the street screaming, if it happened to me. I didn't get the idea of having to show patience, *sabr* and all that.

Amal: Yeah, what good would that do? It would not help in getting her back. My Dad has played a really big part in helping me understand that it's better to go there and show them that I have nothing to be ashamed of. I hold my head high. Going to Jordan and make problems would just make it much harder to ever get her back. He has really been supporting me, my Dad … Now I feel good, Karen, that I at least know I'm doing everything I can. You know I'm not 'extremely' religious, you know me, but still when you believe and you let God into your life, it's such a *warm* feeling inside … I don't know when I will get her back, I hope I will, *insh'Allah* – if it doesn't happen in this life, then …

For a long time Amal's only updates on social media were pictures of her daughter. In the Snapchat platform, though, you can only share what is in the moment and Isra was not in the moment with Amal. She would still send snaps with Isra indirectly, her absence present: a picture of the drawings and letters that Isra's classmates had made for her; the framed compilation of pictures of herself and Isra that she had hung up on the wall; the necklace with her daughter's name in gold letters she received from girlfriends on her birthday; and snaps of Amal herself at events and celebrations with a text across the pictures reading, 'First Ramadan without my Isra', or the like, decorated with emoticons expressing sadness. Other snaps would show the everyday life that Amal was living – without her daughter physically present.

Digital technologies and dreams as open-ended future-making

Feminist media scholar Laura U. Marks traces how Arabic philosophers synthesized Greek philosophy with Qur'anic thought, 'developing a psychology from Aristotelian sources and a cosmology of emanation from Neoplatonic ones' (Marks 2016: 3). Contemporary Muslim scholars continue to develop the concept of the imaginal realm, and Marks argues that it describes a progressive collective imagination (ibid.: 4). In William Chittick's words, drawing from Ibn al-Arabi:

> The rational faculty ('aql) works by a process of stringing concepts together and drawing conclusions, 'reflection' (fikr). In contrast, the imaginal faculty (khayâl) works by an inner perception that perceives ideas in sensory form. Hence imaginal perception may be visual, but this vision does not take place with the physical eyes; it may be auditory, but things are not heard with the physical ears. Again, dreams prove that everyone has nonphysical sense experience. (Chittick 1994: 70)

And as underscored by Corbin: 'Of course, the forms and figures of the mundus imaginalis do not subsist in the same manner as the empirical realities of this physical world' (Corbin 1976: 10). Experiences pertaining to the imaginal realm are real, but on a different plane than the realities of the physical worlds, consequently, the sense experience is nonphysical – as in a dream.

The alam al-mithâl is also described as the world of 'Images in suspense' (mothol mo'allaqa) (Corbin 1976: 10). The analogy of images in suspense is the reflection in a mirror describing the relation of images to the empirical world. In this I find a resemblance to the 'selfies' and other digital images in social media that my interlocutors share with others, particularly in the Snapchat platform, where an image shared will cease to exist after maximum ten seconds. Marks points to a move where contemporary Western thought, tired of the sovereign subject, is trying to conceive of an extra-subjective reality that binds individuals ethically to others (Marks 2016: 4). Henry Corbin suggested the 'the imaginal realm' or 'mundus imaginalis' as the proper trans-lation of *alam al-mithâl*, as he saw it as problematic that 'the term *imaginary* is equated with the *unreal*, with something that is outside the framework of being and existing … I had to find a new expression to avoid misleading the Western reader, who, on the contrary has to be roused form his old engrained way of thinking in order to awaken him to another order of things' (1976: 3–4).

The concept of the imaginal realm offers a way to engage with what lies beyond and between the intelligible and sensible/corporeal, adding a different dimension to the work on the imaginary in continental philosophy and anthropology.[5]

Conclusion

Why do we do what we do as anthropologists? More specifically, why do *I* recount such a disconcerting case of a Muslim interlocutor's moment of impasse? When confronted with disconcerting and unsettling events that seem impossible to come to terms with for those involved as well as the anthropologist, such as the case of the kidnapping I have recounted here, the commitment to the ethnographic encounter and a future-orientation is imperative. 'Meeting each other across serious oppositional difference doesn't resolve into some kind of dialectical resolution' (Haraway 2016: 212), and/but we need to 'think collectively even when answers seem impossible' (Mahmood 2012: xxviii).

I believe (following Brit Ross Winthereik, personal communication) that there is a special generosity to be found in subjecting ourselves to the question of how we inhabit infrastructures for seeing, thinking and knowing. My starting point is from the trajectory of a Western, scientific tradition with all that it entails. 'Allowing' myself to inhabit the infrastructure of the digital technologies as part of fieldwork, and experiencing dreams as entangled in fieldwork, open up different ways of knowledge-making and consequently future-making. This, then, is a tentative proposal for a responsive open-endedness as future-making.

Miyazaki (2014) underscores that the response and replication he calls for entails anthropological commitment to analytical openness, and resides in 'the cultivation of an outward orientation toward, and a willingness to receive and respond to others' (Miyazaki 2014: 526). Through looking at the infra-structure of images, I have shown how dreaming and digital technologies are ways of enduring hardships patiently and of simultaneously seeking to facil-itate a better future. Amal employed digital technologies, sending out images of herself enacting/being the good Muslim woman and mother. I have sought to demonstrate how we can explore dreams and digital technologies such as Snapchat and Instagram as future-making devices, and thus as techniques to interrogate the future anthropologically.

Through what I view as digital tactics, Amal sought to create images with relational and future-making power. The digital technologies and social media platforms seem to be more 'plastic' than the dream images, which can be invited, experienced and responded to but rarely created. Dreaming, lobbying with family members, and cultivating and enacting *sabr* – through digital technologies among other things – are forms of action apparently more powerful than approaching the Danish authorities in Amal's case. But as Amal pointed out herself, when discussing my understanding of her reactions, she was acting as both Dane and Muslim, as she *is* both: what I have elsewhere alluded to as a 'composite habitus' that is symptomatic of all 'modern subjects', but arguably experienced more radically at times by my interlocutors, young Muslim women, children of immigrants, citizens of Denmark (Waltorp 2015). As I see it, this unsettles future scenarios and 'clash of civilizations' proponents. Ideas, images and people travel and morph slowly through encounters and this is what anthropologists work with across scales and worlds.

Acknowledgements

I thank Christian Suhr, Stefania Pandolfo and Iain Edgar for drawing my attention to the importance of dreams in fieldwork.

Notes

1 The fieldwork period was effectively extended by visits to interlocutors in Copenhagen, United Arab Emirates, Iran (2015) and Jordan (2016).

2 Viber is an instant messaging and Voice over IP (VoIP) app integrating instant messaging, images, video and audio. FaceTime is a videotelephony, but the term 'facetiming' is used by interlocutors also for Viber, and Skype.

3 The WhatsApp application integrates photos, text and small videos.

4 So-called snaps are sent from the Snapchat-photo messaging application that allows users to take photos, record videos, add text and drawings, and send them to a controlled list of recipients. The content is deleted after a set time limit of maximum 10 seconds.

5 For a review of work on the imaginary, see Sneath, Holbraad and Pedersen (2009).

References

Bateson, G., 2000 [1972]. *Steps to an Ecology of Mind: Collected Essays in Anthropology, Psychiatry, Evolution and Epistemology*. Chicago and London: The University of Chicago Press.

Chittick, W., 1994. *Imaginal Worlds: Ibn Al-'Arabi and the Problem of Religious Diversity*. Albany: State University of New York Press.

Corbin, H., 1976. *Mundus Imaginalis: Or, the Imaginary and the Imaginal*. Ipswich: Golgonooza Press.

Edgar, I., 2004. *Guide to Imagework: Imagination-Based Research Methods*. London: Routledge.

Edgar, I. and D. Henig, 2010. 'Istikhara: The Guidance and Practice of Islamic Dream Incubation Through Ethnographic Comparison'. *History and Anthropology* 21 (3): 251–62.

Hannerz, U., 2015. 'Writing Futures: An Anthropologist's View of Global Scenarios'. *Current Anthropology* 56 (6): 797–818.

Haraway, D., 2016. *Manifestly Haraway*. Minneapolis and London: University of Minnesota Press.

Hirschkind, C. 2006. *The Ethical Soundscape: Cassette Sermons and Islamic Counterpublics*. New York: Columbia University Press.

Huntington, S., 1993. 'The Clash of Civilizations?'. *Foreign Affairs* 73 (3): 22–49.

Jacobsen, B. A., 2012. Islam i Danmark. *Religion i Danmark 2012: en e-årbog fra Center for Samtidsreligion,* M. Nielsen (ed.), 111–15. Aarhus: Center for Samtidsreligion, Aarhus Universitet.

Mahmood, S., 2009. 'Religious Reason and Secular Affect: An Incommensurable Divide?' In T. Asad, W. Brown, J. Butler and S. Mahmood (eds), *Is Critique Secular? Blasphemy, Injury, and Free Speech*, 64–100. Berkeley: University of California, Townsend Center for the Humanities.

Mahmood, S., 2012 [2004]. *Politics of Piety: The Islamic Revival and the Feminist Subject*. Princeton and Oxford: Princeton University Press.

Marks, L. U., 2016. 'Real Images Flow: Mullâ Sadrâ Meets Film-Philosophy'. *Film-Philosophy* 20 (1): 24–46.

Mische, A., 2009. 'Projects and Possibilities: Researching Futures in Action'. *Sociological Forum* 24 (3): 694–704.

Mittermaier, A., 2012. 'Dreams from Elsewhere: Muslim subjectivities beyond the trope of self-cultivation'. *Journal of the Royal Anthropological Institute* 18: 247–65.

Miyazaki, H., 2004. *The Method of Hope: Anthropology, Philosophy, and Fijian Knowledge*. Stanford, CA: Stanford University Press.

Miyazaki, H., 2014. 'Insistence and Response: On Ethnographic Replication'. *Common Knowledge* 20 (3): 518–26.

Pink, S., H. Horst, J. Postill, L. Hjorth, T. Lewis and J. Tacchi, 2016. *Digital Ethnography. Principles and Practice*. Los Angeles and London: Sage.

Rytter, M. and M. H. Pedersen, 2014. 'A decade of suspicion: Islam and Muslims in Denmark after 9/11'. *Ethnic and Racial Studies* 37 (13): 2303–21.

Sneath, D., M. Holbraad and M. A. Pedersen, 2009. 'Technologies of the Imagination: An Introduction'. *Ethnos* 74 (1): 5–30.

Suhr, C., 2013. 'Descending with Angels: The invisible in Danish psychiatry and Islamic exorcism'. Unpublished PhD thesis. Department of Culture and Society, Aarhus University.

Waltorp, K., 2015. 'Keeping cool, staying virtuous: Social media and the composite habitus of young Muslim women in Copenhagen'. MedieKultur: *Journal of Media and Communication Studies* 58: 49–67.

Werbner, P. 2004. 'The predicament of diaspora and millennial Islam. Reflections on September 11, 2001'. *Ethnicities* 4 (4): 451–76.

8

Future in the ethnographic world

Débora Lanzeni and Elisenda Ardèvol

Introduction

In this chapter we propose an approach that treats future as an analytical tool that emerges in the context of ethnographic work. This involves a concept of future that is produced as the outcome of a mutual engagement between the ethnographer on the one hand, and on the other the people and things who are part of our ethnographic worlds. In doing so we draw on the example of how this approach was developed and mobilized in an ethnographic project undertaken in, and with participants of, the world of digital technology design. In this world, future is in the making, and ethnography has a specific mode of knowledge production that actively participates in this worldmaking (Pink 2014). Future does not exist outside the world we inhabit and there is no singular, universal future. As suggested by Hodges (2014), in both our ethnographic and analytical practice we need to seek concepts that are actively produced through everyday life, rather than treat concepts as things that can *stand* for everyday life, as empty forms awaiting content.

In this chapter we discuss how we came to conceptualize the future on the terms of technology developers and designers, in a way that is rooted in anthropology, but empirically informed and interdisciplinary in scope. Here, future, rather than a ready-made concept that can be applied to ethnographic analysis, has emerged as something that has to be conceptualized and contextualized through vernacular doings and understandings.

Unlocking the future

Researching a phenomenon that media news, advertising companies, marketing managers, speculative designers, urban planners, start-up CEOs and so on, speak about as something that is not yet here, but coming soon, seems somewhat complicated. This is even more so when we tackle this question through ethnography, which is usually situated in a continuous present or devoted to analysing what has already happened in the recent past (Ingold 1996). Moreover, it seems difficult to grasp what this 'something' is. The developers of smart technologies themselves often say that what is announced through media channels as the last novelty is already 'over'. For them it is nothing more than a vestige of the past years of work in their labs, or at most, the past potential of what they have in hand today (the next future of others [us]). As Lucy Suchman quotes from her research at Palo Alto, 'future arrives sooner here' (2011: 2), creating a kind of spatial and temporal distance in relation to a universal chronological time. This perspective presents Silicon Valley as singular place inhabited by an elite that already lives in the future while others (the lay people, the periphery) are still living in the recent past. This raises a series of questions about how we situate future temporally: Do we live in different times? Does future arrive sooner there? What does 'future' mean for the people involved in producing our next futures? Obviously, designers do not believe that they are living in the future, in a different time to ours. They know that some of the things they are doing now will be part of our futures, while others will not. But they work for the future; they know they shape the things to come.

Design research has been well aware of the importance on digging into the future for long time now. Design is a future-oriented activity as many scholars have noted across design research and in science and technology studies (Williams 2008; Nowotny 2011; Dourish and Bell 2011; Gunn et al. 2013; Pink 2014). Technological visions have many faces and illuminate different future worlds, but technological futures that we envisage might not manifest themselves as expected.

In design, visions of future find their ground on *things*, how things will be after the design process, and the role of the specific thing at hand when it will be out in a different social context (Gunn et al. 2013). But in technological design *things* are bound to a broader process where visions of future are also produced, and which is inseparable from the design context and the specific market that this 'thing' is designed to participate in.

Therefore to study how 'innovation' emerges ethnographically, for example in an urban lab in Barcelona, we need to unlock 'future' by situating it in the mundane terrain of the developers' activity. The visions of the future and the daily management of the future in fablabs feed into concepts used in the technology market, but these are not the same thing. Futures that matter inhabit the very processes of making technology possible. Visions of future interpellate what in the market is seen as innovation in dialogue with design processes that obviously are never linear, or new. That is, to comprehend how designers conceptualize 'innovation' and strategically play with its meanings it is necessary to understand that future is not just a temporary moment in a line. Rather we need to acknowledge that there are several futures, which interweave with each other to simultaneously bring these native notions of innovation into play while also confronting them.

For example, Luc became a tech evangelist in addition to other projects related with smart technologies he was carrying out. Speaking of his involvement he said, 'I believe in this. Telling Debora that I organize these meetings because what I want is to bring in the ones that are interested in technology for the future.' He explained that to be an evangelist is a way to open the market. This involves not simply seeking to make people understand what smart technology is, but mainly to help companies understand the roles they can play in the development of the Smart Tech field. Large companies such as Intel, have their evangelists, too. For instance, tech evangelists are responsible for going to hackathons and new platforms designed to promote the virtues that technology brings. Specifically smart technologies are attached, on the one hand, to the creation of an internal market (which encourages companies to develop them) and on the other, to an external market (which encourages society to be open to receive these technologies). This is based not only on what these technologies make possible, but reflects a situation where in order for these technologies to participate in the future, the future needs to be projected into (and by) them. The role of the evangelist is therefore integral to the design of smart technology as it is aligned to visions of the future, and is designed for a 'world to come', and for an emerging market (Lanzeni 2016b).

Future is made and fixed in mundane social and digital-material life, as Watts (2015) explains for the mobile industry. The common sense definition of *innovation* is, with reference to the market, is built on this everyday future making. However in order to understand how other processes are bound to vernacular understanding of futures, we need to reconsider the temporality of future. This allows us to examine how design processes enact certain notions of future that, for the market, are linked to innovation but for the designers themselves are strategically used but never conceptualized as such (Lanzeni 2016a). Existing studies of technological futures however do not attend this tension between vernacular understanding of future and the visions of a future for the specific project at hand, which we argue is at the core of the actual making of technology.

No future for you: Then, you have to make it

In *DIY Citizenship* (2014) Ratto and Boler have highlighted the contemporary call to make things by ourselves in order to fully participate in the social fabric, across fields such as technology, medical care or, even, biology. This idea is well known and circulates in the makerspaces and in the fablabs where the development of smart technologies is happening. One of these spaces is MOB makers of Barcelona. Some evenings the co-workers of MOB make space in their schedules to organize talks and meetings about their interests. Internet of Things, 3D printing and DIY are the hottest topics but food, social economy or games are also part of the repertoire and their meetings are open to anyone in the city. One Tuesday evening two years ago, there were two events scheduled at the same time: a Michel Bauwens talk on Peer-to-Peer economy and an Internet of Things (IoT)[1] Barcelona meeting. Bauwens was speaking on the main floor of MOB and the IoT meeting was in the basement where, at that time, the makerspace MADE was located. From the stairs both the speakers at the IoT meeting and Bauwens's very passionate speech were audible. On the first floor, listening to Bauwens, was an assorted group of academics, designers, eco-activists, and people who self-labelled as hackers and makers. They were paying careful attention to the presentation, which aimed to introduce the public to a new kind of economy that was flourishing all over the world. Meanwhile, in the basement, most of the attendees were seeking hints and tips about new technologies, as Marc, who was the event's main host and a very well-known engineer in the IoT scene, usually says: 'We are a bunch of people that have in common an interest in learning how make good technology.' The presentations ranged from 'how to calibrate a spectrometer' to 'the management of an IoT start-up', but all of them included technical explanations and a personal introduction by the speakers. 'The market' appeared in both events: on the first floor as a common enemy for a healthy social future, in the basement, as something to reach with a myriad modes and strategies, ranging from a start-up to the deployment of a smart homemade sensor that enabled citizens to measure their own local environment. A newcomer to the co-working scene at that moment could have easily understood both events as two unconnected meetings that barely had anything in common, with such different communities and presentation formats. Yet sooner or later that impression would have changed as the speakers advanced over time into the more practical elements of their performances. Within seconds, the newcomer would have begun to hear phrases like 'we need to do it by ourselves', 'the citizens have to embrace technology as makers not as consumers', 'the future has been compromised by the governments and the multinationals without scruples'. In other words, two very dissimilar speeches finally melted into the same words which were delivered in what at first glance appeared to be almost opposite contexts. One could say that on the first floor these ideas were genuinely radical, while in the basement they represented a second-hand appropriation by mainstream capitalism. Nevertheless this would be a clumsy interpretation and would involve the imposition of the moral values of the observer onto the events. Moreover we note that there was no clear boundary between the two floors, and people moved freely between the two events. It is significant that in both events, 'future' was seen as something that had to be built, technology was seen as constitutive of that future, the citizens responded to take part in defining it, and the particular way future was being built was crucial. The two events were part of the same scene, and despite their apparent differences, they are implicated in the same sets of consequences.

Similar themes emerged in other ethnographic encounters. World Mobile Congress in Barcelona took place in February 2014, and the Mini Maker Faire, in June of the same year. One is a large international congress that sits at the core of the technology industry: the other is a local version of a global action consisting of a craft and artisanal faire pivoting around smart and digital technologies, and with many international participants. Initially these likewise appear to be opposed contexts, where similar technologies and their related meanings were performed by attendees and organizers. At both events the technological future was propelled and topped as 'the' theme but differently enacted.

There is no doubt that imagery of future is part of the marketing of digital technologies, and it was a very visible component in the stands of the companies in the World Mobile Congress. The congress was full of images of how bewildering our technological future might be. However, unexpectedly, this context also called on anyone concerned about the world we live in to get involved in its making. Most of the images and slogans reflected the potential of smart technologies to help regular people to take part in the fabric of the future in an easy and affordable ways. The two biggest companies in this business sector were located in a pavilion where visitors could go to participate in workshops and 'speed dating' with them about the kind of mobile industry it would be worth developing for the future, and learn how to collaborate to make such future practicable.

Meanwhile, in the Mini Maker Fair, future was also part of the imagery but rather than representing technology companies already established in the market, it presented crafted technological artefacts which had been made to be understandable and reproducible by non-experts as well as experts. In the corridors of the venue people walked around stands holding not only 'Do It Yourself' smart technology projects but artisan objects and a myriad of 3D printing designs. All of these claimed to have gone through the same process of working with a citizen driven idea and open production. Technology designers as well as artisans were discussing the kind of software that allows them to 'hack' or improve a 3D printing, while a visitor asked the organizers how they could start to work in an open science project led by the person on a stand selling hand-made drones for watching nocturnal life or taking care of urban vegetable gardens. In this event the urgent call to 'make the future' was likewise at the fore, but unlike the congress, here making the future was put into practice, and was evident throughout the Fair. Open technology futures were set out on every stand. Its call for the future was for both advocates and makers to continue their work, to keep the future alive.

In these two scenarios, the possible world that the mobile market invoked and the possible world that maker environments promote are emplaced in different imaginaries of future. Nevertheless they are made by/through the same contested technologies and means as well as supported by the same visions of making. In the design of smart technologies – for market or for common good – the future is not anymore *there*, and it is not available for anyone. It could only exist through envisaging a possible world through making it. In these two contexts, the way to understand and perform the future is through making technology rather than understanding the future itself as a temporal moment that will come sooner or later, or as a realm that has to be boosted though, or filled with present actions. Imaginaries and visions of future are part of the production of the collective future. Future for them all must be a collective endeavour, which occurs in the act of making technology work.

Those situations illuminate a common understanding of what 'future' means in the development of smart technologies in different Urban Labs, designers and companies across the world that meet in Barcelona for different purposes. The 'maker scene' (Lindtner 2015; Lanzeni 2016b) that encompasses the development of smart technologies made by people who aim to make things themselves, and want to open technology to everyone, in order to change the world for the better and share a common understanding of future. This is attached to how they relate to the 'market scene' and to the market oriented design of smart technologies by employees or by independent designers involved in projects framed by local and international for-profit companies and start-ups. These two scenarios are also usually described as almost separate universes in literature about smart technology design, and the contemporary production of technology by hackers, free software communities, makers and DIY advocates (Coleman 2013; Light 2014; Kelty 2008; Ratto and Boler 2014), or professional designers and technology developers at large (Suchman 2007 2011; Lange 2012; Strengers 2013; Watts 2015; Gunn, et al. 2013). Yet ethnographic research shows that these scenarios are in fact entangled and that they share an understanding of future, which is both rooted in the ways they develop technology and makes technology development possible.

The future is (not) a strange land

In anthropology, the future has often been displaced by a focus on the past-present. Yet, the way that we relate past and present also inevitably has to do with the way past and present relate to the future. Thus, any study about past-present or present-future relations bears an inescapable connection to past-present-future relations. To paraphrase L. P. Hartley, that 'The past is a foreign country' (which is also the title of David Lowenthal's great treatise about the past), the future in anthropology has conventionally appeared as a 'strange land' that it seems impossible to step into when standing in the present.

The future takes different forms in the different attempts that anthropologists have made towards analysing it. In earlier work this was manifested for example in Alfred Gell's (1992) focus on the anthropological study of time, and the work of Nancy Munn (1992), as discussed in the introduction to this book. However, more recently time-future related studies have proliferated, with a particular concern for people's expectations, and how people orient themselves in relation to the unknown future. These works range from the sociology of expectations (Brown and Michael 2003; Adam 2009) to human geography (Thrift and French 2002; Anderson 2007; Zook and Graham 2007; Kinsley 2012) and anthropology (Moore 1990; Maurer and Schwab 2006; Bell 2011; Nielsen 2011; Suchman 2012), and many other works related to technology studies and design (Bowker and Star 1999; Dourish and Bell 2011; Fuller 2011; Mackenzie 2012). In addition, in the last five years in the social study of new technologies there has been a focus on technology and space (through notions of cyberspace, media space, media ecology and digispace, etc.), often inspired by Doreen Massey's (2005) discussions of the space-time relationship.

Munn (1992) has argued that the space-time dynamic is usually understood in the social sciences in relation to the actions, the actors and the objects of study. Space and time are taken either as cognitive categories that work such as theoretical constructs used by researchers and applied to the social forms we study. Therefore, the production of knowledge about time and place and the different analyses that are made are usually coupled to theoretical and empirical arguments that precede them.

In contrast to these socio-cognitive approaches, the emphasis on time as experienced, or time that can be experienced, has been a constant concern of anthropology (Gell 1992). This phenomenological perspective also paves the way to consider time as a subjective experience, alongside the idea that time is something that can be counted (and thus, is objective); this dual conception of time has been used to build time as a cultural category rather than being solely something of the physical world (Fabian 2014). This latter approach has become a kind of sociological common sense that has leaked into most of the contemporary studies that attempt to analyse notions of time and space in relation to new technologies and media. However an analysis of the origins of the common sense demonstrates how anthropology has backed certain images in relation to time in order to avoid *apriori* typifications. Munn (1992) distinguishes two movements in anthropology: one refers to the quality of *time* and the other is the *temporary movement*. These are not mutually exclusive but both are based on two common sociological understandings that are recurrent in the study of the visions about the future to our knowledge. The concept of the quality of *time* is based on Durkheiminan notions of social time and personal time, which distinguishes between subjective and collective mental perceptions of time. The *temporary movement* is based in the course of activities, events and units that are likely to be recorded by people. This time is collective and responds to human action and social behaviour with a particular passage of time or related to a specific event (such as a birthday, or a ritual of transition). Both are based on cultural perceptions of the passage of time; the first refers to 'activities' (reckoning time) while the second refers to experience derived from immersion in activities (*inner durée*). These two images have survived and have become quasi qualities of our contemporary notion of time. Nevertheless spatial and temporal dimensions cannot always be unravelled, it is essential to understand this entanglement (Munn 1992: 94), and to account for how other categories, such as materiality, are also inseparable from everyday life and our conceptualizations of 'lived' time. Thus, the conceptualization of *lived time* enables us to imagine other conceptions of time that are not subject to these binomial categories: either subjective experience or objective countable duration. Moreover, this freeing of the concept of time from its reference to duration and subjective experience, allows us to explore how future is present in its vernacular forms among smart technology developers, where it exceeds its temporal-spatial categorizations.

Active futures

'The river is the only thing that separates my company and here … I do firmware here and there.' Tom was answering Anne's question about the differences between his everyday work in his company and what he was doing at the time in the London Open Data Hackathon. Tom develops firmware (enduring software programmed into a read-only memory) in a company that makes 'resources for Smart City makers'. He makes shields that connect sensors to each other, to a diverse infrastructure network and to the Internet. Tom's company was regarded by the 'local maker community' as the best in the 'British maker market'; and provided most of the shields that participants were using to build *kits for grab data from London network railways*. At the beginning of the first day of the hackathon, Tom expounded to his group the leitmotiv of what they had to develop in response to the challenged posed by the organization: 'They are asking us to create new devices for the future of public data ... that help people to engage with their city and its infrastructure. What we will do is keep our *shit* ongoing, so let's connect the Bombay shield with the sensor platform that the train company bring and then convert the wagon vibrations in data ....' The rest of that day and next day Tom and his three workmates worked on making from scratch the shield that they produce in their company, so they could connect it to the sensor platform that the municipality of London use to measure seismic movements. Anne, who was working as host of the event, was walking around the working groups and collecting impressions of what the participants were doing so she could do a wrapping up at the end of the hackathon. When she arrived at Tom's group she asked what kind of innovation they were working on; one of the participants, Peter, said, 'Perhaps we may show you.' The members of the group were working around group an octagonal table, over which there was a set composed of the shield with three sensors connected, a laptop and two very old accelerometers. Peter started talking about how in using the accelerometers they had recalculated vibrations from the railway platform that they received in real time and connected it to the shield that could combine this with other environmental (noise and light) measurement devices. Ann then asked what was new about this arrangement and how it could help improve Londoners' experiences of everyday commuting. 'Well, what we are doing is a concrete way to processes the data that is already there,' Tom said, looking at Peter. 'So, the municipality has the platform, we have the shield, all of us have the accelerometers, and what we are doing is combining the maps of route and distances with the amount of everyday passengers and with the vibrations, so we will know in which areas the train is triggering more tremblings ... so we can calculated in which areas they need new lines of trains ....'

'But this information is already there, so what is innovative and open here?' Ann insisted. 'We are using something that municipality is not using that it is very important to know, where is more need of trains ... that is open, isn't?' Pete replied. 'I think the challenge of this hackathon was to create a *new tool* that helps people to manage their own data and have a nicer commuting experience, right?', said Ann, demonstrating that she was worried about the performance of the team, and continuing, 'OK, then when the municipality gets *this shit* done come to visit me to the nursing home!'

What the group was doing is perceived as part of what could be made here and now to propel people into an improved future that would fulfil the vision of 'a nicer commuting experience enhanced by technology'. Based on the concrete things they had at hand (Bombay shield, accelerometers, the railway platform, etc.) intertwined with the designers' vision of future concerning the role that data plays in technology development they sought to make 'something that only would be useful when [it] enables other uses of the infrastructures'. Therefore they continued making and exploring existing technology by making new connections while keeping in mind others people's future visions. However the designers could not make the future that they had been challenged to create by the hackathon, since future for them was only reachable though making the actual technology at hand, which would eventually become *future*. Innovation then is not understood here as introducing new things (which is a waste of time), but as improvising and improving with what you have at hand.

For these designers, because future is linked to a very material practice (applications, a platform, multiple ways of connecting the same shield, etc.), it can only be reached through action. This specific form of action is connected to certain visions of future, which involve doing what can be achieved with the technologies at hand, is also related to visions of desirable future (a nicer commuting experience, a safer life through technology, etc.). Yet within this vision, what future will be like is unknowable, and designers, managers and lay people acknowledge that the majority of the image of future that are implied may never come about.

Therefore smart technology design is a future oriented practice linked to visions of future that are shared social imaginaries concerning what technology could make possible (Dourish and Bell 2011; Kinsley 2012). It tends to be combined with social imaginaries about the capacity to solve problems through technology, or a 'solution paradigm' and cutting-edge images (of unknowable but imagined futures) that are used to project the technology into the world. These three interrelated dimensions were evident in ethnographic fieldwork (Lanzeni 2016b) where making technology emerged as, rather than being action in the present, action that brings into existence the vernacular understandings and the experience of the future. As we have shown, future is part of making technology in many different ways. Moreover, it operates in practice in everyday life. As Ahmed has noted, orientation matters (2010) and in design and technology development actions and thoughts of the future are oriented towards the making of 'things'. As outlined below, following the logic that seems mark design processes, challenged 'future' through native conceptions involved in making and doing, can open a fruitful analytical path and tangentially illuminate the significant role that the 'future' has in creating everyday social worlds for technology developers. Future here goes beyond the past-present-future tenses. Future is not only a category of time but instead it articulates several dimensions. In the case discussed here, these are orientation for design, and a possible, collective, social and unknowable future (Lanzeni 2016a). If we release future from its temporal constraints, we can open a fruitful analytical path that demonstrates the role of 'future' in creating everyday social worlds.

By putting the materialization of smart technologies at the centre of the analysis of a vernacular understanding of future we do not intend to eliminate time as a relevant category, but to open up alternatives ways of understanding the meaning the future and how it is practiced, lived and enacted by people. This includes the possibility of investigating other categories that emerge as a key to understanding our partners in ethnography and in turn enrich our research. By divesting (if only temporarily) the processes of design and technology making from the imagery of time it is possible to enable native categories to come to the fore and therefore to open up alternative ways ways of doing and thinking to those that have conventionally dominated anthropological-ethnographic practice and theory. In other words, we argue for an anthropological approach that focuses on the heterogeneous processes through which vernacular future and technological making emerge in life.

Conclusions

In this chapter we have approached the notion of futures ethnographically, as a lived category that should not be pre-configured. Thus we call for a fresh dialogue around the future as a category of thought, to avoid the imposition of our existing concepts and common sense understandings of time onto the sites of our ethnographic fieldwork and analysis.

Here we have conceptualized the vernacular future of smart technology designers as always existing within the realm of action. As we have seen, for smart technology developers action goes hand-in-hand with the envisioning of possible worlds and possible worlds open up the conceptualization of the technologies that are in the processes of being. Future in the ordinary life of the designers we have been working with is not reducible to the pursuit of an improved world or to a specific temporal moment that is coming or that is reachable. Future is something alive which only exists thought the processes by which it is made in the form of technology.

We have revealed how future as an analytical category can be productively related with ours and other vernacular categories of thought and as actions in the world. In doing so we have followed five steps. First, we resituated future in the ordinary world we live in; people are 'in' time, rather than simply conceiving or perceiving it (Munn 1992). Second, we sought to avoid a priori typifications that do not fully embrace the complexities of future constructions in multiple actual contexts; for instance, we evaded using future to describe an historical era or to characterize societies, professions or tasks by tempo or duration (Suchman 2011). Third, we placed future in its past-present-future relations, looking not only to 'the past in the present' but also to 'the future in the present', and how these relations are lived in the ethnographic context we engaged with, in order to chart how this category is related with other categories, actions and situations in the flux of everyday life (Nielsen 2011). As a fourth step, we show how future is not only a time tense, mode or aspect ('I will do that in the future'), but rather can be the product of an action ('I am making the future'), a state of being ('this is a thing of the future'), a site ('the future is around the corner'), something that acts and moves ('the future is coming soon'), something that needs to be fed ('I do this for the future'), and so on. Moreover as we have shown through ethnographies of smart technology designers, future is something that can be made. Future, we argue, as an analytical category can be released from its restrictive lodging in time relations, and, when this theoretical movement is grounded in ethnographic knowing and experience, it allows us to understand how future operates, lives and is lived in every ethnographic context. Finally, we undertook a fifth methodological movement to acknowledge that by learning others' futures in this way we are also actively intervening (with them) in future making, whatever that means. As Tim Ingold (2013) remarks, knowing from the inside is learning from others what they have to teach us and involves becoming wayfarers with them. In this wayfaring we did not seek to know what future really is, but to enhance future with other understandings and in doing so to open up future as an analytical tool of inquiry. Through these five movements we propose that we need to construct open categories of thought in order to an alternative methodological path through which to work with the future ethnographically (and anthropologically).

Acknowledgement

We thank Sarah Pink for her comments on this chapter and to the correspondents in the field, whose names have been changed in order to keep their privacy. This chapter presents selected findings from Débora Lanzeni's PhD thesis: *Future Makers; un estudio etnográfico sobre los procesos de diseño de Smart Things/ Smart Citizens y sus visiones de futuro* (2016), and it is part of our current research in the project D-Future; *Future Practices: Spaces of Digital Creation and Social Innovation* founded by Ministerio de Economía y Competitividad (MINECO) – Ref. CSO2014-58196-P.

Note

1 The Internet of Things (IoT) is the network of physical objects – devices, vehicles, buildings and other items – embedded with electronics, software, sensors, and network connectivity that enables these objects to collect and exchange data. Source Wikipedia.

References

Adam, B., 2009. 'Cultural Future Matters: An exploration in the spirit of Max Weber's methodological writings'. *Time & Society* 18 (1): 7–25.

Ahmed, S., 2010. 'Orientations Matter'. In D. Coole and S. Frost (eds), *New Materialisms: Ontology, Agency and Politics*, 234–57. Durham: Duke University Press.

Anderson, B., 2007. 'Hope for nanotechnology: Anticipatory knowledge and the governance of affect'. *Area* 39 (2): 156–65.

Bell, G. and P. Dourish, 2010. *Telling Techno-cultural Tales*. Cambridge: MIT Press.

Bourdieu, P. and L. Wacquant, 1995. *Respuestas: Por una antropología reflexiva*. México: Grijalbo.

Bowker, G. and S. Star, 1999. *Sorting Things Out. Classification and its Consequences*. Cambridge: MIT Press.

Brown, N. and M. Michael, 2003. 'A sociology of expectations: Retrospecting prospects and prospecting retrospects'. *Technology Analysis & Strategic Management* 15 (1): 3–18.

Coleman, E. G., 2013. *Coding Freedom: The Ethics and Aesthetics of Hacking*. Princeton, NJ: Princeton University Press.

Dourish, P. and G. Bell, 2011. *Divining a Digital Future: Mess and Mythology in Ubiquitous Computing*. Cambridge: MIT Press.

Fabian, J., 2014. *Time and the Other: How Anthropology Makes its Object*. New York: Columbia University Press.

Fuller, M., 2005. *Media Ecologies: Materialist Energies in Art and Technoculture*. Cambridge: MIT Press.

Fuller, M., 2011. 'Boxes Towards Bananas'. In M. Shepard (ed.), *Sentient City*. New York: MIT Press / Architectural League of New York.

Gell, A., 1992. *The Anthropology of Time: Cultural Constructions of Temporal Maps and Images*. Oxford: Berg.

Gunn, W., T. Otto and R. C. Smith (eds), 2013. *Design Anthropology: Theory and Practice*. London: A&C Black.

Heilbroner, R. L., 1967. 'Do machines make history?'. *Technology and Culture* 8 (3): 335–45.

Hodges, M., 2014. 'Immanent anthropology: A comparative study of "process" in contemporary France'. *Journal of the Royal Anthropological Institute* 20 (S1): 33–51.

Ingold, T., 1996. *Key Debates in Anthropology*. London: Psychology Press.

Ingold, T., 2013. *Making: Anthropology, Archaeology, Art and Architecture*. London: Routledge.

Kelty, C., 2008. *Two Bits: The Cultural Significance of Free Software and the Internet*. Durham: Duke University Press.

Kelty, C., 2013. 'There is no free software'. *Journal of Peer Production* 1 (3).

Kinsley, S., 2012. 'Futures in the making: Practices for anticipating "ubiquitous computing"'. *Environment and Planning A* 44 (7): 1554–69.

Lange, P., 2008. 'Interruptions and intertasking in distributed knowledge work'. *NAPA Bulletin* 30 (1): 128–47.

Lange, P., 2012. 'Doing it Yourself With Others'. *New Media and Society* 14 (3): 533–8.

Lanzeni, D., 2016a. 'Smart Global Futures: Designing Affordable Materialities for Better Life'. In S. Pink, E. Ardèvol and D. Lanzeni (eds), *Designing Digital Materialities*, 70–96. London: Bloomsbury.

Lanzeni, D., 2016b. *Future Makers. un estudio etnográfico sobre los procesos de diseño de Smart Things/ Smart Citizens y sus visiones de futuro*. Doctoral dissertation, IN3-UOC, Barcelona, Spain.

Light, A., 2014. 'Citizen Innovation: ActiveEnergy and the Quest for Sustenible Design'. In M. Ratto and M. Boler (eds), *DIY citizenship: Critical Making and Social Media*. Cambridge: MIT Press.

Lindtner, S., 2015, July. 'Hacking with Chinese characteristics: The promises of the maker movement against China's manufacturing culture'. *Science, Technology & Human Values* 40 (5): 1–26.

Mackenzie, A., 2012. 'Set'. In C. Lury and N. Wakeford (eds), *Inventive Methods: The Happening of the Social*, 48–60. London: Routledge.

Massey, D., 2005. *For Space*. London: Sage.

Maurer, B. and G. Schwab (eds), 2006. *Accelerating Possession: Global Futures of Property and Personhood*. New York: Columbia University Press.

Moore, H., 1990. 'Visions of the Good Life: Anthropology and the Study of Utopia'. *Cambridge Anthropology* 14 (3): 13–33.

Nielsen, M., 2011. Futures within: Reversible time and house-building in Maputo, Mozambique. *Anthropological Theory* 11 (4): 397–423.

Nowotny, H., 2011. *La curiosidad insaciable: la innovación en un futuro frágil (Vol. 6)*. Editorial UOC.

Pink, S., E. Ardèvol and D. Lanzeni (eds), 2014. *Designing Digital Materialities*, 1–43. London: Bloomsbury.

Ratto, M. and M. Boler (eds), 2014. *DIY Citizenship: Critical Making and Social Media*. Cambridge: MIT Press.

Strengers, Y., 2013. *Smart Energy Technologies in Everyday Life: Smart Utopia?* Basingstoke: Palgrave Macmillan.

Suchman, L., 2002. 'Located accountabilities in technology production'. *Scandinavian Journal of Information Systems* 14 (2): 7.

Suchman, L., 2007. 'Agencies in technology design: Feminist reconfigurations'. Unpublished manuscript.

Suchman, L., 2011. 'Anthropological relocations and the limits of design'. *Annual Review of Anthropology* 40: 1–18.

Thrift, N., 2008. *Non-representational Theory: Space, Politics, Affect*. London: Routledge.

Thrift, N. and S. French, 2002. 'The automatic production of space'. *Transactions of the Institute of British Geographers* 27 (3): 309–35.

Wajcman, J., 2008. 'Life in the fast lane? Towards a sociology of technology and time'. *The British Journal of Sociology* 59 (1): 59–77.

Wallman, S. (ed.), 1992. *Contemporary Futures. Perspectives from Social Anthropology*. London and New York: Routledge.

Watts, L., 2015. 'Future Archaeology Re-animating Innovation in the Mobile Telecoms Industry'. In A. Herman, J. Hadlaw and T. Swiss (eds), *Theories of the Mobile Internet*. London: Taylor & Francis.

Williams, R., 2008. *Notes on the Underground: An Essay on Technology, Society, and the Imagination*. Cambridge: MIT Press.

Zook, M. A. and M. Graham, 2007. 'Mapping DigiPlace: Geocoded Internet data and the representation of place'. *Environment and Planning B: Planning and Design* 34 (3): 466–82.

9

Researching future as an alterity of the present

Sarah Pink, Yoko Akama and Annie Fergusson

Introduction

In this chapter, we introduce an approach to ethnographic practice that focuses on how possible alterities are sensed, imagined and might be realized. In doing so we treat the future as an alterity of the present, rather than something viewed as if from afar. In doing so we suggest that as an alterity of the present, the future is 'other' in that it is both imaginable but unknowable. This, we argue, offers a beneficial way to frame futures in the context of research that seeks to inform, make or understand changes or interventions with people. Our approach blends ethnographic, documentary video and design research in order to shift our terms of engagement with participants and temporalities. We propose that if ethnographic practice (in dialogue with disciplinary theory) is to be fruitfully engaged for collaborative change-making, it needs a methodology that enables researchers to exceed the aim beyond knowing as (and what) others do. Instead, a contemporary approach to ethnographic practice needs to depart from just the known, to consider the uncertainty of the sensory and emotional possibilities of what could or should happen next. Such an approach, we suggest, needs both researchers and participants to imagine possibilities of futures as an alterity of the present, rather than as a distant eventuality. In this chapter, we present an example of how we have put this into practice. The aim of the chapter is therefore not so much to present the findings of a project as something that has been 'discovered' but rather, through a discussion of how we worked with one research participant, to demonstrate the possibilities of the research practice.

To explore with participants the question of how experiences that seep out of the temporality of the present might *feel,* we call for the use of methods and technologies that afford researchers ways to learn and communicate beyond empirical note taking and writing. Therefore we explore the use of video (and/or film) as it has been associated with the production of ways of knowing and understanding the experiences of others that are intimate (Biella 2008), tactile (Marks 2000; MacDougall 1998, 2005) and empathetic (Pink 2015). Moreover because our methodology seeks to blend disciplinary approaches, the anthropological convention of the lone ethnographer is also abandoned. We reflect not on how a single researcher can learn and communicate about other people's experiences and imaginations, but we examine how working in interdisciplinary teams requires us to create/make both forms of documentation to share ways of knowing across persons and disciplines, and methods that blend disciplinary approaches. The blending of the recording techniques of video ethnography (Pink 2013) and phenomenological approaches to ethnographic documentary (e.g. MacDougall 1998, 2005) with design research practices of material documentation (Akama, Pink and Fergusson 2015) creates an ethnographic process which involves shared ways of knowing and audio/visual sensibilities, and becomes more than/ different to any of these three practices when undertaken in isolation.

Blending and unknowing

Our work builds on and advances two key issues that have become part of the way in which ethnography has recently been discussed. First, the increasing 'popularity' of ethnography outside anthropology, which is of concern to anthropologists (see Ingold 2014) who believe that a theoretical-ethnographic dialogue (Pink and Morgan 2014) is generative of 'theoretical insights that could not have been generated in any other way' (Mitchell 2010: 1). We agree with this position but call for it to be disassociated from the long-term fieldwork method as the definition of anthropological practice. Definition via the 'immersion' involved in the long-term fieldwork has already been challenged, for instance through the notion of multi-sited ethnography (Marcus 1995), which leads to shorter fieldwork and methods such as 'interviews, focus groups, life histories, etc' (Mitchell 2010: 7). Yet such methods remain conventional and, we argue, methods that draw from creative practice traditions beyond the social sciences are owed more consideration as techniques that *exceed and alter* the ways of knowing produced by conventional methods, rather than seeking to replace the long-term immersion methods of traditional anthropological ethnography. Short-term ethnography is not a quick and superficial cut to the same findings of a long observational stay, but is constitutive of a different type of encounter, engagement and depth (Pink and Morgan 2014). Its practice has distinct epistemological and ontological framework, which can involve interventional and participatory approaches, such as asking participants to give tours, perform tasks, or to speculate and imagine through material artefacts. Researchers in design anthropology (e.g. Gunn and Donovan 2012; Gunn et al. 2013) also practice ethnography in ways that are inflected with influences of other disciplines. Likewise, we push this further by discussing a blending approach between design, video documentary and anthropological ethnography, whereby anthropological ethnography remains distinctive through its ongoing ethnographic-theoretical dialogue. We advance a call for an open approach to the shape of ethnographic techniques and the temporalities they entail.

Second, the emphasis on ethnographic knowing in twenty-first century anthropological literatures (e.g. Harris 2007; Pink 2015) signals how knowing, and how ethnographers learn to know *with* others (see Ingold 2008) is emergent from ethnographic practice. However research that address questions of change, futures and anticipated but as yet not experienced alterities, needs to investigate beyond what can be known (or on what participants think they know), and shift its focus toward what cannot yet be known and the uncertain. A focus on the condition of not knowing and the uncertainty through which we move forward exists in discussions of maker practice. For instance, Stephanie Bunn, writing of the sensory embodiment of skill in craft work, has discussed the work of the woodworker and writer David Pye who 'sums up this intuitive mastering beautifully as the "workmanship of risk" as opposed to the "workmanship of certainty" which refers more to machine production or "knocking out" work in quantity'. Bunn writes that 'Pye states that true workmanship only happens when "the quality of the result is continually at risk during the process of making" (Pye 1968: 20) '... It is a moment of stepping forward into the unknown. You cannot hold onto what you know, or look back' (Bunn 2011: 24). This willingness to constantly step into the unknown, the uncertain and the risky, is also common to many art, design, theatre, music and other craft-oriented research practices (Barret and Bolt 2007). We advance this discussion by exploring the application of this way of thinking to ethnographic practice, to see it as a 'craft of making' ways of knowing in collaboration with others. Thus as opposed to seeing research as following a 'research design' we might see such research *as making* the methods for exploring uncertainty.

Therefore we discuss how to open out from 'ways of knowing' to explore the 'not known', through short-term ethnographic encounters, and by probing through inviting participants to respond to a speculative question asked in situ. In doing so we have welcomed participants not knowing or not being sure about something as a route to speculative ways of knowing. That anthropological ethnographers would be alert to finding the unexpected will be obvious to some readers; the serendipity (e.g. Okely 1994) of ethnographic learning is well established. However we suggest pushing this further to interrogate the qualities of unknown and uncertainty and make it the site/material for curiosity. While not knowing and speculation is always rooted in existing ways of knowing, speculation has particular characteristics that shift the research agenda. It needs to be theorized as a practice of reconfiguring, adapting and crafting that accommodates risk. To research speculatively we need to engage beyond the certainties of what we and research participants (think we can be certain that we) know or have known in the past. This implies the making of ethnographies that focus towards the future (Gunn and Donovan 2012; Pink 2014), the possible (Halse 2013) and the imagination (Crapanzano 2004). This means shifting the temporal site for ethnography from the unknown to the yet to come.

Fab pod futures

We now explore our approach in relation to a specific project – Fab Pod Futures, part of the Design+Ethnography+Futures research programme (http://d-e-futures.com/). Design+Ethnography+Futures explores the relationship between ethnography and design through a series of themes including uncertainty, disrupting and making. First, we introduce the Fab Pod and our project, and drawing on examples of research encounters with Shanti, one participant, we demonstrate how the methodology has played out in practice. As noted above, we stress here, that our intention is not to report on the findings of the research, but to reflect on the process of the research technique as it was played out with one participant in order to be able to give continuity to the different stages of our encounter. To conclude we argue for blended practice – an approach to researching and imagining that engages practice-based techniques in dialogue with a theory of uncertainty and a penchant for the unknown.

The Fab Pod is situated on the ninth floor of RMIT's Design Hub, an award winning building, inhabited by staff from RMIT University since 2012. It has ten floors, six of which are made up of open-plan 'warehouse room' work space, alongside 'long room' corridors. Two of the authors witnessed its construction. We had begun to sense that there was some debate over how it was experienced as a meeting space, and we were interested in unpacking this. However, the core aim of our project was to learn about the possibilities (both speculative and actual) that had been created by the Fab Pod's design, and how they could play out into future uses and meanings.

The Fab Pod was designed by architecture and spatial sound research colleagues at the Royal Melbourne Institute of Technology University (RMIT) University, as a meeting room to be used in the Hub's open plan workspace. The makers describe it as 'a prototype meeting enclosure located in an open knowledge space ... developed to address acoustic performance ... bringing together existing knowledge of acoustic diffusion, cnc prototyping and digital workflows and craft traditions of making' (Williams et al. 2013). At a creative writing workshop that formed part of our research process (Carlin et al. 2015), Jane Burry, one the Fab Pod's architect, explained how the inspiration for its acoustic design, which uses hyperbolic structures, had come from their work on Antoni Gaudi's Sagrada Familia Cathedral in Barcelona.

Fab Pod Futures began with meetings with two colleagues: Jane Burry, the architect and Xiaojun Qiu, the acoustic engineer who had undertaken measurement studies of the Fab Pod's acoustic performance. The Fab Pod was both an architectural design prototype and a research project in acoustic design, but had not yet achieved an optimal level of acoustic privacy (Qiu et al. 2015). We had learned through experience that there was something unusual about the acoustic properties of the Fab Pod, which had not always

FIGURE 9.1 *Two faces of the exterior of the Fab Pod. Photo by Kyla Brettle. Creative commons license 2014*

FIGURE 9.2 *Working inside during the Essaying the Fab Pod workshop. Photo by Kyla Brettle. Creative commons license 2014.*

met users' expectations for acoustic privacy. To a certain extent, these starting points indicate a process of ethnographic evaluation of how the Fab Pod prototype was experienced by users, to produce insights for making a better meeting room. While our findings do generate such insights, during the research process this was an idea that we sought to disrupt, since we were seeking to undermine the very assumption that it was a meeting room, in order to engage its materiality and sensoriality to invoke ideas that were beyond what it was meant to be and known to be like. Therefore, we treated the Fab Pod as a design probe through which to learn about the potential of designed enclosures, and to some extent about open plan work places. Our work was also an experiment in how to learn about engaging people in fields of potentiality through an artefact.

Knowing in ethnography

Above we noted the focus on knowing in anthropological discussions of ethnographic methodology, around the first decade of the twenty-first century. This literature was part of a move towards situating knowing as incremental, ongoing and as a process that also impacted on other disciplines. The idea that knowing was learned through and generated through practice was disseminated widely through the influential work of Lave and Wenger (1991) and Wenger (1998) on 'communities of practice'. For anthropologists the question of knowing became central to understanding how ethnographers may understand the people they work with in fieldwork (e.g. Harris 2007) and how they distinguished between the knowledge that might be crystallized in representational texts of scholarship, and the ongoing process of embodied and non-representational ways of knowing. Video thus could be used as a medium through which to explore with participants, not simply the knowledge that they could articulate and represent in words, but the ways of knowing in and with things in the world that are performative, sensory and embodied, and perhaps never spoken about (e.g. Grasseni 2004; Pink 2015). Some such approaches have also developed in organization studies, which due to the site of our fieldwork is relevant to account for. In the field of organizational aesthetics Antonio Strati has argued that organizations are not 'exclusively cognitive' constructs but derive 'from the knowledge creating faculties of all the senses' (2000: 13, cited by Warren 2002: 227). Davide Nicolini, Silvia Gherardi and Dvora Yanow have stressed 'knowing in organizations' (2003), and Samantha Warren has advanced this field through a focus on the 'interplays between consumption, aesthetics and organization' with an interest in the 'experiences and feelings' (2002: 231) of employees. By asking her participants to photograph their experiences of their working environment Warren was able to understand how they sensed and felt the work environment, noting how their photographs often referred not to visual sights or forms, but to invisible referents, 'the intangible and largely ineffable experiences of the photographer' (2002: 233). Warren's work illustrates an understudied area in organization studies, and endorses the need for us to take seriously the argument that knowing in organizational environments is embodied, sensory and atmospheric.

The first stage of our Fab Pod Futures research process was focused on bringing to the fore two existing ways of everyday knowing the Fab Pod. To do this we focused on two themes: *First Encounters*; and *Knowing through Contact*. Video recording provides an ideal and a reason to be with and follow the traces of participants around their worlds (Pink 2007; Pink and Leder Mackley 2014). As such, being with people with video, and to video record them as they (re)inhabit, show and experience their environments, their activities and memories is a way of engaging with participants through a shared encounter. However in this case, sharing goes beyond the relationship between the participant and researcher *in situ* since, in teamwork, the research design, tasks, theoretical conversations and analysis are distributed between researchers. This creates a research context which is generative of co-produced ways of knowing that involve assemblages of different researchers, disciplines, participants and materials, what Pink (2015) has elsewhere called an 'ethnographic place'.

The Fab Pod futures video ethnography

We used video ethnography precisely to explore the Fab Pod, across three themes, each of which represented a different temporality and was broadly divided into: how participants had 'met' and learned about the Fab Pod in relation to the building it is part of; how they had experienced the Fab Pod as users; how their expectations as *users* had been framed, and the disappointments and the pleasure these led to; and to speculate with participants

FIGURE 9.3 *Sarah and Annie video record, reflected in the door (left), while Shanti reached out to the building with her hands to explain how she had contemplated its exterior (right). Video still. Copyright Sarah Pink 2014.*

about possible futures or alternatives for the Fab Pod. We wished to undermine its identity as a meeting room, and to collaborate with participants to refigure what they might do with it. This final stage deliberately sought to open up ways of thinking about the Fab Pod as possibly being something else and in doing so, to understand its potentiality beyond the purposes for which it was already being judged.

The first steps of our Fab Pod Futures project were taken outside at the door of the Hub. We asked participants to recollect the first time they came to the building and to then re-trace with us, on video, the route they had taken to encounter the Fab Pod on the ninth floor. Using the building as a prompt, we invited participants to narrate how they felt and what they thought in those moments prior to encountering the Fab Pod.

Shanti recounted, how on arriving, she was not quite sure how to navigate her way to the ninth floor. Smiling as we stepped into the lift, she recalled, 'And I was excited. I was wearing a blue coat. I remember. I remember what I was wearing … I felt excited in a really positive way, not in a scared or anxious way.' As we stepped out of the lift into the Long Room on the ninth floor Shanti continued to describe the 'delicious sense of anticipation of what was going to unfold in this quite beautiful space'.

Shanti led us next to the Fab Pod. She had arrived at the building after the Fab Pod was constructed, and had encountered it as already part of the environment she would work in, obscured from view from her desk by a partition. She told us that 'One of the first things we would have looked at

FIGURE 9.4 *Imagine the feeling of anticipation on walking down the corridor towards the door around the corner at the end. Video still. Copyright Sarah Pink 2014.*

would have been the Fab Pod … I don't remember exactly what happened, but I do remember going along the floor, and thinking "no one else works here because there was like no one else around, but there was this sort of Fab Pod there"'. Shanti did not know about the Fab Pod before she entered the main open-plan area called a Warehouse space. She opened the large glass door and led us in, like other participants, lowering her voice as she entered. She reflected on how 'you come into this space, right, and your voice drops', and that this generates awareness of where others are and of their conversations, thus bringing to the fore the acoustic environment of the open-plan room. This, she said, constituted the 'moment of being at work' – a shift in embodied sensibility to the environment of a work(ing) place which felt different to the entrance area and the lifts. As she commented, re-enacting this process, it enabled her to articulate this experience, in that she 'hadn't realized until we came through that door … that's the moment, I think you move … well I sort of move into a more, a stiller kind of state, maybe its the quiet that does that'. The quiet, she said, was 'quite palpable'.

Shanti recalled her first encounter with the Fab Pod, as an experience in knowing and feeling: 'When I first saw it … it made me laugh because it was like this crazy design thing … there's this object that's modern looking, and kind of strange … what I think of as designed.' At first, 'you don't really know what it is'. She told us how they had gone in, put the lights on and then come out, which was part of the 'tour' that she later repeated whenever she hosted visitors to the Hub. Sarah asked if she had touched it the first time she saw it. Shanti was not sure, but said she would have wanted to, and that she often wants to touch it, going on to show us how she likes its 'furry' blocks.

The auditory, tactile, visual – multisensory – ways that Shanti recalled her first encounter of the Fab Pod and the environment in which it is situated, invites us to reflect on how, when going beyond the conventions of participant observation, an interventional video ethnography can enable participants to (re)create embodied and articulated ways of knowing about past experiences. They explored both what they felt they knew and the embodied, sensory and affective ways in which they had known. Yet, implicit in ethnographic practice is both the impossibility of knowing exactly what others know, and the notion of ethnographic fictions (Clifford 1986), each of which contest the likelihood that we will ever know, or communicate accurately to others, what participants in our research have experienced. We have engaged Shanti's words and video stills to open up the possibility of imagining through her recollections of experiences and ways of knowing, but invite readers to reflexively imagine the rest.

The next stage in our encounters with participants focused on their experiences as users of the Fab Pod. We do not dwell on this here but note that we approached participants' experiences as users through the Fab Pod as

FIGURE 9.5 *Shanti reached out to touch the Fab Pod's furrier shapes. Through this gesture she demonstrated the feeling of being drawn to it, which encouraged us to empathize with this feeling. It is shown here to invite readers to engage with the experience. Video still copyright Sarah Pink 2014.*

an artefact. We learned about different uses for it, sometimes as a meeting room or as a design object to show on tours. In each case we realized that how important it was to to *be in* or to show the Fab Pod. Knowing what the Fab Pod was about, at least in part knowing through the experiences of its qualities and affordances, some of which, due to its design intent as an acoustic space, were pre-framed as sonic.

By moving beyond an observational approach in our encounter with Shanti, and inviting her to recollect her experiences, we have shown how we invited participants to speculate about their past experiences with the Fab Pod. This is on the one hand a critical response to the observational mode of traditional ethnography, and on the other it is an insistence on the relevance of the historicity of contemporary and past ways of knowing to the future orientation of design. Here the role of ethnographic knowing in design is not in understanding how and why design artefacts are used, and suggesting how they might be improved so as to be more satisfactory (or marketable). Instead, the focus is on exploring speculatively how this artefact can participate in the generation of possibilities for human experience, activity and environment. In the next section we take this further through a focus on not knowing.

Ethnography of the not known

Having established what participants thought they knew about the Fab Pod, our next step involved inviting them to speculate about the Fab Pod from new starting points. In this approach we concur with Gatt and Ingold (2013: 141) who wish to depart from 'thinking about anthropology ... as the description and analysis of what has already come to pass', calling 'for a discipline of anthropology conceived as a speculative inquiry into the conditions and possibilities of human life'. We approached this in two ways: through our Essaying the Fab Pod creative writing workshop and publication (Carlin et al. 2015) in an eBook created by Adrian Miles; and by taking a future-focused stance in our video ethnography, discussed below. We detail the latter below.

As outlined in the introduction to this book, there has recently been an increasing move towards anthropologies of futures. Particularly relevant for the discussion here are social science literatures that show how forms of future thinking impact on us as academics working in institutional settings, and have documented and analysed tendencies towards risk-averse or predictive approaches to futures within society (see Pink 2017). Critical approaches call for academics to be engaged more actively with futures. For instance Collins (2008: 8) has argued that anthropology should 'gesture to radical alterity' in its treatment of the future and sociologists have critically revealed how futures are constituted across a range of societal practices and discourses (e.g. Adam and Groves 2007). These sites for discussing futures invite us to ask how – if futures are so central to social research and theoretical agendas – might we research them ethnographically? How might we seek, invoke and research embodied ways of knowing the yet to come, the imagined, or the possible? Concerning how the Fab Pod might be re-thought or differently experienced, concepts of potentiality and the possible offer one way to consider these questions,

Drawing on their anthropological study of biomedicine, Taussig and colleagues (2013) discuss the 'anthropology of potentiality'. They suggest that 'As a conceptual apparatus, potentiality does complex work: to imagine or talk about potential is to imagine or talk about that which does not (yet and may never) exist' and that, 'In some respects, potentiality can be understood as the partner to, or flip side of, "risk" – also defined as a set of possibilities – though it has yet to be theorized in the same way' (Taussig et al. 2013: xx). Like Bunn (2011), their reference to risk and the uncertainty associated with it has positive connotations and potentiality might be engaged 'productively'. They argue for a study of potentiality that should be reflexive about the 'tacit assumptions' underpinning it and the power dynamics that frame it, by focusing on the specific rather than the universal and allows for subjectivity (Ibid.: xx).

The growing field of design anthropology has highlighted the concept of the possible, and ways of engaging with the future that disrupt the practices and principles of traditional ethnographic practice. Ton Otto and Rachel Charlotte Smith (2013: 3) point to how 'anthropology lacks tools and practices to actively engage and collaborate in people's formation of their futures' whereas the discipline of design has always been oriented towards the future. Approaches in participatory design have been catalytic in informing the design anthropology discourse to enable change-making practices in response to social concerns and people's wellbeing. For example, Akama's (2014) work with regional communities in Australia assisted residents to imagine unexpected incidents of natural disasters through 'what if' scenarios that prompts them towards collective preparedness. Instead of prototyping designs in artificial labs and isolated environments, such case studies in participatory design are deliberative in its intervention to provoke alternative ways of imagining and taking action. In other words, there is a 'pursuit of how to best bring people into the design of the invisible, mediating structures around them' (Light and Akama 2014: 153) to enable people to participate in the making of their own futures. In a context where Ingold has argued that 'Anthropology's obsession with ethnography, more than anything else, is curtailing its public voice' and that 'the way to regain it is through reasserting the value of anthropology as a forward-moving discipline dedicated to healing the rupture between imagination and real life' (Ingold 2014: 383), these moves to future-focused ethnographic techniques pave the way to research what is not yet known in ways that are co-directed by participants and researchers.

Likewise we explored, with participants, ways of imagining possible, embodied and sensory experiences of future environments, atmospheres, relationships and relationalities. Like design anthropology where futures and possibilities are explored through both social and material assemblages, in Fab Pod Futures, we sought to engage objects for embodied imagining of a socio-material future.

In this research process, we understand the body and its relationship to the environment as productive of an affective sense or perception of an atmosphere of another alterity. In a way similar to theorists of atmospheres (Böhme 1993), we see this sense or perception as emergent from the relationship between the environment of the present and a human capacity to imagine (in cognitive and embodied ways) what it would feel like beyond the present. Importantly, in a practical sense this means bringing together the materiality of the present with the imagining, sensory, embodied, affective selves of research participants. In this stage of the research we asked participants to re-imagine their encounters with the Fab Pod, by posing questions that consistently removed elements that underpinned the identity of the Fab Pod as an acoustically designed meeting room. We tested possibilities, some as simple as asking what they would do with the Fab Pod if they could take it home, and others more interventional such as inviting them to imagine the Fab Pod as like the 'Tree of Souls' from the feature film *Avatar* and thus the life-source of the Design Hub Building. Significantly, there was a noted shift in how participants engaged when we focused on these imaginative questions. For instance, in dialogue with Shanti, we began to speculate based on her suggestion that the Fab Pod had a sense of non-permanence about it. She wondered if one day she would arrive at work and it would have been taken away. Our speculations ranged from how Shanti thought it had been constructed, how it would be removed in pieces of the right size to go out of the doors, and how she imagined it would be stored, somewhere, out of public view, because 'it wasn't specifically enough purposed to have a place to stay' – in that they 'wouldn't know what to do with it' or it having expired as a design object, in that what had been researched through it had been learned.

If the above emphasizes the limits for the Fab Pod in its current use, Shanti's discussion of how it would feel in other contexts brought to the fore the generative qualities and affordances that she sensed its interior had. For instance, if she could take it home, she would 'make it its own space that either individuals or a group, as a family, we could go to have quiet, cuddly time ... watch a movie, cuddle in there ... read, maybe listen to music with headphones on' – with 'beanbags or a shag pile carpet' 'I think you want to do quiet, sort of physical attitudes of repose ... if there was a giant beanbag.' When we suggested that it might stay in the Hub as something akin to the 'Tree of Souls' from the film *Avatar*, Shanti's comments told us about how her experiences of encountering the Fab Pod in the hub suggested possibilities for its exterior. She suggested that 'it would be almost something you would come to as an object to worship ... the first thing that implies to me is that you are not going in it, you are surrounding it ... if you're having ceremonies for example, where you were recognizing the wonderful ambiguity of this object, then you would be gathering around it ... and to focus people's gaze inward on it'. She mentioned that there might be some 'special' people who could go inside 'and do mysterious unknown things in there', which could be glimpsed in through the windows. Sarah replied that this often does happen when people come on tours of the Hub and see the Fab Pod, indeed as a 'public face', it is a key moment in tours of the building. When we asked Shanti what she would do if the Fab Pod was her office, she returned to the qualities of its interior, saying it would be like a 'cocoon' which for her working style she would find very appealing. She would not be prepared to share it, because 'there is something enclosed about it, which is not just a physical enclosure, it is a contemplative enclosure' and sharing it with someone at work would be 'too intimate' and 'intolerable'.

As for other participants, the Fab Pod was not a meeting room. For Bianca, who had also been a Fab Pod user, for example, standing in its interior became a probe for connecting its affordances and qualities with imagining its possibilities. Bianca, who had earlier noted the scifi affordances of the Fab Pod suggested that 'aliens would probably like this kind of environment, or some kind of frog amphibian man'. She continued to share: 'it kind of feels like frog eggs ... its sort of got that kind of "am I going to emerge as another being?" ... it's the green and the circles and the fact that light is slightly transferred and it's not, its muted, but it's still there ... it's kind of like looking out through lots of eggs'. Bianca's narratives resonate in several ways with those of the participants in our *Essaying the Fab Pod* (Carlin et al. 2015) workshop. Indeed, we argue that ethnographies, even when undertaken with the presentist capacity of video to record what is happening right now, can be coaxed into ambiguous temporalities. In some ways, imagining future alterities is what people do in many contexts, as diverse as renovating a house or participating in forms of activism. If so, the challenge we face as researchers involves developing ways to bring attention to this future orientation that acknowledges our interventions and to critically examine our approaches. In other words, we need a shift from purely attempting to understand how participants imagine alternatives to consider how we (participants and researchers) imagine in ways that make futures together. The implication is that we need to define our role in the inscription of futures with our research participants in ways that trouble traditional paradigms.

Conclusion

We have used our discussion of a methodology of ethnographic, design and video practice to critique traditional anthropological ethnography in its past-orientation, claiming that this renders it difficult for it to participate in change or future-making. Our methodology constituted a technique that was not simply video making, ethnography or design inflected by its partner practices. But rather a blended practice, that was grown in dialogue with a theory of knowing and of the future as an alterity of the present.

Such blending also distinguishes our work from classic anthropology. Our approach to knowing is generated not by the lone ethnographer – the assumed protagonist of much writing on ethnographic knowing and indeed of most anthropological writing about ethnographic fieldwork at all, including that of the reflexive turn of the 1980s. In the context of design anthropology which involves teamwork and interventionist, Otto and Smith have suggested that this brings a 'distinct style of knowing' (2013: 10) whereby 'the production of knowledge involves more than thinking and reasoning: it also comprises practice of acting on the world that generate specific forms of knowledge' (2013: 11). Interdisciplinary and team ethnography makes knowing through dialogue or in dialogue, between participants and between researchers, between practice and theory and between disciplines.

In this chapter, we have presented one possible way to research the future, as an alterity of the present. However the question remains open: we propose putting the question 'what does a future alterity feel like' at the centre of investigations of imagination, the possible, the not yet to come or be. By putting the emphasis in this way on the embodied, sensory and affective ways in which the future becomes part of the present, we open up an alternative way of thinking about what the future means.

References

Adam, B. and C. Groves, 2007. *Future Matters: Action, Knowledge, Ethics.* Leiden: Brill.

Akama, Y., 2014. 'Passing on, handing over, letting go – the passage of embodied design methods for disaster preparedness'. Paper presented to Service Design and Innovation Conference, Lancaster University, UK, 9–11 April 2014.

Akama, Y., S. Pink and A. Fergusson, 2015. 'Design + Ethnography + Futures: Surrendering in Uncertainty'. Paper presented to CHI '15, Seoul, Republic of Korea, April 18–23.

Barret, E. and B. Bolt (eds), 2007. *Practice as Research: Approaches to Creative Arts Enquiry.* New York: I.B. Tauris & Co.

Biella, P, 2008. 'Visual Anthropology in a Time of War'. In M. Strong and L. Wilder (eds), *Viewpoints: Visual Anthropologists at Work.* Austin: University of Texas Press.

Böhme, G., 1993. 'Atmosphere as the Fundamental Concept of a New Aesthetics'. *Thesis Eleven* 36: 113–26.

Bunn, S., 2011. 'Materials in Making'. In T. Ingold (ed.), *Redrawing anthropology.* Farnham: Ashgate: 21–32.

Carlin, D., Y. Akama, S. Pink, A. Miles, K. Brettle, A. Fergusson, B. Magner, A. Pang, F. Rendle-Short and S. Sumartojo, 2015. 'Essaying The Fabpod: An improvised experimental collaborative account of the uncertain cultural life and futures of the fabpod'. *Axon Journal* 8.

Clifford, J., 1986. 'Introduction: Partial Truths'. In J. Clifford and G. Marcus (eds), *Writing Culture: The Poetics and Politics of Ethnography.* Berkeley, CA: University of California Press.

Collins, S. G., 2008. *All Tomorrow's Cultures: Anthropological Engagements with the Future.* Oxford and New York: Berg.

Crapanzano, V., 2004. *Imaginative Horizons.* Chicago: University of Chicago Press.

Gatt, C. and Ingold, T., 2013. 'From Description to Correspondence: Anthropology in Real Time'. In *Design Anthropology: Theory and Practice*, W. Gunn, T. Otto and R. C. Smoth (eds). London: Bloomsbury.

Grasseni, C., 2004. 'Video and Ethnographic Knowledge: Skilled Vision and the Practice of Breeding'. In S. Pink, L. Kürti and A. I. Afonso (eds), *Working Images*. London: Routledge.

Gunn, W., and J. Donovan (eds), 2012. *Design and Anthropology*. Surrey: Ashgate.

Gunn, W. T. Otto and R. Smith (eds), 2013. *Design Anthropology: Theory and Practice*. London: Bloomsbury Academic.

Halse, J., 2013. 'Ethnographies of the Possible'. In W. Gunn, T. Otto and R. C. Smith (eds), *Design Anthropology: Theory and Practice*. London: Bloomsbury.

Harris, M., 2007. 'Introduction: Ways of Knowing'. In M. Harris (ed.), *Ways of Knowing, New Approaches in the Anthropology of Experience and Learning*. Oxford: Berg.

Ingold, T., 2008. 'Anthropology is *not* ethnography'. *Proceedings of the British Academy* 154: 69–92.

Ingold, T., 2014. 'That's enough about ethnography'. *Hau: Journal of Ethnographic Theory* 4 (1): 383–95. Available online: http://dx.doi.org/10.14318/hau4.1.021 (accessed 20 October 2016).

Lave, J. and E. Wenger, 1991. *Situated Learning: Legitimate Peripheral Participation*. Cambridge: Cambridge University Press.

Light, A. and Y. Akama, 2014. 'Structuring Future Social Relations: The Politics of Care in Participatory Practice'. Paper presented to Participatory Design Conference, Windhoek, Namibia, 6–10 October 2014.

MacDougall, D., 1998. *Transcultural Cinema*. Princeton, NJ: Princeton University Press.

MacDougall, D., 2005. *The Corporeal Image: Film, Ethnography, and the Senses*. Princeton, NJ: Princeton University Press.

Marcus, G., 1995. 'Ethnography in/of the World System: The Emergence of Multi-sited Ethnography'. *Annual Review of Anthropology* 24: 95–117.

Marks, L., 2000. *The Skin of the Film*. Durham and London: Duke University Press.

Mitchell, J. P., 2010. 'Introduction'. In M. Melhuus, J. P. Mithcell and H. Wulff (eds), *Ethnographic Practice in the Present*, 1–15. Oxford: Berg.

Nicolini, D, S. Gherardi and D. Yanow (eds), 2003. *Knowing in Organizations*. New York: M. E. Sharpe Inc.

Okely, J., 1994. 'Vicarious and Sensory Knowledge of Chronology and Change: Ageing in Rural France'. In K. Hastrup and P. Hervik (eds), *Social Experience and Anthropological Knowledge*. London: Routledge.

Otto, T. and R. C. Smith, 2013. 'Design Anthropology: A Distinct Style of Knowing'. In W. Gunn, T. Otto and R. C. Smith (eds), *Design Anthropology: Theory and Practice*. London: Bloomsbury Academic.

Pink, S., 2014. 'Digital-Visual-Sensory-Design Anthropology: Ethnography, imagination and intervention'. *Arts and Humanities in Higher Education* 13 (4): 412–27.

Pink, S., 2015. *Doing Sensory Ethnography*. London: Sage.

Pink, S. and K. Leder Mackley, 2014. 'Reenactment Methodologies for Everyday Life Research: Art Therapy Insights for Video Ethnography'. *Visual Studies* 29 (2): 146–54.

Pink, S. and J. Morgan, 2013. 'Short-term ethnography: Intense routes to knowing'. *Symbolic Interaction* 36 (3): 351–61.

Qiu, X., E. Cheng, I. Burnett, N. Williams, J. Burry and M. Burry, 2015. 'Preliminary Study on the Speech Privacy Performance of the Fabpod'. *Acoustics 2015, Hunter Valley.*

Strati, A., 2003. 'Knowing in Practice: Aesthetic Understanding and Tacit Knowledge'. In D. Nicolini, S. Gherardi and D. Yanow (eds), *Knowing in Organisations.* New York: M. E. Sharpe Inc.

Warren, S., 2002. 'Show me how it feels to work here: Using photography to research organizational aesthetics'. *Ephemera: Theory and Politics in Organizations* 2 (3): 224–45.

Wenger, E., 1998. *Communities of Practice: Learning, Meaning, and Identity.* Cambridge: Cambridge University Press.

Williams, N., J. Cherrey, B. Peters and J. Burry, 2013. 'FabPod: A Prototypical Design System for Acoustically Diffused Enclosures'. In M. Stacey (ed.), *Prototyping Architecture: The Conference Papers.* Building Centre Trust, London.

10

Speculative fabulation: Researching worlds to come in Antarctica

Juan Francisco Salazar

Introduction

Antarctica has been imagined and fantasized for millennia, yet it has remained – until now – off-limits to the ethnographic imagination. In this chapter I reflect on a specific aspect of my on-going research and many years of short-term ethnographic fieldwork in the Antarctic Peninsula: the making of the documentary film *Nightfall on Gaia*[1] (2015), which, I argue, illustrates a creative approach to researching futures anthropologically and engaging with an anthropology of extreme environments.

An overarching aim of my research endeavour in the Antarctic has been to better understand how humans are learning to live on the Ice. That is, how humans have come to inhabit an extreme environment that was almost completely out-of-bounds as recently as little more than 100 years ago. For the most part Antarctica has been depicted as a last wilderness, as a continent of science, a place inhabited by fictional characters, as a tourism hotspot, a natural resources frontier, and a space of geopolitical influence, interest and manoeuvring. This chapter situates Antarctica anthropologically through accounts of how transient communities think and perceive the Antarctic world they inhabit and how this world inhabits them. It describes how people living there imagine and explain how the future of the Antarctic is unfolding through a situated, and embodied approach to knowing – and being in – these emerging polar worlds. This chapter is thus a reflection on these experiences in experimenting ethnographically and creatively with anticipatory and speculative narratives of life in Antarctica and how we are beginning to imagine – and inhabit – an anthropogenic Antarctica. The main interest is to offer a 'critical description' (Tsing 2013) of distinctive forms of sociality and subjectivity emerging in Antarctica as a way of suggesting a future ethnographies approach. Drawing on Anna L. Tsing's notion of critical description entails asking urgent (critical) questions and immersing oneself into being curious about how humans and other species 'come into ways of life through webs of social relations' (Tsing 2013: 28).

In this particular case the urgent questions have to do with the predicament that humanity is no longer able to control most of the feedback effects derived from its own actions. Human activity has so profoundly impacted geology and atmospheric cycles that a new geological unit has become necessary to account for measuring the impact of human activities on Earth systems. The Antarctic continent and surrounding ocean are undergoing a profound transformation impelled largely by accelerated change in its ecosystems dynamics. Scientists are painting a sober picture of an unfolding and relent-lessly unravelling future where changes will only intensify considerably in the next fifty years. These changes are also linked to shifting geopolitical under-currents, improved technological and logistical capabilities, intense human activities in the continent and surrounding ocean, and increased interest in its bio-resources. The scope and intensity of human activities in the southern polar region has changed dramatically over the past 100 years and Antarctica is becoming an 'anthropogenic landscape' where the challenges of inten-sifying human activities entail that the current governance system may be insufficient to meet the environmental protection obligations set out under the Madrid Protocol twenty-five years ago. In this regard, Antarctica presents an inherently futures-oriented problem and one of the most serious tests of our collective and coordinated capacity to exercise foresight. Not only to protect these fragile environments, but also to rethink our species as part of and in relation with nature, and to mobilize novel experiments with living differently in the Anthropocene.

On the one hand this entails looking at how Antarctica shapes the future of the planet, but also to speculate how Antarctica can be thought of not only as a laboratory for science, but as a laboratory for thinking alternative ways of living in the Anthropocene.

Discussing the film *Nightfall on Gaia*, a speculative documentary film that I completed in 2015 after four years returning each summer to do ethnographic work in the Antarctic Peninsula, the chapter foregrounds a concern with the relational conditions of life in extreme environments. It also recognizes the future as a deeply relational category that invites facing non-tangible and yet to be worlds: worlds that are nevertheless immanent to the present as they uphold real and material weight in the here and now. As I develop in more detail in the pages that follow, the film seeks to speculate futures through the enactment of a form of generative ethnography. The plot brings together a fictional character in the year 2043 with glimpses of life in the Antarctic in 2012–14 which are treated both as ethnographic fragments and research events which Mike Michaels drawing on Isabelle Stengers (2010) describes as 'open, unfolding and oriented toward the not-as-yet' (Michaels 2016: 100; Stengers 2010). The film was initially conceived as a form of 'immersement' and 'atmospheric attunement' (Stewart 2011) into human and more than human life in the Antarctic. However, it grew into a speculative engagement with Antarctica that sought to identify something beyond the imaginaries of my interlocutors, who were a diverse group of transient and semi-permanent populations of scientists, military, teachers, families, logistics personnel and tourists. It sought to find events that could be narrated with a 'speculative intent' (Michaels 2016). Drawing on the centrality of the speculative as 'a multi-form worlding practice' (Haraway 2013), that is, of being in and making of Antarctic worlds, my concern has been to explore how futures are imagined and hoped for in relation to how novel forms of sociality emerge in extreme environments. These futures are performed and given substance through material entanglements and lively engagements with the more than human world.

Creative experimentations in 'futures anthropology'

As discussed in the Introduction to this volume (Pink and Salazar), since the 1970s anthropologists have highlighted that anthropology's forte has always been disciplined hindsight (Riner 1987) primarily as a consequence of anthropology's inability to describe, critique, and interrogate futures without being imbricated in those same discourses (Collins 2007). Perhaps to an embarrassing extent, thinking about time in anthropology has been far less illuminating about the future than about the past (Guyer 2007) given that anthropologists have consistently engaged with futurity in shreds and patches (Munn 1992). It is not entirely clear whether this has been solely the result of the futility of anthropology's key methodological techniques in analysing or venturing into the future (Heemskerk 2003). Here, in the context of the emergent interest in researching futures across a range of disciplines, I propose that the speculative might be a useful approach for thinking future ethnographies of both a people yet to come and for understandings of present and future 'more-than-human sociality' (Tsing 2013). In this specific case this entails examining ethnographically a range of social practices for inhabiting the extreme, including the very particular and contingent cultural dynamics among international scientific and military stations in the South Shetland Islands, Antarctic Peninsula. It also involves examining concomitant processes of 'making Antarctica familiar' (Bureaud 2012), where living in Antarctica becomes not only a mode of transforming Antarctica into a habitable world – a terraforming process of sorts – but also a way of opening up ways of thinking more than human sociality on Earth and beyond.

While speculation has often lingered at the margins of established histories of knowledge production in both the 'natural' and 'social' sciences, significant exceptions are certainly not hard to find. Speculation takes place across a range of knowledge practices concerned with the uncertainty of unfolding futures, such as commodity futures, predictive genomics, climate change modelling or astrobiology to name a few. Most importantly in relation to this chapter, speculation has gained theoretical traction in disciplines as varied as continental and pragmatist philosophy, speculative design, fiction and literary theory, as well as social science fiction studies. Across a range of social sciences, particularly those inflected by phenomenology, object-oriented ontologies and feminist new materialism, the speculative is being taken up as a practical-theoretical approach to reconceptualising problems and seeking more imaginative propositions. As I explore in the following pages, speculation acts as a means for asking more inventive questions about life in Antarctica.

Consequently, this project plunges into uncertain futures by foreshadowing possible worlds to come in Antarctica. It seeks to re-shape what an Antarctic politics looks and feels like on the ground, or on the Ice, by jostling documentary film and ethnography in new ways. I draw on Donna Haraway's ambivalent and ambiguous notion of 'speculative fabulation' (2013, 2016), to argue that in coupling arts practice and cultural research though 'material-semiotic entanglements' of the factual, the fictional, and the fabulated, both the filmic and the ethnographic become correlated to interact with each to enact a realism of the possible. This enables an account of how the Ice, as an everyday extreme, confronts its inhabitants with problems of survival and habitation that can be scientifically, ethically and temporally scaled outward. Such predicament of inhabiting the extreme makes visible big quandaries about the future of habitable conditions for earthly life. Moreover, when modulated by the speculative it invites a recalibration towards a future-facing cultural inquiry that enables research to follow forked directions, to both respond and anticipate phenomena that may not simply be held, observed and acted upon. In this particular instance the film embraces speculative fabulation and mobilizes it as an ethnographic method for researching worlds to come in Antarctica. In this way both ethnography and documentary film become entangled as a mode of practice to be effected as creative treatment of possibility and potentiality, not just actuality.

Anticipating Antarctic futures

Anticipation has recently been considered 'a regime of being in time', and as some have provocatively pointed out it seems more and more likely that 'one defining quality of our current moment is its characteristic state of anticipation, of thinking and living toward the future' (Adams et al. 2009). In such a perspective, anticipation as an affective state or disposition acquires epistemic value when a mutual adjustment occurs between future expectations and contingent dynamics – as a process through which the present is transformed, intervened in and ultimately governed in the name of the future. According to geographer Ben Anderson futures are 'disclosed and related to through statements about the future (or what he calls styles); rendered present through materialities, epistemic objects and affects (what he terms practices); and acted on through specific policies and programmes (what he names logics)' (Anderson 2010: 779). He outlines three types of anticipatory practices: those of calculating futures; of imagining futures; and of performing futures, each of which produces different pre-emptive and precautionary logics.

The geophysical and life sciences have been anticipating a sober picture of the future of the Polar Regions for some time now, with widespread ecosystems change and both the Arctic and parts of the Antarctic Peninsula warming at twice the rate of the rest of the planet. Since the International Geophysical year of 1957–8 international science has deployed an anticipatory practice of calculating futures through a range of styles and epistemic objects, to the point that both the Arctic and the Antarctic befit long-lasting sources of imagery of amplified environmental change and have become the spatial setting for climate crisis discourses and affects. The human as geological force field is significantly pervasive in the poles as evidenced across a range of phenomena including melting and calving of glaciers and ice-sheets, rapid spread of invasive species, and also – as in most other parts of the planet – high concentration of CO_2 and aerosol pollutants in the atmosphere or ocean pollution and ocean acidification.

Antarctica has thus become an anthropogenic landscape where ever-intensifying human activities are prompting doubts about how current governance system are turning to be insufficient to meet the environmental protection obligations set out under the Protocol on Environmental Protection to the Antarctic Treaty signed in 1998 (which may be opened for review in 2048).

Antarctica is thus an inherently future-oriented matter of concern due to inevitable crossings of thresholds in Earth systems and the shift into whole new systemic states, both of which set out a serious test of our collective and coordinated capacity to exercise foresight. An exercise that not only demands action to protect these fragile yet resilient ecologies, but which also invited a rethinking of multispecies life in extreme ecologies.

The scope and intensity of human activities in the Antarctic has changed dramatically over the past 100 years, including a rising interest in resources together with growth and diversification of existing commercial activities, such as fishing and tourism. In the Antarctic context 'resources' include 'minerals, meteorites, intellectual property of Antarctic bio-prospecting (the quest to find commercial uses for bio-resources), locations for scientific bases, marine living resources, and preferred access to the continent for tourism' (Brady 2010: 759). In the past decade or so there has been a broadening awareness of the potential of the polar regions as global political spaces as well as sources of valuable resources. Like the Arctic, Antarctica has sprung up as a geopolitical space, where investing in Antarctic science is often an anticipatory logic to signal presence and influence in Antarctic decision-making and future geopolitical settings.

In an exercise of synthesis of future scenarios in Antarctica, Tin et al. (2014) for example examined a series of prevalent scenarios to offer three alternative scenarios for Antarctica. The first, utopia, where there is no interest in resources and internal influence; second, nationalism and economic globalization on the opposite side – with a future of unlimited exploitation of resources and external influence; and third, in between these more extreme possible scenarios, a cluster of three business-as-usual scenarios: slippery slope, self-control and low interest. In the first case, by extrapolating current trajectories into the future, Tin, Liggett, Maher and Lamers (2014) argue that there will be an expansion of virtually all anthropogenic activities in the Antarctic over the next fifty years, predicting that synergistic and cumulative impacts will exacerbate existing threats and reduce the resilience of ecosystems to further anthropogenic threats. In anticipatory horizon scanning exercises like this one, business as usual futures are pre-empted on the basis that sovereignty disputes, scientific endeavours and tourism will continue to define the logic of engagement with the Antarctic region. If we were to apply Anderson's framework we would see how within these business as usual settings the future of the Antarctic is expected to be driven by two complementary logics: one of economic resource exploitation and national sovereignty interests, where bioprospecting continues to develop in a vacuum of regulation, parties continue to position themselves for a future lifting of the mining ban, and tourism and fishing industries continue to expand. And a second, opposing view: that of an Antarctic sanctuary, where

Antarctica becomes a common heritage for all of humanity and where the trend towards environmental protection through current governance arrangements prevails into the future. These preferred and aspirational futures carry with them a problematic vision in which Antarctica remains a 'wilderness' where there is little impact of human presence; where human footprint shrinks thanks to the development of new technologies and infrastructures. The big elephant in the room is therefore the failure to foresee any materialization of human settlements in the coming decades, a process that in my view has already started.

Nightfall on Gaia and a poetics of 'tomorrowing'

The Antarctic Peninsula is the northernmost part of the mainland of Antarctica and is where I conducted fieldwork and produced the film titled *Nightfall on Gaia* (Salazar 2015b). The peninsula has been since the 1940s part of disputed and overlapping sovereignty claims by Argentina, Chile and the UK. None of these claims has international recognition under the Antarctic Treaty System (ATS). The ATS, which provides a high-level forum for cooperation and a regime of governance, was negotiated and signed by twelve countries in the midst of the Cold War (1959) and entered into force in 1961. Since then it has provided a mechanism and a regime for governing the Antarctic based on science and international collaboration.

The Peninsula offers some of the most dramatic scenery in the whole of the Antarctic continent and boasts a huge level biodiversity, particularly in the South Shetland Islands. Located across the Drake Passage, roughly 1,000 kilometres south of Tierra del Fuego, the southern-most tip of South America, King George Island is one of the South Shetland Islands and is one of the areas experiencing the most rapid and pervasive global warming on the planet comparable only to certain places in the Arctic. King George Island has been pictured as a 'mesocosm of the change that is occurring in response to climate warming and a test-bed for predicting future responses to climate change' (Kennicutt 2009). The island is dominated by a pervasive ice cap with more than 90 per cent of the island being glaciated. However, the Fildes peninsula, on the southern end of the island, is in fact one of the largest ice-free areas in the maritime Antarctic, and together with adjacent coastal zones of the island has high levels of biodiversity. Eighty-seven per cent of the island's glaciers have retreated over the past fifty years. The island is host to fifteen international research stations as well as a military-civilian permanent village – Villa Las Estrellas or The Stars Village – with families, a school, a community gym and a small supermarket. The area is home to about 200 inhabitants all year round and up to 2,500 people in summer including scientists, visitors and tourists. Figure 10.1 shows the Chilean Julio Escudero Station where I stayed during the fieldwork seasons of 2012, 2013 and 2014.

After visiting this place for the first time in 2011 to conduct a series of digital storytelling projects (Salazar 2013; Salazar and Barticevic 2015) and after undertaking a critical examination of a range of anticipatory logics deployed by science and international governance in Antarctica since 1959, I felt frustrated that it wasn't enough to capture the scale, the magnitude of this affective becoming: 'a world in the making in an extreme environment that could have been but never was' as Xue Noon, the main character in *Nightfall on Gaia* says. Perhaps enough to understand who goes there today and why, but not enough to capture a glimpse of a possible people to come – let alone of a polity to come, yet unformed and unnamed.

Travelling to Antarctica for the first time in 2011 was also a big wake-up call on the state of affairs of what it means to live in an extreme environment and a corroboration that any understanding of a becoming is always a becoming with other species. During many moments it didn't feel too different with how outer space travel and exploration is often imagined: the affective division of labour; the performance of communal tasks; the hierarchical social context; how our bodies swiftly acquired a different rhythm under the three layers of clothing; or the permanent feeling of being outside of Earth. My main preoccupation was with how to research Antarctic futures anthropologically, if this was a viable option, and how I could combine the ethnographic and speculative to recalibrate the research into a future-oriented inquiry. A key challenge was how to develop a critical account – or at least a glimpse – of these Antarcticans, by definition ontologically agile but not automatically attuned to multispecies entanglements; and how they become 'agents of anticipation' (Mackenzie 2013) in places where human habitation has been barely possible until now. Critical in this instance means looking at the shaping of Antarctica into an inhabitable world beyond the realm of seasonal scientists and logistics

FIGURE 10.1 *Exterior view of Julio Escudero Station in King George Island. Photo by Juan Francisco Salazar.*

FIGURE 10.2 *Exterior of a living quarter at the Russian Station Bellingshausen. Photo by Juan Francisco Salazar.*

personnel and questioning ethnographically how things might be otherwise than previously assumed or commonly foreseen. The environmental historian Tom Griffiths observed that these emergent human communities living in the Antarctic are 'a peculiar civilisation where the workings of history might be laid bare' (Griffiths 2008: 4). This affective future orientation of a peculiar community-to-come on the Ice comes out strongly in the ethnographic material. To me this is indicative of how specific sites are becoming places for human sociality, or perhaps a pre-figurative configuring of sociality 'taking-place' in precarious cultural spaces, most of which seem still more like national enclaves (Figure 10.2).

Four periods of ethnographic fieldwork were undertaken in the Antarctic Peninsula during the summer seasons of 2011 to 2014, totalling sixteen weeks. The latest phase of the fieldwork included three weeks aboard the Chilean Navy Ship *Aquiles* and five weeks in the Julio Escudero Research Station in King George Island (Figure 10.3) and other five scientific research stations in the Fildes Peninsula – Bellingshausen Station (Russia); Great Wall (China); King Sejong (South Korea); Artigas (Uruguay) and Presidente Eduardo Frei and Villa Las Estrellas (Chile) all in King George Island.

Ethnographic participant-observation was carried out during field sampling by marine biologists and during conversations and meetings on-board the ship and the stations. In-depth ethnographic interviews, semi-structured interviews and informal interviews were carried out with eighteen scientists (across marine microbiology, astrobiology, ecology, glaciology) both

FIGURE 10.3 *Teachers and students at School F-50, Villa Las Estrellas. Photo by Juan Francisco Salazar.*

on-board the ship and at the research station (Salazar forthcoming 2017). These research interviews were framed from the beginning and used afterwards in the film as 'agential conversations', purposely meant to interfere with the 'contexts they sought to understand' and create 'situated moments of reflection, connection, and disruption' (Müller and Kenney 2014), not only with scientists but also with doctors, teachers, children, logistics personnel, Chilean Navy and Air Force officers, and tourists in King George Island.

'Disparate times call for disparate methods' is how Mackenzie Wark (2015: 1) opened his book *Molecular Red* to call attention to the worldmaking capacities of methods. Engagements with Antarctica require disparate methods: novel reinventions of embodied and social presence, ecological limits, and imaginaries of human becoming. Wark calls for a shift from the 'molar' to the 'molecular' (Wark 2015: xvi). The molar are the 'big-bodied entities' which in this case might be the Antarctic Treaty System, the National Antarctic Programs, government departments and non-state actors who clash and antagonize on questions of territorial sovereignty, environmental conservation, fishing quotas or tourism regulation. The molar, Wark argues, corresponds to 'signification that delimits objects, subjects, representations and their reference systems'. The molecular order on the other hand, is one of 'flows, becomings, phase transitions and intensities' (Ibid.). I would place the prefiguring of novel modes of subjectivity and sociality emerging in Antarctica in this order. The collaborative labour of scientists and logistical-technical labour produce a very concrete worldview of what it is like to inhabit the Antarctic. This worldview is often analogous with outer space colonization (the techno-scientific-military complex). It is precisely here where speculation in the molecular mode might conjecture about what other sorts of human and more-than-human ecologies are possible in extreme environments (such as Antarctica or outer space) that might engender values and relations in which the 'naturecultures' of inhabiting the extreme can be enacted and imagined differently.

Speculation is thus central to my research, and I am still testing, experimenting and putting it to work in different, sometimes contradictory ways. I would note that anticipation differs from speculation in subtle yet important ways. Anticipation, as a lived condition or orientation, always demands a response in the present; it is the future materializing in the present, which gives way to a series of anticipatory regimes. Etymologically anticipation concerns a taking care of (preparing for) ahead of time. In contrast, the etymology of speculation relates to 'observing from a vantage point', from the Latin verb *speculari*, from the Latin specula 'watchtower'. In other words, a vantage point for grasping alternate futures. Thus, the anticipatory gaze is ultimately fixed on the present while the speculative gaze is entrenched on the future. So the visionary elements within the speculative dimension are different than in anticipatory practices since they open up the possibility of 'extracting from the present certain immanent potentialities that may be capable of opening up a transition into otherwise unlikely futures'.

A key entry point into the speculative, both in the ethnographic account and the film, was to engage with Donna Haraway's ambiguous and ambivalent notion of *speculative fabulation* (Haraway 2013). The way to grasp Haraway's impulse is, I think, as a kind of chimera – a single organism composed of cells from different zygotes. As Haraway herself explains (2013), a hybrid infused by Alfred N. Whitehead's speculative pragmatism filtered via Isabelle Stengers' (2011) notion of 'speculative thinking'; mixed and situated in feminist speculative fiction (Ursula K. Le Guin) and ultimately morphed by the US academic, feminist theorist and writer Marleen Barr into feminist fabulation. SF implies the tight coupling of writing and research, where both terms require the factual, fictional, and fabulated; and where both terms are materialized in fiction and scholarship. In the process philosophy of Whitehead – and as developed later by Stengers – the speculative acquires renewed expediency as a set of responses, as members of the *Unit of Play* at Goldsmiths, University of London put it, 'to phenomena that cannot be held, or observed or acted upon'.[2] But these set of responses are indeed as Cecilia Åsberg, Kathrin Thiele and Iris van der Tuin argue 'a very material process, a performative process of the world, a form of worlding itself' (Åsberg et al. 2015: 152). This is what Haraway refers to as a SF mode: a process of worlding and a 'potent material-semiotic sign for the riches of speculative fabulation, speculative feminism, science fiction, speculative fiction, science fact, science fantasy … and string figures' and also means 'so far, opening up what is yet-to-come in protean entangled times' pasts, presents, and futures (Haraway 2013: 10).

In light of these perspectives, the process of making *Nightfall on Gaia* became a form of situated knowledge-making, or in Haraway's terms, of doing things 'in the SF mode'. By this I mean a new way of organizing knowledge about the Antarctic, where both ethnographic knowledge and film practice might meet. Conceived in this way, the fascinating aspect of speculation as method is the particular way it might propel cultural research in general and anthropological research in particular 'to follow forked directions' as Celia Lury and Nina Wakeford argue 'to trace processes that are in disequilibrium or uncertain, to acknowledge and refract complex combinations of human and non-human agencies, supporting an investigation of what matters and how in ways that are open, without assuming a single fixed relation between epistemology and ontology' (Lury and Wakeford 2012: 19). In other words, speculation transforms a fieldwork site into a 'garden of forking paths' (Borges 1962) where the factual, the fictional and the fabulated become entangled across possible and impossible worlds that exist simultaneously within future contingents. Once again, as Åsberg et al. would argue, speculation implies 'both the envisioning of a different world and a challenge to taken-for-granted knowledges by way of situating them in specific historical, sociocultural, material and bodily contexts (2015: 153).

In order to turn these ideas into practice I opted for a speculative experiment: the making of a feature length documentary film: *Nightfall on Gaia*. The film was shot entirely in the Antarctic Peninsula during four fieldwork trips between 2011 and 2014, apart from a couple of scenes (set in the near future), which were filmed at a studio in Sydney. I argue that the film seeks to demonstrate a performative anticipatory practice (in reference to Ben Anderson 2010), which embodies the speculative mode to foster what I call a 'poetics of tomorrowing'. This is a call to conceive documentary film practice not as a creative treatment of actuality but 'creative account of possibility' (Salazar 2015a), and in this sense one of the things I tried to explore was how to make the film work as a diffractive reading (Barad 2007) how Antarctic futures might look and feel like. What I mean here by a diffractive reading is a way of avoiding images of Antarctica as static representations of Antarctic wilderness or scientists at work, to productive accounts of multispecies ecologies, hence moving from the binary and oppositional to the multifarious and differential, from critical reflection after the fact, to critical, embedded involvement in the there and then.

Hence, the diffractive moves the speculative mode beyond an enumeration of possible Antarctic futures or even a representation of a set of plausible futures of Antarctica, towards an embodying of an 'as if' future. By arguing that documentary film should not be confined/defined as 'the creative treatment of actuality' (as defined by John Grierson in the 1930s) but as 'creative treatment of possibility (Salazar 2015a), my purpose is certainly to provoke, by arguing that as a mode of practice and desire both documentary media and ethnographic practice must not be limited by an emphasis on representing the past and documenting the present, and might be reinvigorated by being an anticipatory practice for presenting and embodying possible and preferred futures. Thus the film is a response to what Åsberg, Thiele and van der Tuin call, 'current re-emergence of a feminist (Whiteheadian) philosophical urge to speculate' and follows 'a methodological line of flight that emphasises practice and situatedness' (2015: 163).

In her 'Cyborg Manifesto', Haraway (1991) contends that the boundary between science fiction and social reality is 'an optical illusion'. In the case of *Nightfall on Gaia*, the erasure of this boundary between ethnography, science fiction and social reality also becomes an illusion in both the film and the ethnographic account. At the core of this experiment in speculative anthropological storytelling is the fictional/fabulated character of astrobiologist Xue Noon in the year 2043. She is of Maori background, works at the NASA Jet Propulsion Centre and is leading a team undertaking extremophile bioprospecting in Antarctica as preparation for the first manned expedition to Europa – one of the moons of Jupiter. She finds herself stranded in the fictional GAiA International Antarctic Station. This is not a random fact, but a critique of the fact that at the time of making the film there was no International Antarctic Station, as compared, for instance, with the International Space Station. As the polar night closes in, Xue Noon connects herself to the artificial intelligence system of the research station to scavenge digital memories and archives. As a figure resembling that of the cyborg, I wanted Dr Noon – as the AI calls her – to open up new imaginative possibilities for thinking about what Antarctica is becoming, by refiguring and embodying a different structure of feeling – the negotiation that results from different ontologies but also kinds of labour in Antarctica. First, Xue Noon is a cyborg-punk-looking androgynous figure with a Maori background and she is a top scientist in her field. She is not a cybernetic organism in the strict sense. She is presented as having a hybrid human-machine consciousness. She is a Matakite, a seer into the future and the past in traditional Maori society, daughter of another Matakite woman. She is a fabulated character of fiction as well as social reality, created from ethnographic interviews with astrobiologists and marine biologists as well as the personal life story of the award winning Maori performer Victoria Hunt who plays the role of Xue Noon (Figure 10.4). In this sense Xue Noon is a personal and modest homage to the tradition of feminist speculative fiction and I wrote her character as a result of long and intense moments during fieldwork following Antarctic microbiologists in sampling fieldtrips, observing their practices of DNA sequencing, engaging with them in undergraduate teaching; following them at international conferences; and looking at plans by NASA to send a manned expedition to Europa in the 2040s.

As such, the ambition here is to propel the film work as a kind of material-semiotic experiment in 'inventive methods' (Lury and Wakeford 2012), which pushes us to acknowledge the inseparability of epistemology and materiality when we look for techniques for researching futures. Functioning then as a sort of 'thought experiment', useful to problematize in provocative ways a time of planetary transition such as the Anthropocene, the film invites viewers not only to critique and respond constructively to the current predicament of socio-ecological change, but also to both anticipate possible effects of global change processes and speculate in the subjunctive mode about the 'what if' and the 'not as yet'. Therefore the film attempts not only to depict fragments of the lives and visions of human communities living in the Antarctic Peninsula. Set across multiple temporalities (2013 and 2043) it also fabulates with fragments of a future, by juxtaposing fictional/fabulated characters, events, places and phenomena with observational material, and with ethno-graphic interviews with a range of transient and semi-permanent dwellers, including people who have lived in Antarctica for six months a year for the past thirty-three years. The film thus becomes a kind of probe, a 'diegetic prototype' (Kirby 2011) that for a moment suspends disbelief about possible

FIGURE 10.4 *The fabulated character of Xue Noon (Victoria Hunt). Photo by Juan Francisco Salazar.*

futures, not only to tell a story, but also in order to narrate a world made out of fragments of stories, events and phenomena. Engagement with the future often rests on tacit knowledge. Yet, futures are not merely imagined; they are also made. The film is concerned then with the 'what if' and the 'not as yet', but ultimately with the 'about to be' and in search of a people to come. In such a way, both as final product and as process of storytelling, *Nightfall on Gaia* enacts a form of generative ethnography to speculate futures with, as a kind of *modest witnessing* (Haraway 1997: 269), where ethnography remains open to and aware of its partiality and subjectivity. In opening up a speculative orientation it aims to offer some coordinates for understanding how people envision the making of extraterritorial spaces social. As a filmic+ethnographic account (not an ethnographic film in the traditional definition) of the 'spectral gatherings' (Thrift 1999) of Antarctic life, the film tries to capture the many different things and forces that gather, some of which we know about, some not, some of which may be just on the edge of awareness (Anderson and Harrison 2010), and some of which may probably exist across multiple simultaneous temporalities and time-space dimensions (Figure 10.5).

For me then, speculative fabulation as method and *poiesis* enacts a realism of the possible to account for how the Ice, as an everyday extreme, confronts its inhabitants with problems of survival that make visible big predicaments about the future of habitable conditions for earthly life and the transgressing of planetary boundaries. The film's ending is confusing and for some frustrating in that it doesn't guarantee an outcome or an explanation. It hints though a subtle critique: we must think how to overcome that scientific

FIGURE 10.5 *A scene from the film* Nightfall on Gaia. *Photo by Juan Francisco Salazar.*

or 'scientistic' worldview that sees the Antarctic as a source of data, so that new arrangements of relationality can be envisioned. Xue Noon engages the AI system to hold the past, present and future in attention simultaneously. Also important is how the film as device deploys an 'ethnographic sensibility' (van Dooren and Rose 2016), in that it attempts not to be a detailed revealing of another's (human) way of life, but an opening into a lively world of relationships between humans and the non-human or more than human. The film thus wants to be a resource of hope to open up to multispecies stories and the relationality of life in anthropocenic environments. In *Nightfall on Gaia*, this framing asks viewers to speculate a future moment in which the Ice is at an end due to a massive solar storm, but leaves it open to the imagination whether this is in fact due to resource exploitation as a consequence of the end of the Antarctic Treaty, or even as a consequence of science/instrumentality gone awry – that the human-AI interface has turned out badly.

Conclusion

Given the growing interest in anticipation and speculation in social and cultural research, the aim of this chapter has been to examine how speculative fabulation can be mobilized as an ethnographically inflected method to attend to epistemological, ontological, ethical and political implications of doing research in a site like Antarctica. In so doing, I wish to, first, invite a dialogue into the expedience of the speculative for anthropological research as a productive mode of thinking, feeling and knowing that might offer new perspectives from which to tackle otherwise seemingly intractable matters of concern in uncertain times. And second, invite readers to reflect on an experiment in inventive methods whereby documentary film and ethnographic practice are brought together into a speculative mode that might illustrate the 'worldmaking' role of speculative ethnographic approaches.

New ways of knowing Antarctica also mean new ways of acting on/in it, and the mode of colonization of the Antarctic may well serve both as harbinger of future conditions of life on Earth as well as a proxy for planetary space exploration. In tracing this relational trajectory of Antarctica as 'that place outside the circuits of the known world that both precedes the moon as a destination of otherworldly knowledge and is coterminous with "outer space"' (Glasberg 2012: 34), speculation is a trope to engage with the emergence of 'an extra-terrestrial mode of thinking about the planet' (Helmreich 2012: 1133) where Antarctica is that liminal space: not completely Earthly and partly extra-terrestrial. Antarctica turns out to be not only a laboratory for science, but also a laboratory of ideas for thinking life in extra-terrestrial Earths, but at the same time an extra-terrestrial mode of thinking Earth. In this way, I think speculation regains its meaning as a form of observation engaged from a different vantage point, where Antarctica itself becomes a place of speculation, an ecological watchtower.

In this case the vantage point is not only for observation but also for intervention. As Adam and Groves (2007) have argued, researching futures entail acknowledging the 'uneven relation between acting, knowing and taking responsibility' for the future, or in other words between doing, knowing and caring. In this chapter I have addressed the making of anthropologies in relation to the future in a geo-political moment in which questions of what the future might be appear to overshadow events right now. I began this chapter with a note on how critical work in anthropology can be relevant to tackle urgent questions. My hope is that *Nightfall on Gaia* – as an example of an ethnographically informed film in the SF mode – captures this process as one that requires both an attitude of urgency as well as contemplative understanding (Figure 10.6).

There is a need for increased public understanding of how processes of global change in the Polar Regions are adding new and even more intractable dimensions and casting doubt over the future of these regions. As the Antarctic becomes peopled, as new life forms with potential commercial and health applications are discovered, and as Antarctica potentially becomes a new commodity and resources frontier, it is imperative to develop novel future-oriented approaches that can open up alternative modes of knowing-making

FIGURE 10.6 *Juan F. Salazar filming in Fildes peninsula, King George Island. Photo by Juan Francisco Salazar.*

that construct multiple, often contested, narratives of the future, and prepare to take action in the present in anticipation to those futures.

Notes

1 See www.nightfallongaia.net for more details or watch the film at https://vimeo.com/juansalazar/nightfall (accessed 23 September 2016).

2 Speculation in Social Science: Novel Methods for Re-Inventing Problems. British Sociological Association Annual Conference, 25 April 2014, http://www.gold.ac.uk/unit-of-play/events/speculation-bsa-abstracts/ (accessed 23 September 2016).

References

Adam B. and C. Groves, 2007. *Future Matters: Action, Knowledge, Ethics*. Leiden: Brill.

Adams, V., M. Murphy and A. E. Clarke, 2009. 'Anticipation: Technoscience, life, affect, temporality'. *Subjectivity* 28 (1): 246–65.

Anderson, B., 2010. 'Preemption, precaution, preparedness: Anticipatory action and future geographies'. *Progress in Human Geography* 34 (6): 777–98.

Anderson, B. and P. Harrison, 2010. 'The Promise of Non-representational Theories'. In *Taking-place: Non-representational Theories and Geography*, 1–36. Farnham: Ashgate.

Åsberg, C., K. Thiele and I. van der Tuin, 2015. 'Speculative before the turn: Reintroducing feminist materialist performativity'. *Cultural Studies Review*, 21 (2): 145–72.

Barad, K. M., 2007. *Meeting the Universe Halfway: Quantum Physics and the Entanglement of Matter and Meaning*. Durham, NC: Duke University Press.

Borges, J. L., 1962. 'The Garden of Forking Paths'. *Labyrinths: Selected Stories and Other Writings'*. New York: New Directions Publishing.

Brady, A. M., 2010. 'China's rise in Antarctica?' *Asian Survey* 50 (4): 759–85.

Bureaud, A., 2012. 'Inhabiting the Extreme or Making Antarctica Familiar'. In J. D. Marsching and A. Polli (eds), *Far Field: Digital Culture, Climate Change, and the Poles,* 187–97. Bristol: Intellect Ltd.

Collins, S. G., 2007. 'Le temps perdu: Anthropologists (re)discover the future'. *Anthropological Quarterly* 80 (4): 1175–86.

Dooren, T. van and D. B. Rose, 2016. 'Lively ethography'. *Environmental Humanities* 8 (1): 77, fig. 94.

Glasberg, E., 2012. *Antarctica as Cultural Critique: The Gendered Politics of Scientific Exploration and climate change*. London: Palgrave Macmillan.

Griffiths, T., 2008. 'The Cultural Challenge of Antarctica: The 2007 Stephen-Murray Smith Memorial Lecture'. *The La Trobe Journal* 82: 4–14.

Guyer, J. I., 2007. 'Prophecy and the near future: Thoughts on macroeconomic, evangelical, and punctuated time'. *American Ethnologist* 34 (3): 409–21.

Haraway, D., 1991. 'A Cyborg Manifesto: Science, Technology, and Socialist-Feminism in the Late Twentieth Century'. In *Simians, Cyborgs, and Women: The Reinvention of Nature*, 149–81. New York: Routledge.

Haraway, D., 1997. *Modest_Witness@Second_Millennium.FemaleMan©Meets_OncoMouseTM*. London: Routledge.

Haraway, D., 2013. SF: 'Science fiction, speculative fabulation, string figures, so far'. *Ada: A Journal of Gender, New Media, and Technology*, 3. Special Issue on Feminist Science Fiction. Available online: http://adanewmedia.org/issues/issue-archives/issue3/ (accessed 23 September 2016).

Heemskerk, M., 2003. 'Scenarios in anthropology: Reflections on possible futures of the Suriname Maroons'. *Futures* 35 (9) 931–49.

Helmreich, S., 2012. 'Extraterrestrial relativism'. *Anthropological Quarterly* 85 (4): 1125–39.

Ingold, T., 1995. 'Building, Dwelling, Living: How Animals and People Make Themselves at Home in the World'. In *Shifting contexts. Transformations in anthropological knowledge*. M. Strathern (ed.), 57–80. London: Routledge.

Kennicutt, M. C., 2009. 'King George Island and SCAR science'. Available online: http://www.scar.org/scar_media/documents/publications/King_George_Island_Science_Kennicutt.pdf (accessed 25 January 2016).

Kirby, D. A., 2011. *Lab Coats in Hollywood: Science, Scientists, and Cinema*. Cambridge: MIT Press.

Lury, C. and N. Wakeford, 2012. *Inventive Methods: The Happening of the Social*. New York and London: Routledge.

Mackenzie, A., 2013. 'Programming subjects in the regime of anticipation: Software studies and subjectivity'. *Subjectivity* 6 (4): 391–405.

Michaels, M., 2016. 'Speculative Design and Digital Materialities: Idiocy, Threat and Com-promise'. In S. Pink, E. Ardèvol and D. Lanzeni (eds), *Digital Materialities: Anthropology and Design*, 99–113. London: Bloomsbury.

Müller, R. and M. Kenney, 2014. 'Agential conversations: Interviewing postdoctoral life scientists and the politics of mundane research practices'. *Science As Culture* 23 (4): 537–59.

Munn, N. D., 1992. 'The Cultural Anthropology of Time: A Critical Essay'. *Annual Review of Anthropology* 21: 93–123.

O'Reilly, J., 2008. 'Policy and Practice in Antarctica'. PhD thesis in Anthropology. University of California, Santa Cruz.

Parisi, L., 2012. 'Speculation'. In C. Lury and N. Wakeford (eds), *Inventive Methods: The Happening of the Social*, 232–43. London: Routledge.

Riner, R. D., 1987. 'Doing futures research anthropologically'. *Futures* 19 (3): 311–28.

Salazar J. F., 2013. 'Geographies of place-making in Antarctica: An ethnographic perspective'. *The Polar Journal* 3 (1): 53–71.

Salazar, J. F., 2015a. 'Science/Fiction: Documentary Film and Anticipatory Modes of Futuring Planetary Change'. In A. Lebow and A. Juhasz (eds), *Companion to Contemporary Documentary Studies*, 43–60. Malden, MA and Oxford: Wiley-Blackwell.

Salazar, J. F. (Producer and Director), 2015b. *Nightfall on Gaia* [Motion Picture]. Australia/Chile: Aq Films and Western Sydney University.

Salazar, J. F., 2017. 'Microbial Geographies at the extremes of life: relational trajectories of Antarctica and Outer Space'. *Environmental Humanities* 9 (2).

170   **ANTHROPOLOGIES AND FUTURES**

Salazar, J. F. and E. Barticevic, 2015. 'Digital Storytelling Antarctica'. *Critical Arts: South-North Cultural and Media Studies* 29 (5): 576–90.

Stengers, I., 2010. *Cosmopolitics I*. Minneapolis: University of Minnesota Press.

Stengers, I., 2011. *Thinking with Whitehead: A Free and Wild Creation of Concepts*. Cambridge, MA: Harvard University Press.

Stewart, K., 2011. 'Atmospheric Attunements'. *Environment and Planning D: Society and Space* 29 (3): 445–53.

Thrift, N., 1999. 'Steps to an Ecology of Place'. In D. Massey, J. Allen and P. Sarre (eds), *Human Geography Today*, 295–321. Cambridge: Polity Press.

Tin, T., D. Liggett, P. T. Maher and M. Lamers (eds), 2014. *Antarctic Futures: Human Engagement with the Antarctic Environment*. Dordrecht: Springer.

Tsing, A., 2013. 'More-than-Human Sociality'. In K. Hastrup (ed.), *Anthropology and Nature,* 14–27. London and New York: Routledge.

Wark, M., 2015. *Molecular Red*. New York: Verso.

11

Ethno science fiction: Projective improvisations of future scenarios and environmental threat in the everyday life of British youth

Johannes Sjöberg

Introduction

It's me, James, from the future. The year is 2036. All the houses have gone. They've built some shops over the top of where the houses were. The only thing that is recognizable around here is the pub. The pub has stayed, which is incredibly impressive. They've built more and more units over the whole of Otley Road. It's like one big [commercial] park and it has taken over the whole side by the river. [...] Shipley is almost completely cut off now due to the frequent flooding. Everyone has to take the long road around Bingley to come to Baildon now. They've just ruined it: just ruined it. There are just so many things wrong with it, everybody is fighting for place with everybody. [...] It's horrible [...] It's nothing like it ever was and it'll never be the same again.

This dystopic vision of the future was recorded as part of my ongoing research project *Forward Play*, which commenced in 2014. The objective of the research is to apply and critically examine the use of 'ethno science fiction' as an ethnographic and anthropological film method. In the first of a series of ethno science fictions, I ask English youth living in regions affected by drastic environmental change to improvise their own science fictions, especially with regard to climate change, in order to research and represent young people's perceptions and understandings of the future.

James Hudson-Wright is twenty years old. He lives with his grandmother in Shipley, a town near Leeds in West Yorkshire, in a rented Victorian house originally built to accommodate mill workers during the boom in wool production that took place in Yorkshire in the mid- to late 1800s. Their house is built on the water table of the River Aire, which resulted in the flooding of their house and the entire neighbourhood in 2000 and 2015. During recent years James has seen other drastic changes, including a major property development adjacent to his house. The Victorian textile mill next to his house was torn down and replaced with a parking lot and plans for a commerical development, radically changing the material and social environment of his neighbourhood.

There is ongoing speculation among the local population about the possibility of increasing flood risk from the River Aire. Previous estimates predicted major flooding in the area 'once every fifty years' based on the inundations of 1947 and 2000. However, December 2015 saw the worst flooding in the area in living memory, and climate change has very much been part of the local conversation following these events. Some of those at risk have begun embarking on major flood prevention measures, believing that another flood will happen sooner rather than later.

In July 2014, James and I started to make the film *Call Me Back* (2017) as part of my research into the future. It begins with eighteen-year-old James entering an old style red phone booth next to his house in Shipley (Figure 11.1). He phones his future self and asks a series of pressing questions about the future, including his own life, the local town and the world in general. Exactly one year later I filmed James, who is now nineteen years old, walking into the same phone booth and responding to his past self, revealing changed outlooks and perspectives in the process. Over the course of the year, the shopping centre continues to be constructed and its changing outline can be seen in the background of the phone booth. Documentary shots reveal the changes to the environment surrounding the phone booth and James's home, which he tries to relate to through his phone dialogues with his past and future selves.

In the summer of 2016, James enters the phone booth again. Twenty-year-old James responds to recent developments in his life, including the drastic events of the 2015 Boxing Day flooding of his neighbourhood, and other changes in his life and environment. The imagined forty-year-old James of 2036 also joins the phone calls to tell his previous incarnations about developments in the region over the past twenty years. Finally, sixty-year-old James of 2056 will enter the phone booth reporting back to his younger selves on another twenty years of changes to his life and old neighbourhood.

FIGURE 11.1 *James Hudson-Wright in* Call Me Back *(2017)*

The phone conversations between James and his future selves are intercut with documentary shots of James guiding us through his neighbourhood and scenes showing the drastic changes the area has gone through since 2014. James' greatest passion is music, and the film will be accompanied by songs that James has written and performs to express his vision of the future.

Ethno science fiction

The chapter explores how to apply projective improvisation in ethnographic film to understand how fieldwork informants relate to and imagine the future through a technique I call 'ethno science fiction'. More specifically, ethno science fiction is a co-creative genre of ethnographic film in which the informants express their imagined future through improvisation and other forms of applied theatre and artistic practice.

The method I am proposing offers an alternative approach to ethnographic research on the imagination, and about the future. It is intended to complement existing methods in ethnographic film – such as interviews and participant observation – and combines the traditions of qualitative research in anthropology and creative practice in applied art, in order to challenge positivist research traditions and quantitative methods within Future Studies.

Ethno science fiction is also meant to provide a means of reflexive intervention, conducted with ethical care and anthropological critique in mind. The ethnographic film material is screened back to the participants to facilitate reflection and change, drawing on the film as a sounding board for innovation in times of crisis. I will ask if ethno science fictions could contribute to a 'temporal proximity', encouraging critical debate, speculation and sympathy in relation to the lives of future generations, similar to how ethnographic film traditionally has facilitated cultural proximity through a complex understanding of 'the other'.

The three words 'ethno', 'science' and 'fiction' that constitute the neologism, represent three very specific methodological claims and research interests that sets this film method apart from other science fiction genres. 'Ethno' suggests the same methodological rigour as other ethnographic film methods, including extended ethnographic fieldwork informed by anthropological theory. 'Science' refers to how fieldwork informants relate to scientific predictions of the future. Scientific progress has allowed researchers to predict changes in economy, politics, population, health, geography, climate, etc., with increased precision, and ethno science fiction allows fieldwork informants to critically and playfully engage with these predictions through their imagination. 'Fiction' refers to the human necessity to speculate, to fill the blank canvas of uncertainty with imagined utopias and dystopias.

However, unlike mainstream science fiction in literature and film that is written and produced for the commercial market, ethno science fiction is co-created with the participants to make an imagined future explicit and tangible though projective improvisations. The philosophy of fiction in the practice of everyday life suggests the close link between fictions about the future and how we conduct our lives. Ethno science fiction offers a practical means to reveal these links, not only showing how our imagined futures are realized, but also how they impact on our interpretation of past and present experiences.

Fiction in practice

Ethno science fiction is a development of the ethnofictions of pioneering visual anthropologist Jean Rouch. Rouch asked his West African and French friends and informants to act out and improvise their own and others' experiences in front of the camera, in order to show aspects of ethnographic research that could not be revealed and presented in any other way. Rouch regarded these films as surrealist games inspired by Songhay-Zerma culture. (Henley 2009; Rouch 2003; Sjöberg 2008, 2009a; Stoller 1992).

While contemporary French speaking film critics referred to these films as 'etnofictions' (Fr), Rouch himself saw little value in labelling his film practice (Yakir 1978: 10). On occasion, he did however refer to the films as 'science fictions' (Marshall and Adams 1978: 1005). Rather than attempting to place his films within the pulp genre of science fiction, he used the term ironically and critically. He saw no difference between art and ethnography or fact and fiction in his practice. He regarded his films to be both social science and fiction (Rouch 2003: 185). The reference to science fiction played a part in Rouch's provocative and anti-authoritarian attitude towards positivist and other academic conventions that dominated contemporary anthropology. It was a humorous monkey-wrench intended for the machinery of a social science still grounded in the Cartesian divide between subjectivity and objectivity (Rouch with Fulchignoni 2003: 156; Rouch 2003: 185). Interestingly, similar hermeneutic ideas that would make the inter-subjectivity of fieldwork relationships transparent were later introduced to the discipline through Geertz's interpretative anthropology, which would revolutionize the social sciences more than a decade after Rouch's own forays.

Rouch explicitly encouraged the protagonists of his ethnofictions to act out possible scenarios of the future. In the film *Petit a Petit* (1970), two West African protagonists from his previous ethnographic films decide to fly to Paris to study high-rise buildings and to observe what use Parisians make of them. Rather than a science fiction these films draw on surrealist improvisation techniques. The imagination of the fieldwork informant is expressed through improvised acting. This approach was inspired by griot storytelling of West African culture, as well as surrealist art techniques such as automatic writing and drawing, in order to tap into the creative subconscious of the protagonists (Henley 2009; Rouch 2003; Sjöberg 2008, 2009a; Stoller 1992).

Jean Rouch and co-director Edgar Morin also compared their approach in *Chronique d'un été* (1961) to the psychodrama of Jacob Moreno (Morin in Rouch 2003: 233). Psychodrama is psychotherapeutic techniques developed by the Austrian physician Moreno in the United States from the 1920s and onwards. Rouch and Morin were influenced by their academic and artistic environment, and obviously drew on contemporary ideas. In spite of their frequent references to psychodrama they never seemed to have applied the techniques of Moreno as a consciously preconceived methodology for their films, but rather as a product of the general zeitgeist of the time (Sjöberg forthcoming). The approach to improvised acting in Rouch's films does however recall Moreno's use of enactment in psychodrama: 'There are several forms of enactment – pretending to be in a role, re-enactment or acting out a past scene living out a problem presently pressing, or testing oneself for the future' (Fox 1987: 13). The ethnofictions of Jean Rouch provided a space where the protagonists of the films could live out their dreams and aspirations, as well as their anxieties about uncertain futures, in a surrealist and ethnographic game.

My previous use of Rouch's method of ethnofiction (Sjoberg 2008, 2009a, 2009b, 2011) was in collaboration with transgendered Brazilians living in São Paulo, resulting in the film *Transfiction* (2007). One scene in the film is exclusively concerned with the future where the transgendered prostitute Zilda, played by Savana 'Bibi' Meirelles, meets Philippe, a Frenchman visiting São Paulo. Together they dream about living in Paris together and at the end of the film Zilda moves to Paris to live with Philippe. We follow her to the airport and enter into her utopian vision of her future life in Paris, as represented by dreamy shots of the Eiffel tower, French flags and sunny blue skies. While this 'happy ever after' ending was perceived as less authentic and more clichéd than the rest of the film, it nevertheless offered a faithful account of Bibi's dreams of going to Paris.

More specifically, the main protagonists of the film wanted to create a happy ending to critique and avoid reproducing the stereotypical, often negative, representations of transgendered Brazilians that reduce the complexity of their lived experience to images of suffering, poverty, discrimination and health problems. I asked them to try Rouch's enactments of dreams, similar to when Oumarou Ganda enacts his dreams of being a world champion boxer in *Moi un Noir* (1958). Rather than being presented as an object of study or offering a routine account of social identity, marginalization and his day-to-day life as a migrant worker, Oumarou Ganda tells us who he would like to be and how he would like to live (Sjöberg 2008, 2009a, 2009b). Similarly, Bibi came to use some of the improvisations in the film to paint an image of another life, happier than the reality she had to face as a transgendered prostitute in São Paulo.

The approach behind this filmed scene of the future was inspired by Moreno's psychodrama so as to offer the possibility of testing 'oneself for the future' (Fox 1987:13) through a series of performative and improvised enactments. While Moreno's motivation was to give his patients the courage to dream again, the enactment of the future as part of the ethnographic process provides a possibility to tap into the imaginary world of the fieldwork informants. For Bibi and other trans people in São Paulo, Paris represents a combination of success and possibility. A city of glamour and chic where their female and/or feminine identity (Kulick 1998; Sjöberg 2011) would be accepted and affirmed, ideally in the protecting arms of a wealthy gentleman or handsome dreamy prince who offers unprejudiced and unconditional love. These glimpses of utopia that are created, enacted and reflected on by the fieldwork informants also provide ethnographic research data on their present lives and future existential concerns. For example, it provided me with a tangible and contextual understanding of some of the primary motivations among many transgendered prostitutes to participate in sex trafficking to Europe despite the substantial risks (ibid.).

The political activism of the transgendered fieldwork informants, encouraged me to turn to the techniques of Brazilian theatre director Augusto Boal. Inspired by philosopher Paulo Freire's *Pedagogy of the Oppressed* (1968, 1970), Boal created *Theatre of the Oppressed* (1979) a political form of applied theatre. I had participated in several of his workshops previously and recognized similarities between Boal's Forum Theatre, Moreno's psychodrama and Rouch's ethnofictions. They were all drawing on the process of dreaming to facilitate improvisations with different aims and objectives in mind (Sjöberg, forthcoming). One key technique involved Boal asking members of the audience to present a problem that was then enacted by the theatre ensemble. Other participants in the audience would then suggest solutions to the problem that they then also enacted with the ensemble. The Forum Theatre sparked debate, and also turned out to be particularly useful among illiterate participants that found a useful and effective medium to express and discuss political oppression.

The political documentary dramas of British filmmaker Peter Watkins were contemporary to Boal's theatre practice and were likewise inspired by the political movements of the 1960s and 1970s. *The War Game* (1965) and *Punishment Park* (1971) are often referred to as science fictions about a near future. Watkins filmed his dramas with documentary techniques to challenge the media objectivism of the time. Through documentary aesthetics including, long shots and shaky hand-held cameras, on-location shooting, natural lighting, enactments by non-professional actors and interviews, his intention was to encourage the modernist audience of the time to be critical of facts and claims to objectivity and not take news and documentary media at face value (Watkins 2015).

The War Game depicts a nuclear war in Britain and its consequences. It is based on research that non-professional actors illustrate though scenes showing the repercussions of the nuclear blast. In contrast, the narrative content of *Punishment Park* is based on the improvisations of the participants playing roles similar to their own lives. Like Rouch's films, *Punishment Park* has been compared to psychodrama (MacDonald 1993: 171). In the film, political activists who are opposed to the Vietnam War are arrested when Nixon proclaims a state of emergency. Under a new law they are given the choice of visiting Punishment Park in lieu of prison. The park is situated in the California desert, where they have a tribunal and the convicts are required to cross the desert without food and water in three days in order to avoid prison. The trial and punishment is covered by a European documentary team. The non-professional actors playing the convicts were all activists in real life and drew on their own experience when improvising, resulting in a number of powerful and emotionally resonant scenes. In doing so, a near and plausible future was played out and portrayed on the basis of the actors' own perceptions and experiences.

Moreno, Rouch, Boal and especially Watkins, encouraged participants to elaborate on their future through their imagination, and the participatory theatre and filmmaking allowed them a practical means to try out future scenarios and reflect on them on stage and screen with members of the audience. Peter Loizos calls the acting in Rouchs' ethnofictions 'projective improvisation' (1993: 53). Based on his own experiences of psychotherapy, Loizos meant that the protagonists made 'implicit' information of ethnographic value 'explicit', through the improvisations. The fictional format allowed the protagonists to approach issues of their own life that they usually did not discuss. Rouch saw this as a result of his 'ciné-provocation' where the camera was used as a catalyst to reveal knowledge that usually is taken for granted. Implicit information, involved as part of the existence of the fieldwork informants, usually without being revealed, expressed, or developed (Sjöberg 2009a, 2009b). I distinguish between the descriptive and the expressive function of projective improvisation: the descriptive function is used to show the structure of events that cannot be told in any other way (such as historical or criminal events), while the expressive function of projective improvisation is more relevant for ethno science fictions since it draws on improvisations to get access to the subconscious world of the protagonists (Sjöberg 2008, 2009a, 2009b). Rouch used his surreal games to reveal 'hidden' or 'inner truths' (Morin and Rouch 2003), while Irving (2011) and Rapport (2008) have attempted to use other methods to access, elicit or exteriorize the interior lifeworlds of fieldwork informants that exist beyond third-party observation or are rarely made public. In my own practice, I utilize creative improvisations and different modes of playmaking to trigger the imagination of the protagonists and provide insight into their lived experience and embodied understandings of the world through free associations.

Play and playmaking stand at the centre of the projective improvisations in ethno science fictions. In Huizinga's definition, play constitutes a 'magic circle' (Huizinga 1938, 1955), while for Turner (1964), play creates a 'liminal space' that allows the participants to transgress their own realities.

In my own work, the protagonists of the film are provided with a personal testing ground, where they can play with and live out their own ideas in fictions about a possible future. Consequently, in a recollection of Oumarou Ganda's dream of winning a boxing championship or Zilda's dream about leaving Brazil for Paris, and when James calls himself from 2036 he has realized his dream to leave the town of Shipley to become an international rock star:

> I'm working in music, I'm living elsewhere, I'm miles away. I'm [...] still in a Horror Punk band. We had a resurgence about fifteen years ago and it just catapulted into the limelight, which was like an overnight thing. The one thing we didn't do, we didn't sell out, we didn't sell out to a label. We did it on our own and it was hard work but we have the rewards now. The money, [...] the bits of fame. Not that it's the most important thing, it's just nice to know that I can live comfortably now and do the thing that I love. I could never ever complain about the way things have turned out so far and I just hope that the success just carries on, more for the fact that I love playing the crowds, see the crowds' reactions, the vibe that you get out of it really, the number of shows I've done for free purely because they were enjoying themselves. [...] We made our money, we made millions and millions as a group. We don't ever have to worry [...] about living, about where our next meal is coming from. [...] I'm loving it, absolutely loving it and I don't want it ever to stop. I will push the music, I will write music, I will release solo albums, things like that. [...] Nothing will ever, ever beat moving away from here, that was the thing that shot us to fame.

The liminal space of the ethno science fiction provides a possibility to play with and test boundaries. James's dystopian vision of Shipley in the future and his personal utopia as a rock star after a successful escape from his life in Shipley, represent two extremes that helps him navigate his own life. The fiction he creates allows him to explore and test his possibilities. It is thus important to acknowledge the links between fiction and lived experience. As it is important to recognize how we make our history (Kean 2010) it is also important to recognize the processes of how we make our future.

Fiction in theory

Crapanzano (2004) draws on literature and philosophy to show the structure and process of imagination and boundary formation, and how imagination plays an important role in exploring possibilities. While Crapanzano sets out the theoretical possibilities of the subject, there remains a lack of methods in the social sciences and anthropology to study imagination from an ethnographic, fieldwork based perspective (Harris and Rapport 2015). This is especially relevant when exploring the process of how these possibilities are imagined and created on a personal level in the lives of the fieldwork informants, and more specifically in relation to the future. Ethno science fiction provides one such alternative and acts as a complement to other methods in an attempt to expand the toolbox of ethnographic possibility. The validity of this method is however based on certain theoretical assumptions related to theoretical understanding of imagination and fiction.

The definition of science fiction, as a literary and film genre, is an ongoing and often contested project. The theoretical struggle to define science fiction, as with other genres, is nevertheless helpful in articulating and establishing the shared reality that is created between the author and the audience. Freedman draws on literary historian and critic Darko Suvins' definition of science fiction as determined by the dialectic between estrangement and cognition:

> We may validly describe a particular text as science fiction if we understand the formulation to mean that cognitive estrangement is the dominant generic tendency within the over determined textual whole. (Freedman 2000: 20)

Moreover:

> The first term [estrangement] refers to the creation of an alternative fictional world that, by refusing to take our mundane environment for granted, implicitly or explicitly performs an estranging critical interrogation of the latter. But the critical character of the interrogation is guaranteed by the operation of cognition, which enables the science-fictional text to account rationally for its imagined world and for the connections as well as the disconnections of the latter to our own empirical world.' (Ibid: 16–17)

In this interpretation of the genre, the text could be defined as realistic mundane fiction if there is cognitive account for the fiction without any estrangement, and fantasy if the text estranges without any rational and theoretical legitimacy. Freedman also emphasizes that texts are rarely that clear cut. He means that a genre is a generic tendency that happens within a text, rather than a classification filed under a generic category (ibid.: 20).

James's ethno science fiction phone call from 2036 is based on his cognitive and critical perception of his current neighbourhood. The estrangement consists of his dystopic visions of its transformation into a gloomy place of poverty and exploitation. The ground where his old neighbourhood once stood is now entirely covered with commercial units. The population is poor and the people of Shipley either work in the commercial units or live off government support that they spend in the units:

> Different developers trying to make money, different businesses trying to make money. […] We're all to blame. Everyone living around here is to blame for not standing up when they we're doing it and realizing how wrong it was. It's everybody's fault from around here, more so the people that have built the units, but the people that weren't willing to stand up for what they believed in and what they believed was wrong. […] Politicians are the same old, same old. […] They say they [care], but clearly they don't, they give permission for all these units, all these units [where people] spend their hundred thousand pounds, emptying their wage on it, […] so [that the politicians] can go on holiday three times a year. Most of the people […] are struggling to eat, but yet they have a job, how does that work, how is that fair?

James's ethno science fiction has very strong cognitive links to his current world and worries, where the buildings he grew up with are torn down and replaced with a soulless commercial development, creating a new social environment that he perceives as hostile. He feels that he lacks power to influence the future of his environment, which is controlled by the developers and politicians he distrusts, but the science fiction allows him the freedom to develop and elaborate his critique towards them. In contrast to the cognitive aspects of his ethno science fiction, the 'estrangement' offers a liminal space where he can explore future scenarios without any limitations.

Crapanzano (2004) argues that the process of imagination allows us to explore what lies beyond the 'horizon' in the 'hinterland'. While the boundaries of possibilities usually are represented by cognition in science fiction, estrangement offers the means to also imagine possibilities and hope. In James's imaginative construction of the future, he comes back to Shipley to use the fortune that he has earned in the music business to help young people realize their dreams:

> I know what it's like to be a musician and not earning money, feeling awful and nobody likes your music. [I want to make use of] all of those zeros at

the end of my bank account. I want to put some of that back into people and help more people get out there and do something they love. [I want to help them with] not even just the music, just their dreams, their aspirations, anything they want to do I'm willing to hear about it. You know, I don't see it as a loan, anything like that, I just hope that if I create one success story out of a million, I've succeeded, and I hope that if I ever find myself in trouble, monetary wise for some reason, that that person might do the same for me. [...] And yes, I might have earned a lot of money in what we did but I could have been in a totally different boat and I appreciate that, I think that's why I've come back, that's why I've come to make a difference, to come and show these people I am still the young lad from Shipley. I might have made my money, the money isn't important, the people are.

The ethno science fiction becomes a laboratory where James can try out different possibilities for the future, of how to save his world. James imagination of his future life is not that for from his current life. The imagined possibility presented in the ethno science fiction also becomes a plan and a model to act upon in James's life. In *The Philosophy of 'As If'* (1911) the German philosopher Vaihinger argued that we make up systems of thoughts, models that we treat 'as if' they correspond to our actual real world, to deal with the uncertainty of it; by establishing 'constructs that, from a practical point of view, are useful and necessary, though theoretically they are false' (Vaihinger 1924: 63). For example, Vaihinger observes how scientific models of atoms and molecules in physics can be regarded as figures of the imagination or as fictional, given that we cannot see them, but this does not make such models any less useful:

It is, of course, true that many fundamental scientific concepts are fictional and contradictory and are not a reflection of the world of reality—a world quite inaccessible to us—but this in no way renders them valueless. They are psychical constructs which not only give rise to the illusion that the world is being comprehended, but which make it possible, at the same time, for us to orient ourselves in the realm of actuality. (Ibid: 65)

Crapanzano argues along similar lines by quoting literary critic Starobinski to describe the power of imagination to distance oneself and speculate but also to deal with our real worlds:

Insinuated into perception itself, mixed with the operations of memory, opening up around us a horizon of the possible, escorting the project, the hope, the fear, speculations – the imagination is much more than a faculty for evoking images which double the world of our direct perceptions: it is a distancing power thanks to which we represent to ourselves distant objects and we distance ourselves from present realities. Hence, the ambiguity that we discover everywhere: the imagination, because it anticipates and previews, views, serves action, draws before us the configuration of the realizable before it can be realized. (Starobinski 1970: 173–4, quoted in Crapanzano 2004: 19)

Not only does the imaginative consciousness allow us to transcend (depasser) the immediacy of the present instant in order to grasp a future that is at first indistinct, Starobinski argues, in turn it facilitates our 'practical domination over the real' or our breaking ties with it. (Crapanzano 2004: 19)

Intervention

The ethnographic value of ethno science fiction lies in that the method can contribute with data on (i) how future scenarios are tested and realized through a process of imagination in the present, and (ii) how fictional accounts of the future indicate how past and present experiences are inter- preted. Other applications of ethno science fiction are more controversial from a traditional non-interventional point of view in anthropology. As ethno science fiction encourages participants to imagine their futures, the reali- zation of these fictions is one step closer. It presents a potential for the participants to consider the prospect of realizing future possibilities explored in the ethno science fiction. This entails an interventionist fieldwork research and filmmaking that in turn, brings a range of epistemological and ethical problems. Even if we accept that fieldwork research is inter-subjective, there are limitations for how much anthropologists can impact on the contextual reality of the fieldwork, and still maintain their roles as researchers. And are we ready to shoulder the ethical responsibility for the intervention?

The film *Call Me Back* intersects with my colleague in Drama Stephen Bottoms', research in Shipley 'Towards Hydro-Citizenship' (2014–17) which explores how citizens and communities live with each other and their environment in relation to water (www.hydrocitizenship.com) and waterways (http://multi-story-shipley.co.uk). Intervention is less controversial in theatre and performance studies, and especially applied theatre that aims to facilitate positive change. My own work has thus been a careful balance between the different ethical frameworks of applied theatre and anthropology.

This interdisciplinary negotiation became apparent when the River Aire broke its banks on Boxing Day 2015. Since James's home and neighbourhood is built on the water table of the River Aire it is vulnerable to flooding in two ways: water might enter the house from below the ground through rising groundwater, and also above ground when water from the river surrounds it. Groundwater entered the house in both the 2000 and 2015 floods, while in 2015 overground water from the river also almost reached inside the house. James and his grandmother had to move out of their home for several months and were both shaken by the experience, while the owners had to pay for flood damage to the house.

Scientific experts commenting on the 2015 floods in media emphasised the likely relationship between the recent heavy rain and the global problem of a changing climate. Centre for Ecology and Hydrology (CEH) deputy director Professor Alan Jenkins did for example say that:

> We are absolutely convinced that there is weighty scientific evidence that the recent extreme rainfall has been impacted by climate change. (Cookson 2016)

However, the James of 2036 reads the situation in terms of more local causes:

> About ten years ago [...] they started building all the [commercial] units and it disturbs the land. It ruined the water table and it just causes more and more frequent flooding. Every time the river gets quite high because of the rain [...] it floods further down near Esholt, because they've just built big flood defenses behind the shops. It just pushes the water elsewhere. It has made Esholt a ghost town, everywhere else they've got flood defences to protect the commercial units, not to protect the houses of Esholt that were flooded and destroyed. And they wonder why people left. It's disgusting, it's wrong, it's immoral. That's what it is, it's immoral.

James 2036 sees a clear connection between the flooding and the commercial development that he despises so much. As might be the case with the rest of the world, it is difficult to consider economy and environmental concerns separately when debating the future of Shipley. James 2036 is however more positive with regards to the future of climate change:

> Things have gotten a little warmer. [...] The actions that they've put in place are working. But it's like trying to stop a train down a big hill, you put the brakes on and it's not going to stop instantly. It's going to slow down and it's still slowing down but it's getting to an almost no change. It's almost like the train stopped on the hill. And soon we're going to pull it back up that hill and repair it and try to undo the damage.

The interventional function of ethno science fiction allows us to explore how we relate to scientific predictions of the future. Scientific progress has made it possible to predict changes with increased precision. Ethno science fiction provides an expression for how fieldwork informants relate to these predictions through their imagination. Scientific predictions on climate change and its impact on the population are usually based on statistical data collected over an extended period and are representative of large areas and groups of people. People's individual perceptions and moral understandings are often overlooked in these predictions. Anthropology provides the opposite perspective. The ethnographic tradition of qualitative research relies on methods that foreground people's lived experiences, whereby the life story or words of particular informants are used to stand for and represent a wider social perspective in a metonymic relation of part to whole.

In the production of ethno science fiction, imagined narratives of the future are generated in the tension between the personal imagination of the participants and the predictions of the scientists. In doing so, ethno science fiction films offer an individual perspective on the future that complements scientific predictions and conceptualizations of the future across a range of possible social and cultural scenarios. Environmental instability caused by climate change, including that of flooding, presents an especially interesting focal point in this context. Climate change is perceived as one of the main future threats to humanity among the vast majority of scientific experts and world leaders. This acknowledgement has spurred the release of international resources allowing scientists to predict the consequences of climate change over a long-term perspective with improved accuracy. But what do such predictions, for example in relation to rising water levels and increased flooding, mean locally? And how does this shape people's perceptions and imaginaries of the future among those living in areas prone to flooding whereby climate change threatens the livelihood, housing, health and safety of one's friends, neighbours, relatives and the local population?

Official and governmental reports on the effects of climate change are rarely read and do not play a significant part in the everyday life-worlds of most British people. More immediate concerns such as employment, the local neighbourhood, leisure activities and one's future job prospects are often prioritized. And yet, media coverage about environmental disasters and scientific predictions about future environmental threats still play on the imagination of individuals. Swedish reports, for example, show an increase of so-called 'climate change anxiety' (Lagerblad 2010), which affects the mental health of people and often centres on the responsibility they feel in relation to their own children and future generations. I refer to this relation as 'temporal proximity'. This is reflected in the documentary shots I recorded of James having a phone conversation with his past, present and future selves between 2014 and 2056, which contains many traces of how he relates to change. The content and character of the questions he asks himself indicates that his primary concerns about the future not are about the abstract idea of climate change but rather the health and general well-being of his family, and his own dream of becoming a rock star. This informal ranking of his concerns is comparable to the hierarchy that controls the news presentation in media, depending on the cultural proximity the audience feels in relation to the news topic. Straubhaar explains cultural proximity as '[...] the tendency to prefer media products from one's own culture or the most similar possible culture' (Straubhaar 2003: 85). The media audience might for example be more interested in reading and watching news about a local matter rather than a more serious incident in another part of the world. Ethnographic films have traditionally contributed to cultural proximity among the audience by bridging the different with the familiar, and mediating complex cultural understanding. Similarly, ethno science fictions present the possibility to create complex understanding and sympathy for future generations – a temporal proximity. Abstract ideas about the future become concrete problems and possibilities as they are imagined and discussed with the audience.

Conclusion

In this chapter, I have tried to show how ethno science fiction film can be used as an ethnographic film method. From an interventionist perspective, it also provides a possibility for innovation and solution. Ethno science fiction can be applied as a sounding board for communities to watch and reflect on their imagined scenarios about the future. Often, the imagination of the individual is difficult to include in scientific predictions about the future. Yet, at least eight of the ideas that Jules Verne presented in his science fictions were later engineered, including electric submarines, newscasts, solar sails, lunar modules, skywriting, videoconferencing, tasers and splashdown space-ships (*National Geographic*, January 2011). While it is difficult to evidence the influence that Jules Verne had on the engineers of the above devices, it is also hard to deny the future impact of Verne's creative imagination. Based on similar principles, ethno science fiction facilitates the invention of new ideas in response to a range of subjects and social issues, including climate change and crisis, that are grounded in the individual imagination of the future. Screening the resulting film material back to the people involved, offers an additional practical means for shared reflexivity and dialogue, as the entire community may participate in the sounding board to give feedback and develop new ideas and solutions to problems in times of crisis.

References

Boal, A., 1979. *Theatre of the Oppressed*. London: Pluto Press.

Bottoms, S., 2014–17. 'Towards Hydro-Citizenship'. Available online: www. hydrocitizenship.com (accessed 20 July 2016).

Bottoms, S., 2016. 'Multi-Story Water: Celebrating Shipley and its waterways'. Available online: http://multi-story-shipley.co.uk (accessed 20 July 2016).

Cookson, C., 2016. 'Climate change strongly linked to UK flooding'. *Financial Times*, 8 January.

Crapanzano, V., 2004. *Imaginative Horizons: An Essay in Literary-Philosophical Anthropology*. Chicago: University of Chicago Press.

Fox, J., 1987. *The Essential Moreno. Writings on Psychodrama, Group Method, and Spontaneity*. New York: Springer Publishing Co. Inc.

Freedman, C., 2000. *Critical Theory and Science Fiction*. Hanover and London: University Press of New England.

Freire, P., 1970. *Pedagogy of the Oppressed*. New York: Herder and Herder.

Harris, M. and N. Rapport (eds), 2015. *Reflections on Imagination: Human Capacity and Ethnographic Method*. Farnham and Burlington, VT: Ashgate.

Henley, P., 2009. *The Adventure of the Real: Jean Rouch and the Craft of Ethnographic Cinema*. Chicago and London: University of Chicago Press.

Huizinga, J., 1955. *Homo Ludens: A Study of the Play-element in Culture*. Boston: Beacon Press, 1938.

Irving, A., 2011. 'Strange Distance: Towards an Anthropology of Interior Dialogue'. *Medical Anthropology Quarterly* 25 (1): 22–44.

Kean, H., 2010. 'People, Historians, and Public History: Demystifying the Process of History Making'. *The Public Historian* 32 (3): 26.

Kulick, D., 1998. *Travesti. Sex, Gender and Culture among Brazilian Transgendered Prostitutes*. Chicago: University of Chicago Press.

Lagerblad, A., 2010. 'Klimatångest nytt fenomen i psykiatrin'. *Svenska Dagbladet*, 6 December.

Loizos, P., 1993. *Innovation in Ethnographic Film*. Manchester: Manchester University Press.

MacDonald, S., 1993. *Avant-garde Film: Motion Studies*. Cambridge: Cambridge University Press.

Marshall, J. and J. W. Adams, 1978. 'Jean Rouch Talks About His Films to John Marshall and John W. Adams (14 and 15 September 1977)'. *American Anthropologist* 80 (4): 1005–20.

Morin, E. and J. Rouch, 2003. 'Chronicle of a Summer: A Film Book by Jean Rouch and Edgar Morin'. In J. Rouch. S. Feld (ed. and trans.), *Ciné-Ethnography*. Minneapolis and London: University of Minnesota Press.

National Geographic, 2011. '8 Jules Verne Inventions That Came True', 8 February.

Rapport, N., 2008. 'Gratuitousness: Notes Towards an Anthropology of Interiority'. *Australian Journal of Anthropology* 19 (3): 331–49.

Rouch, J. (Director), 1958. *Moi un Noir* [Motion Picture]. France: Les Films de la Pléiade.

Rouch, J. (Director), 1970. *Petit a Petit* [Motion Picture]. France: Les Films de la Pléiade.

Rouch, J., 2003. *Ciné-Ethnography*, S. Feld (ed. and trans.). Minneapolis and London: University of Minnesota Press.

Rouch, J. with E. Fulchignoni, 2003. 'Ciné-Anthropology'. In J. Rouch and S. Feld (eds and trans.), *Ciné-Ethnography*. Minneapolis and London: University of Minnesota Press.

Sjöberg, J. (Producer and Director), 2007. *Transfiction* [Motion Picture]. Brazil, Sweden and United Kingdom: FaktaFiktion Sweden and The University of Manchester.

Sjöberg, J., 2008. 'Ethnofiction: Drama as a creative research practice in ethnographic film'. *Journal of Media Practice* 9 (3): 229–42.

Sjöberg, J., 2009a. 'Ethnofiction: Genre hybridity in theory and practice', PhD thesis, Drama, Faculty of Humanities, The University of Manchester.

Sjöberg, J., 2009b. 'Ethnofiction and Beyond: The legacy of projective improvisation in ethnographic filmmaking'. Paper presented at the international conference A Knowledge Beyond Text at Centre Pompidou in Paris, November.

Sjöberg, J., 2011. 'Transgendered Saints and Harlots: Reproduction of Popular Brazilian Transgender Stereotypes through Performance on Stage, Screen and in Everyday Life'. In K. Ross (ed.), *The Handbook of Gender, Sex and Media*. Malden, MA and Oxford: Wiley-Blackwell.

Sjöberg, J., forthcoming. '"A Sort of Psychodrama": Applied drama as Ethnographic Method in Jean Rouch's Films'. In R. Sherman (ed.), *In the Wake of Jean Rouch*. London and New York: Wallflower Press.

Starobinski, J., 1970. *Jean-Jacques Rousseau: la transparence et l'obstacle*. Paris: Plon [1957]; Gallimard [1971].

Stoller, P., 1992. *The Cinematic Griot: The Ethnography of Jean Rouch*. Chicago: Chicago University Press.

Straubhaar, J. D., 2003. 'Choosing National TV: Cultural Capital, Language, and Cultural Proximity in Brazil'. In M. G. Elasmar (ed.), *The Impact of International Television: A Paradigm Shift*, 77–110. Mahwah, NJ: Lawrence Erlbaum Associates, Inc.

Turner, V., 1964. 'Betwixt and Between: The Liminal Period in Rites de Passage'. *The Proceedings of the American Ethnological Society. Symposium on New Approaches to the Study of Religion* 4–20.

Vaihinger, H., 1924. *The Philosophy of 'As if': A System of Theoretical, Practical and Religious Fictions of Mankind*. London: Kegan Paul.

Watkins, P. (Director), 1965. *The War Game* [Motion Picture]. United Kingdom: British Broadcasting Corporation (BBC).

Watkins, P. (Director), 1971. *Punishment Park* [Motion Picture]. Chartwell, Francoise.

Watkins, P., 2015. *Media Crisis*. France: Editions L'échappée.

Yakir, D., 1978. 'Cine-Trance: The Vision of Jean Rouch'. *Film Quarterly* 31 (3).

12

Reaching for the horizon: Exploring existential possibilities of migration and movement within the past-present-future through participatory animation

Alexandra D'Onofrio

FIGURE 12.1 *'My future return' (Mahmoud)*[1]

Alex: 'How do you think this moment will be?
Mahmud: An emotional moment … we will feel we have missed each
other too much.
Alex: When do you think this can happen?
Mahmud: The end of next year, hopefully.'

Mahmud is an Egyptian migrant in his mid-twenties for whom the act of
embracing his mother, until very recently, was a practical impossibility. When
we first met, he had already been living illegally in Milan for four years, a
fact which impeded him from travelling and which made him live under the
constant threat of sudden deportation. The only way he could live through
his desired future and turn it into a possibility, was through his imagination.

My research with Egyptian migrants in Milan is a methodological and
existential investigation into people's perceptions of the future and their
imaginative 'lifeworlds' (Jackson 2012) as these influence the narrations of
lived experiences. The ethnographic examples presented in this chapter aim
to show how the future seen through dreams, hopes and fears becomes
almost tangible in migrants' daily chores, plans, actions and storytelling.
Though out of reach for people who perceive themselves as constantly on
the move, the future plays a crucial role in providing a sense of direction
and expectation. It is through the existential possibilities of certain imagined
futures that migrants often redefine who they are and ascribe new meanings
to their past and present circumstances. Therefore, I argue that in order to
understand people's experiences, we need to research beyond what is readily
accessible, as informants often describe intangible phenomena that exist
outside the realms of ordinary perception and disrupt the linear structure of
narrative and the temporal ordering of events. Sometimes a past experience
becomes a re-interpretation of a desired future and a present hardship
provokes a revision of past decisions and future expectations, which redefine
whole life purposes and trajectories.

Understanding my participants' discordant temporalities, experiences
and stories, demands responsive practice-based methods and a different,
non-linear approach to ethnographic representation.

The quest for new methodological approaches also aims at showing that
imaginings are not merely abstract products of people's consciousness but
are embodied and embedded in people's present actions. For example, when
Mahmud managed to legalize his status in Italy, the possibility of going back
to Egypt in the conditions he always had hoped for (as an active breadwinner,
able to marry and take care of his family, to refurbish his parents' house and
to build his own) took a presence in the way he dedicated himself to work
every day, to build some significant capital prior to his return. It would also
be present in his words as he would often tell me 'We are here to build our

future!', interestingly linking his actual labour as a builder and decorator with the practical and imaginative process of giving form to his future. Likewise, all the hardship he went through, starting from the perilous Mediterranean crossing and the subsequent abuse at work, or unemployment, started to make some sense. Although the amount of time that it took for his papers to arrive had often made him feel that he was wasting his life, now he had finally found a purpose in waiting.

So if imaginings are present to us, what qualities does their existence have? What ontological status is accorded to an absence, or to a remote possibility? Understanding the future and the imagination in terms of people's perceptions, is not a theoretical question but a practical, empirical one. In order to relate the future to lived experiences and make the discussion relevant anthropologically, we need to find new ways to interact with the people we work with.

Method and process in context

I first met Mahmud, Ali and Mohamed during Theatre of the Oppressed workshops that I co-facilitated in 2010, as a project of the Fandema group which is a community-based theatre company I founded in 2006. Its members have been asylum seekers, refugees, migrants and Italian activists who have used Forum Theatre[2] to create more public awareness and debate around socio-political issues arising throughout the experience of migration.

Subsequently, as part of my fieldwork between 2012 and 2015, we experimented with various creative methods, starting with already familiar theatre and storytelling techniques. Through games and exercises we focused on physical and verbal, improvisation and representation. The aim was to explore and enact different possible futures and existential options through theatre improvisations. The storytelling workshops were devised with Mahmoud, Ali and Mohamed who narrated a story which was meaningful to them, for the topic or questions they identified with. This process trained them, as storytellers, to select themes, words and moral or existential questions that could engage an audience that didn't have similar experiential or social backgrounds.

The second stage of fieldwork consisted in experimenting with audio-visual methods. Initially my informants were involved in a participatory photography workshop which I co-facilitated, with the objective of exploring autobiographical storytelling through still images. After this process we recorded documentary footage following their wish to re-visit the first places of arrival in Italy. During these journeys I asked them to take photographs of the most significant places as they walked through them to capture in an image and in their improvised speech some of the memories and imaginary future possibilities associated with their past experiences. According to Peter Loizos, this is one of the major innovations that Jean Rouch brought to ethnographic filmmaking 'to convey something fundamental about real lives' (1993: 50) by encouraging informants to improvise their acting in front of the camera in 'ethnofictions' (Sjöberg 2008; Stoller 1992). Similar to psychoanalysis, the protagonists of the ethnofictions would make previously implicit information explicit (Sjöberg 2008), by a process Loizos called 'projective improvisation' (Loizos 1993: 50). When improvising what they say or do in front of the camera, the protagonists express what they would normally take for granted (Sjöberg 2008). As I filmed Mohamed, Ali and Mahmoud react to places that had been meaningful for the beginning of their lives in Italy, I realized how the environment was triggering the associations that my subjects were making. Similar to the process of ethnofictions, the situation triggered another experience that they suddenly remembered, as the unforeseen environment and unrehearsed situation fed the imagination and gave life to new associations (Sjöberg 2009). My own participants engaged in a creative flow that was the outcome of the dialogic relationship between their material surroundings and their subconscious, and also an interplay between memories and imaginings. The photographs from these journeys attempted to capture a still image of this free flow which would have been very difficult to visualize there and then, without interrupting the creative momentum the protagonists were experiencing. Imaginative horizons, in the sense of future envisionings, are by definition in perpetual (trans)formation, and they are unfixable and unreachable projections of people's minds. Their very nature poses a challenge to conventional anthropological methodologies, which heavily rely on observation, interviews and text and 'are often too static to capture the unfinished, transitory, and ever-changing character of people's interior experiences and expressions as they emerge in the present tense' (Irving 2011: 25). In exploring the intangible dimensions of people's everyday lives, as social scientists, we should perhaps engage in a more 'adventurous relationship to the real' (Henley 2010: xiv), as Rouch did using improvised filmmaking and his actors' projective improvisation and fantasy. He often blurred the boundaries between fact and fiction as his ethnographic filmmaking documented the manifestations of the surreal in the forms of the real, in order to produce what he poetically described as 'a postcard at the service of the imaginary' (Fieschi and Téchiné 1967:19).[3] Similar achievements have been echoed by scholars in animation studies (Skoller 2011; Wells 1998; Ward 2006; Honness Roe 2011; Callus 2012), sustaining the argument that the rising interest and the popular acceptance of the hybrid form of animated documentary signals a deepening awareness that the truth claims of non-fiction forms no longer reside in the 'reality effects' of the photographic trace, but rather 'in a developing understanding that the realities that surround us and the events that structure our present are not always visualizable, that their meanings are unclear, and that documentary evidence is not always possible, revealing or clarifying' (Skoller 2011: 207). Hence, the aesthetic and narrative re-elaboration of the memories, feelings, imaginings associated with those places, was carried out at a later stage of the research in a studio, a very different, confined, professionally defined space. After making a careful selection, my informants used some of the images as the visual and the storytelling basis of the painted animation thanks to the collaboration of Francesca Cogni, a professional animator who helped facilitate the process.

This chapter will focus on participatory animation as a practice towards new anthropological directions of envisioning and working with people's, and not only migrants', life stories, which need to encompass future and conditional tenses as much as they do the present and the past. I argue that animation brings an innovative contribution to ordinary ethnographic practices and representations as it creatively engages with people's imaginative possibilities that often lie beyond our grasp. By belonging to a type of film that would not necessarily be of anthropological intent, animation offers the opportunity to expose 'anthropologists and ethnographic filmmakers to ways of using image and sound to create expressive, rather than realist, representations of aspects of human experience and discourse' (Pink 2001: 24). It is in its own power to penetrate an aspect of 'reality', that we may want to find access and an expression to, that social scientists can gain outstanding advantages. In *Understanding Animation* (1998), Paul Wells defines the penetrative character of the animated documentary as its ability to evoke internal spaces of being, to portray what is generally invisible to the naked eye. Thus, the animated film can become the very method that can help us identify and represent particular kinds of experience and perceptions, which do not find adequate expression elsewhere. Being completely constructed, this genre of films also indicates the limits of other methods and forms that claim to be more 'objective' and neutral, but whose truth claims have been highly critiqued and contested in post-colonial and postmodern theory.

The following ethnographic examples aim to show how my methodological experimentation has been also a way to trace the ontological status of my participants' imaginings of the future through creative practice. In the attempt to identify the forms that imaginative possibilities take in people's experiences this chapter will be looking at some basic questions: Where do we find evidence? When is it that they become manifest? What qualities (physical, emotional, mood-like etc.) do they have? And why do certain imaginings appear to some and not others?

Ethnographic background, theory on crisis and imagination
What would you do if one day you fell asleep, and when you woke up
the next day you would see yourself in the mirror ... and cried.
A question goes in your mind; you scream ... who am I?? Who am I??
Am I still who I was or am I divided into two persons?
So what's next?
Hey you in the mirror tell me, explain to me what's going on [...][4]

Ali, Mahmud and Mohamed left Egypt without legal papers when they were
teenagers or slightly older. During the theatre and storytelling workshops they
often referred to their border crossing experience as a critical moment that
split their lives into two very distinct existential moments: the life before the
crossing and the one that unfolded thereafter. Each portion contained its own
imaginative and experiential possibilities.

When we traverse a crisis, which creates a rupture in our structured
normalities, offering an opportunity or imposing an impediment in reaching
our existential objectives, our imaginary worlds become manifest in very
particular ways. Turner's concept of social drama echoes here, as conflict and
crisis come to interrupt the continuous flow of social processes, of rituals and
performances that mitigate differences into the smooth surface of a shared
community. This moment is 'one of those turning points [...] of danger and
suspense, when a true state of affairs is revealed' (Turner 1974: 39) allowing
the underlying structures of inequality to emerge. In this sense, the Universal
Declaration of Human Rights is an act of civilisation attempting to mitigate the
disparity between different citizens of the world, recognizing to 'Everyone [...]
the right to leave any country, including his own, and to return to his country'
(Article 13.2). But the true state of affairs, as Turner would put it, is completely
different. In Egypt, as in all African states, only some people, belonging to
the upper and middle classes, are granted travelling visas by the European
embassies. The majority of the citizens belonging to the poorer working class
are denied the right to travel to Europe and are thus forced into the smuggling
routes at the risk of their lives. Such critical moments are charged with
contrasting feelings of excitement, fear, frustration and angst, revealing the
power of specific imaginations about the future to cause action or paralysis.

The almost palpable dimension of the possibilities that unfold in front of
people standing at a crossroad determines the way they are going to feel
about what will happen next, the choices they will make. Whether directed
by chance or by a conscious decision, the stronger the 'reality' of those possibilities, or impossibilities, the more passionately these will take over people's
present perceptions of self and their world views.

Like Michael Jackson's work with Sierra Leonean migrants (2008), my
fieldwork has been considering how migrants' imaginative possibilities

become particularly fervent during critical transitions (such as sea crossings, escapes from reception centres and legalization processes) and have a hold on their immediate reality. Having acknowledged this, how do these other possibilities affect people's actions and decisions in crucial moments? How does it affect the way they re-interpret their own life trajectory (from present to past and then to future)?

The relationship between the so called reality and our images of what lies beyond the horizon is one of 'interdependence' (Crapanzano 2003) because as much as dreams, projections, calculations, and prophecies may give form to 'the beyond', the images that are created also form and inform people's experiences. What is particularly interesting about this dialectical relationship is the role played by what lies beyond the horizon, 'the possibilities it opens up to us, the licit or illicit desires it provokes, the plays of power it suggests, the dread it can cause – the uncertainty, the sense of contingency, of chance – the exaltation, the thrill of the unknown, it can provoke' (ibid.: 14).

Concurrently, the irreality of these possibilities affects how people reconstruct their autobiographical stories, the interpretations of their immediate experiences and perceptions, and the decisions and actions they put forward.

During border crossings and on escape routes, people's imaginative horizons were importantly also providing the direction. This dialectical tension which Crapanzano so poignantly describes as 'the paradoxical ways in which the irreality of the imaginary impresses the real of the reality and the real of reality compels the irreality of the imaginary' (ibid.: 15) is at the heart of my research.

Although both Jackson and Crapanzano have made a case for engaging analytically with the imaginative realms of our informants, this inquiry has been extending their concept by encompassing the realms of the future (as perceived from the present, or the past, in its direct, conditional and past forms) but most importantly through the methodological investigation of a practice, which also gives the initial ontological quest its relevant epistemological turn.

Ali

During the legalization process, following an amnesty decreed by the Italian government in September 2012, my informants expressed the wish to film their return to their places of arrival in Italy. The amnesty after many years of uncertainty served to revive their hopes as they had the chance to redeem themselves and their future was again vividly re-inhabited by possibilities.

Interestingly though, it was not just the future, in the sense of the forward tense, to be the focus of their talking, but also their past was being recovered, as memories would re-emerge in the light of the changed circumstances.

For Ali however, the decision of returning to Porto Nogaro, a port near Udine in northern Italy where he had abandoned the merchant ship he was working on, had to take into account how he felt about his present and how close he perceived to be in realizing his dreams about the future. This place was invested by symbolical connotations due to the meanings ascribed to it through Ali's narration of his past. Going back was not a simple action to carry out.

Although at the beginning he himself wished to travel soon after he received the residence permit, his initial enthusiasm was soon deadened by the difficulty in finding a job in the midst of the Italian economic crisis. So our journey was postponed until Ali could tell me that the right time had arrived.

'I want to go to the port that brought me into Italy and say – "Bless this port!" – instead now I'm almost regretting having come. I want to go there as a complete man, as a man satisfied with himself.' Work and the ability to compare himself to the successful professional lives of his siblings and friends back home, were fundamental to Ali's conception of manhood.

A year later, when Ali was managing two different jobs we finally arranged to do the shooting in and around Porto Nogaro. We decided to shoot at dawn, closer to the time he had escaped and his excitement was evident by the detail and the drama he put into his narration. His body moved swiftly amongst the goods on the quay, along the wall, beyond the gates, behind the bushes, re-living the excitement of that moment where he had bravely taken hold of his life. At times he would stop, take a picture of a specific place and think aloud: 'Why didn't I go right instead of left? Why did I take this street down? I don't know myself ….' As we retraced Ali's escape, his body began to stiffen and his movements became quicker and quicker. For a second he would look ahead and then suddenly look back towards the port, until we finally came to the first side street he took during his escape.

> From this point onwards we stopped looking at the port. From this street it started … this line separates that side [the side of the port] from this side with its future. Past and future. The street if you look at it from here, it doesn't tell you anything. Because it was exactly like this, empty and dark. You're entering a street as if you were entering a forest. In darkness, there was no light.

During shooting Ali photographed the street as he remembered it (Figure 12.2). Some months later, when he was animating that moment, he drew what suddenly crossed his mind when a set of car lights pointed into his direction.

Without even knowing whether it was a police car, as soon as he noticed the lights his imagination immediately drew three possible future scenarios. If caught, he would be sent back to the ship, imprisoned or repatriated.

FIGURE 12.2 *Ali imagines himself imprisoned after seeing the car lights.*

The technique, which would enable Ali to draw over the image he had captured, without altering it, was to paint on glass. We built a light box together, which was composed by a drawer, a small table lamp and a glass picture frame. The photograph, printed in black and white to allow the contrast of the coloured animation to emerge further, was attached to the interior side of the glass frame providing in transparency a constant reference to Ali's drawings. A still camera, fixed to a tripod and tilted facing down towards the frame, was connected to the computer and to the software which commanded the shutter to close when the frame was ready to be photographed. The image then was automatically imported on the software's timeline (Figure 12. 3).

While animating, to convey how intensely he experienced his imaginative possibilities at that given moment, Ali wiped his body off his original position (in the street, when he first saw the car lights), and re-drew it directly in his imaginative 'bubbles'. Once again indicating that the 'reality' of his imagination existed not just in abstract terms, but was made present and embodied through his nervous system.

In order to avoid being caught and identified, Ali got rid of his Egyptian passport in the bushes anticipating, thus, the future in a present action. By predicting what could have happened, Ali legislated his behaviour. His quick decision making, as much as his experience as a whole, was influenced by stories he had heard by acquaintances, who had previously taken

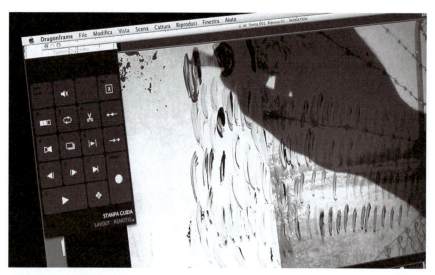

FIGURE 12.3 *Screenshot of animation in progress.*

such a risk and knew how to warn and advise others. Out of repetition and exchange, stories of people crossing borders illegally have become part of a collective history which acts as reference to new migrants' experiences. David Carr would say that the past is also present to us in the world we experience. As a phenomenologist he argues that the historical past is not just the subject matter of historians, as a time we can 'bracket' away from our present. We live the historical past, as we have a 'non-thematic' or 'pre-thematic' awareness of it, which means that it acts also as a horizon and 'background for our present experience, or our experience of the present' (1986: 3).

Similarly, I argue the future acts upon our present functioning as a 'foreground' to our everyday experience. In Ali, the consequences of getting caught were transformed vividly into a bodily experience by his imagination of a possible near future. Hence we could say it is part of the human condition to legislate, decide, perceive and narrate as if the future was already part of our lived experience. As Ricoeur (1984) has argued, our experience of time is essentially characterized by 'discordance': the present is past, at the same time it's projected forward and then again, as other examples from the field will show, accompanied by other conditional possibilities. It is then through narrative (in the form of story and storytelling, and here also of animation) that we bring 'concord' to the dissonance, as it is our primary way of organizing our experience of time. Therefore, not only can narrative elucidate our pre-theoretical past (Carr 1986: 5), but it can also do the same with our imagined possibilities of the future.

FIGURE 12.4 *Ali imagines his future return to Porto Nogaro.*

As Ali and I started returning to the harbour from the side street where he had thrown his passport and uniform, he stopped again in front of the main entrance of the port and told me that he now wanted to take another picture.

This time it's not a picture of the past. This picture is for the future. [...] I don't want to enter this port on foot again. I want to enter it with my own car. Perhaps with the shipment papers of some goods. Which goods, I don't know. The important thing is to do a job like that. I would love to do it.

He later added that his newly acquired residence permit allowed him to project himself and capture this image of the future.

When animating this picture and by re-claiming some sort of belonging to the place, Ali decided to rename the port with his name (Figure 12.4).

Jackson recognizes the existential qualities of storytelling 'as a vital strategy for sustaining a sense of agency in the face of disempowering circumstances' (2002: 15). Ali's wishful animated anecdote about his future, enabled him to actively re-elaborate events in a story, and no longer to live those events in passivity.

Mohamed

Mohamed wished to distinguish himself from other fellow villagers that had migrated like him to Italy, by asserting that what motivated him to cross the sea was to achieve something for himself, study and gain experience of the world. The idea of making money to show off back home through brand new cars and freshly built houses, was certainly part of the collective motivation of migrating but during the legalization process his original dream of getting himself an education in Europe, became more and more compelling and close.

Mohamed disembarked in Sicily, at the harbour of Agrigento at the age of seventeen. Ten years had passed before he managed to return to the places he had first seen with the eyes of a much younger and inexperienced man. Even so, the memories of those days were still so fresh and vivid, and he had become nervous and anxious about our journey. He told me he was worried about the possibility of not being able to recognize the places he had passed through, but also, as evident in the reflections that emerged while we were filming, he was also becoming uncomfortable with the idea of coming to terms with what had happened in his life since then. He was aware of the fact that his dreams as a teenager, which had driven him to undertake such a life threatening and transforming journey, did not coincide in the least with what had actually taken place. As soon as we started visiting the harbour and walking through the streets, Mohamed became visibly excited and emotional. He photographed the harbour and the pier where he first set foot.

Then he wished to visit the centre for minors where he had spent fifteen days before deciding to escape to reach Milan, which was his final destination. That place, he realized, was where he could have started a completely different life had he decided to stay and not escape. If he only had understood that he had a chance to get some schooling and a temporary paper, perhaps he would have found the patience to wait. But he wished to be free to decide for himself, 'without feeling obliged to stay closed up in that place in the middle of nowhere … I couldn't tell with my eyes that I had reached Italy. I wanted to get to Milan. That was the place I had left my home for.'

But now that we were retracing his steps the suspicion that things could have gone down an easier route if he had acted differently began to haunt him. While we were walking around the buildings where other young people were being lodged he would talk to one of the social workers and myself and say: 'If I only knew it was going to be so hard after I escaped … that I was going to lose ten years of my life … no, I should've stayed! Now I know it for sure. Things would be different now …'

Here, Mohamed came face to face with his other possible life. Where he would have had the chance to learn the language, create other contacts,

FIGURE 12.5 *Mohamed imagines receiving his residence permit at the reception centre.*

and not live as an outcast as he had done for ten years (Figure 12.5). This imaginary possible life probably has accompanied Mohamed all the time, as when asked about the future he would plunge into confusion and sadness. He realized he had lost too much time of his youth, which was the time appropriate according to him for dreams and for developing his knowledge. On top of that he lamented the idea of having lost proximity to his family, to his people, to whom he once was, and now was unable to change his situation. Jackson also encountered similar feelings and perceptions in his Sierra Leonean informants: '[…] constant exposure to a negative social environment will easily lead one … to a nagging guilt that the price of one's own improved chances in life is the loss of one's kith and kin and one's heritage' (2008:70).

Mahmud

Mahmud, first thing after getting his papers, wished to go back to visit his family because, as he said, not being able to return for so long was a defining aspect of being, or *becoming* a migrant, adding that there is a difference between travelling and migrating: 'When we were in our country we used to say we were going to travel. But then during the journey, this turns into migrating. Because many years pass and we can't go back. That is how a journey turns into migration.' As a defining feature of an undocumented migrant's identity therefore, Mahmud was saying that at the same time as they were losing the proximity to their own familiar people and places, they were also losing a part of their future which would have included being able to visit their families whenever they wished, to feel connected to their places of origin. In Mohamed's and Mahmud's words it is possible to trace the sense of loss they have developed for a future that they will never get to know.

Mahmud boarded a plane for the first time in his life with me, on our flight to Lampedusa, a now famous small island in the middle of the Mediterranean where so many undocumented migrants following the smuggling routes disembark on. Since Lampedusa is the southernmost part of Italy, and the closest European island to the African continent, many boats carrying undocumented migrants and asylum seekers that enter international waters, try to disembark there or in Sicily and end up being detected by the Italian coastal guards.

In April 2015 Lampedusa was the site of one of the most tragic shipwrecks in the post-war history of the Mediterranean, when more than 900 immigrants drowned.

Mahmud had been on a similar journey, ten years ago, when he too was only seventeen. While we were in Lampedusa he expressed the desire to film the dawn from up a cliff. He said it was so lovely to observe the sea from land.

> It's not like being in the middle of the sea, on a small boat with 40 people, where all you can see *is* the sea. There, the water comes and hits you, there's no need to go and touch it … the water is beautiful from a beautiful beach, from a mountain, from a big nice ship!

One of the images we photographed on that cliff ended up on our animation light box. Mahmud thought he could tell part of the story of the crossing by animating the photograph of himself looking at the sea (Figure 12.6). Francesca, our professional animator, asked him whether he wanted to start from the 'beautiful sea, seen from land', in order to recall what he had said at the time, so he decided to start the animation with the sun rising.

The attention he gave to detail was impressive. The more Francesca and I tried to simplify the act of drawing, the more Mahmud came up with quite elaborate aesthetic ideas. In the picture he stood there still, like in real life and watched, and not until the sun moved up in the sky did he move his arms in a relaxed position of admiration. Then slowly, as he was starting to remember the quality of the sea when he saw it from the boat, his colours became thicker, and the sea started surrounding him. Suddenly he stopped and said,

FIGURE 12.6 *The beautiful sea, seen from land (Mahmoud).*

'I don't remember anything anymore.' We persisted for a while in asking him questions thinking they might help unblock his memory: 'What happened there? What part of the story would you like to tell now?' He replied, 'While I was there I didn't wish to keep these memories; I didn't want them to stay with me. It was horrible … It took me so long to forget, and now you come and ask me to tell you the story.' After a reflective pause, we felt we had to reassure Mahmud and clarify that the purpose of our work was not to dig out discomforting traumatic memories. Although I knew Mahmud very well, and had previously discussed my ethical concerns with Francesca and all participants of this research, I felt obliged to remind Mahmud that there was no need for us to continue to work on this story if he wished to stop. The fact that he resisted giving testimony to what had happened was integral part of the process and he had the freedom to twist or conclude the story in any way he preferred. Moreover, the creative practices we had been engaging with had been used ethically so that my participants could co-direct their narration and use fiction and metaphors whenever they wished to avoid descriptive accounts of troublesome experiences.

Finally, Mahmud abandoned the brush, and coloured his fingers with some paint and began to smudge the colours and the lines on the picture. As he began mixing the colours little by little an image seemed to start emerging.

Slowly, they became clearly visible. Two faces, with watery eyes and contours. Mahmud then spoke up: 'It's Mum and Dad. They are crying for their son who's in the middle of the sea.' (Figure 12.7)

I realized only later that I had learned something very valuable from Mahmud about the relationship we had developed throughout our research.

FIGURE 12.7 *Mum and Dad (Mahmoud).*

The fact that he had control over the animation process also helped him to feel in the right position to re-negotiate and resist the claims that Francesca and I could have made about his process of remembering, and the ways in which he would have recounted this experience in the future. What was more relevant to him was not the exact description of his terrifying journey but the devastating effects it must have had in his parents' thoughts and feelings. Was he trying to relive this experience as seen through the watery eyes of his parents? Did his imagining at that time, of their faces and their worries, prevail over his individual recollection of the crossing? It can be argued that, deciding to substitute his personal perspective with theirs, he is making a claim over whose experience he believed best represented the drama of that moment.

In analysing the process of making *Running for Freedom* (2003/04) a film about refugees coming to London, Piotrowska makes an argument for hybrid forms to be used for representing, and I would add, for researching, people's traumatic memories and experiences. In asking herself the question of what happens when our subjects' narrative breaks down, she realizes that 'Some things, that are too intimate or too traumatic are best left alone – or to fiction' (2011: 337). By using live action together with animation she allowed for the fictional and symbolical recuperation of language, as the participants to her film found a way of telling part of their story. If it hadn't been for animation, Mahmud would have most probably felt more uneasy. But he had always been very keen to tell and share his own experience in the form of stories. He would often tell me how he wished to bring part of his documentary to his family, in Egypt, and in future share it with his own children. Even enriched by fictional or more metaphorical content, he would always refer to the account he made as 'real'. Post-structuralist philosopher Jaques Derrida offers a defence of fictionalized accounts based on lived experiences, which attempts to bring fantasies and fears closer to one's life experiences. Animation within documentary, gives this possibility as it is completely 'created' by the work of imagination. Moreover, lies, fiction and imagination have the potentiality of creating something 'anew' (Ricoeur 1984), which takes us safely beyond an uncomfortable, and often unethical research of truth claims. This isn't to say, Paul Ward warns us, that the claims represented are thereby completely invalidated: 'on the contrary, it might well be the case that an animated documentary manages to reveal *more* of the "reality" of a situation than any number of live-action documentaries. Animated documentaries want to engage with the world in all its complexity and contradiction' (2006: 89).

When reflecting on the process of animating, Mahmud told us that he hadn't imagined it would turn out the way it did. Every time he was adding something, he said, the next step would come into his mind, by itself, as if it would appear into his imagination. After the workshop, Francesca added something she herself had realized while working with this technique: 'This technique enables imaginary perceptions to emerge step by step as one draws … Sometimes I get so immersed, imagining my characters and their actions, that then it's kind of automatic for me to do certain things that I wouldn't have seen otherwise.'

Conclusion

The reflections and considerations that have emerged from the ethnographic context created by the filmmaking and the animation process, have led me as a researcher to recognize the value of the animated film as a creative method. It is capable of venturing within the realm of future existential possibilities, which are crucial in providing guidance and a reference in the lives of people that have experienced migration. The animation process has shed light onto the workings of imaginings related to possible futures and the impact these may have on people's lived experiences and decision-making. Furthermore, animation has also provided Ali, Mahmud and Mohamed with a narrative form that gave them the creative possibility to reproduce the experience of the different temporal tenses, as sometimes overlaying or complementing one another, as discording and contrasting on other occasions. For its very nature, this hybrid form also has a tendency to facilitate the development collaborative working methods, which is a beneficial characteristic for all anthropological methods. Ward considers this a vital point to make when we consider that the topics of animated documentaries are precisely the supposedly incommunicable thoughts and concepts, belonging to people's experiences and perceptions. This is the reason why these films could not exist without the direct involvement of the people they 'are about' (Ward 2006: 94). One could say that making an animated documentary is a perfect fit for the anthropological agenda, as 'these films are not just attractions, they are forms of knowledge' (Skoller 2011: 209). Even more so, during the animation stage, we went through a learning process together, where we saw memories and imaginings taking forms totally unexpected to us, and where knowledge was negotiated and collaboratively created.

Notes

1 A frame from an animation scene (Figure 12.1) Mahmud created regarding his future, in response to my question: 'What would you do after you get your permit of stay?' The image portrays a young man embracing his old mother. One can tell it is a very emotional and dramatic moment, from the expression of the woman's face. Mahmud himself found and downloaded this image from the internet.

2 Forum Theatre is a technique pioneered by Augusto Boal, the author and creator of Theatre of the Oppressed.

3 In Henley 2010, xiv

4 Original title of the song, using social networking transliteration – *Hate3amal eih?* (What will you do?), interpreted by the very popular Egyptian singer, Sherine. This song was chosen for its lyrics by Ali, during our initial session of theatre workshops, as he saw it as representing what he feels happens to him when he is facing a critical moment in his life.

References

Carr, D., 1986. *Time, Narrative and History*. Bloomington, IN: Indiana University Press.

Crapanzano, V., 2003. *Imaginative Horizons: An Essay in Literary-Philosophical Anthropology*. Chicago: University of Chicago Press.

Henley, P., 2010. *The Adventure of the Real: Jean Rouch and the Craft of Ethnographic Cinema*. Chicago: University of Chicago Press.

Honess Roe, A., 2011. 'Absence, Excess and Epistemological Expansion: Towards a Framework for the Study of Animated Documentary'. *Animation: An Interdisciplinary Journal* 6 (3): 215–30.

Irving, A., 2011. Strange 'Distance: Towards an Anthropology of Interior Dialogue'. *Medical Anthropology Quarterly* 25 (1): 22–44.

Jackson, M., 2002. *The Politics of Storytelling – Violence, Transgression and Intersubjectivity*. Museum Tusculanum Press, University of Copenhagen.

Jackson, M., 2008. 'The Shock of the New: On Migrant Imaginaries and Critical Transitions'. *Ethnos: Journal of Anthropology* 73 (1): 57–72.

Loizos, P., 1993. *Innovation in Ethnographic film: From Innocence to Self-Consciousness.* Manchester: Manchester University Press.

Piotrowska, A., 2011. 'Animating the Real: A Case Study in Documentary Animation'. *Animation: An Interdisciplinary Journal* 6 (3): 335–51.

Ricoeur, P., 1984. *Time and Narrative.* Chicago: University of Chicago Press.

Sjöberg, J., 2008. 'Ethnofiction: Drama as a creative research practice in ethnographic film'. *Journal of Media Practice* 9 (3): 229–42.

Sjöberg, J., 2009. 'Ethnofiction and Beyond: The Legacy of Projective Improvisation in Ethnographic Filmmaking'. Paper presented at the international conference *A Knowledge Beyond Text* at Centre Pompidou in Paris, November 2009.

Skoller, J., 2011. 'Introduction to the Special Issue, Making It (Un)real: Contemporary Theories and Practices in Documentary Animation'. *Animation: An Interdisciplinary Journal* 6 (3): 207–14.

Stoller, P. 1992. *The Cinematic Griot: The Ethnography of Jean Rouch.* Chicago: Chicago University Press.

Turner, V., 1974. *Dramas, Fields and Metaphors: symbolic action in human society.* Ithaca, NY: Cornell University Press.

Ward, P., 2006. *Documentary – the Margins of Reality.* New York: Columbia University Press.

Wells, P., 1998. *Understanding Animation.* London and New York: Routledge.

13

Agency and dramatic storytelling: Roving through pasts, presents and futures

Magdalena Kazubowski-Houston

The scene

Christmas tree lights flickering in the corner. A cat sleeping on a still-warm stove. Randia, an elderly Polish Roma[1] woman, and I are sitting in her living room, sipping hot tea. It's Christmas Day. Randia is alone and claims that no one will visit her today. Her children haven't called. I am holding a dramatic storytelling session with her to learn about her life in Poland after her children moved abroad. We are narrating a script based on her life experiences; more than a recitation of lines, this involves full-fledged acting in which Randia and I assume the roles of different characters. Today Randia, playing Córka, enthusiastically tells her friend Ela (played by me) about her plans to move to England and live with her children there. She is full of anticipation; the future belongs to her. But after the session wraps up, she says, 'Only my cats and me. ... There is no future.' What does it mean to own the future while in character but then see no future outside of it? This chapter explores dramatic storytelling as a framework for researching, imagining and intervening into futures.

In recent years, anthropologists have been reflecting on how anthropology might engage with futures. Studies consider, among others, how different futures are imagined, assembled and contested in the global present (e.g. Roy and Ong 2011); futures as 'the capacity to aspire' to a more just world (Appadurai 2013); futures as imagined risks, dangers and catastrophes (e.g. Giddens 2000); futures as nostalgia, hope, despair and panic (e.g. Miyazaki

2004); and futures as consequences of, and effects on, the present (e.g. Nowotny 1994). This project is particularly important in our uncertain present, with its looming environmental disasters, violence and poverty, refugee crises and privatization and deregulation. While anthropologists are increasingly concerned about the discipline's moral responsibility to intervene in futures, scant attention has been paid to how to do so through ethnographic practices and techniques.

This chapter is a step in this direction, asking: how might a transdisciplinary ethnographic practice, such as dramatic storytelling, provide embodied and affective 'routes to knowing' (Hogan and Pink 2010: 158) how futures are lived, imagined, produced and disrupted in people's everyday lives? How might such storytelling foster agentic practices of reimagining and transforming futures? And with such methods, how might we re-envision a collaborative, deeply reflexive and engaged interventionist anthropology of futures? This chapter draws on the emergent interest in the imaginative, experiential, sensory and embodied realms of everyday experience (e.g. Hogan and Pink 2010; Irving 2011; Rapport 2008); studies of affect (e.g. Coole 2005; Massumi 2002; Stewart 2007); and recent ethnographic experiments situated at the intersections of imagination, performance-centered research, and storytelling (Conquergood 1988, 1991; Crapanzano 2004; Kazubowski-Houston 2010; Madison 2010; Robertson and Culhane 2005). I suggest that agency can materialize in the context of dramatic storytelling by generating 'affective interiorities', an intersubjective process that can act upon futures. By 'affective interiorities', I mean people's more articulated and conscious inner dialogues, feelings, sensations, moods and urges, as well as their more pre-reflective, subliminal bodily feelings, sensations, and moods (Irving 2011; Massumi 2002; Stewart 2007). I explore how these might materialize in interactions between the ethnographer and interlocutor, and how, in a dramatic storytelling context, ethnographers may engage with such futures imaginatively and collaboratively with our interlocutors.

My interest in futures arises as part of my larger research project on post-EU accession migration, and its impact on the lives of Poland's non-migrant elderly Roma women. In Poland and other Eastern European states, the lives of elders have been tremendously affected by the transnational migration of young and middle-aged adults. Many elderly people have been fending for themselves since Poland's accession to the EU in 2004, which opened access to Western labour markets, and the 2007 Schengen Treaty, which eliminated tourist visa requirements for Polish citizens (White 2011). Romani elders are one of the social groups most affected by these migrations (Kazubowski-Houston 2012), and ongoing socioeconomic transformations have seen Romani minorities' quality of life deteriorate. Negative stereotypes, combined with economic crises and resurgent Polish nationalism, have increased acts of prejudice, marginalization and violence against the Roma (Jasinska-Kania

2009). Consequently, nearly 60 per cent – in some regions up to 90 per cent – of Poland's Roma migrated to Western Europe. Many of the Roma I have worked with report that some Romani communities in Poland are now populated primarily by the elderly, often widows, who are unable to travel abroad due to their advanced age and/or ill health (Kazubowski-Houston 2012; Zwiazek Romow Polskich 2012). However, my interest in futures also arises from my personal life, as my mother in Poland was diagnosed with a serious illness. She never wanted to relocate to Canada and now was too ill to be approved for Canadian landed-immigrant status. I faced an uncertain future of juggling my university job and family responsibilities in Canada with the care of my mother in Poland.

Since 2001, I have been conducting fieldwork in Elbląg – a mid-sized city of 130,000 people in northern Poland – located in the Warmińsko-Mazurskie *voivodeship* (region), which has one of the country's oldest populations, an unemployment rate of approximately 20 per cent (between 2010 and 2015) (Powiatowy Urząd Pracy w Elblągu), and high migration rates among the Roma (Kazubowski-Houston 2012). My two main research participants have been Randia, in her late sixties, and Maria, in her mid-sixties. Both women are widows, and most of their children and relatives have emigrated to Western Europe. Their pensions are meagre, and they live in decrepit government-subsidized apartment blocks. They both suffer from heart disease, diabetes, high blood pressure and depression. Randia recently lost most of her vision to diabetes.

We adopted dramatic storytelling as an approach to ethnographic research, because it turned out that, in a small Roma community, issues of confidentiality were paramount. The women were reluctant to discuss many aspects of their lives in interviews, and were concerned that pseudonyms alone would not guarantee their anonymity. Our storytelling sessions took place over a period of five years, wherein each woman met with me individually to narrate impro-vised dramatic scripts based on her life experiences; these were recorded with a digital voice recorder. Frequently, the women stepped into character by assuming different voices and physicalities, and treating me as an audience member or as another character in the play (Kazubowski-Houston 2012). They acted in a style that I refer to as psychological realism[2] and, later in the process, even adopted elements of magic realism[3] (Ahmadzadeh 2011: 289).

Imaginative ethnography

Our approach to dramatic storytelling was a form of imaginative ethnography, bridging storytelling and performance-centered research (performance as an ethnographic research process and means of representation). Attuned to our interlocutors' 'imaginative lifeworlds' (Irving 2011: 22) – the diverse, messy, incidental, improvisational, and generative processes that constitute people's inner experiences, social practices, and relations with us as ethnographers – imaginative ethnography embraces collaborative, embodied and critical research methods that draw from ethnography, anthropology and the creative arts (see Kazubowski-Houston forthcoming).

In the last few decades, performance has garnered much interest as a form of ethnography. This trend has arisen out of the desire to transform traditionally hierarchical interactions between ethnographer and informant (Yeich 1996), and to find ways to disseminate knowledge more effectively and accessibly than through conventional scholarly publications (Denzin 2003; Mienczakowski 2001; Saldaña 2003). Many scholars see the collective nature of performance as facilitating more collaborative research relation-ships, wherein the ethnographer and interlocutors can co-create both the research process and its performance (Conquergood 1988; Culhane 2011; Fabian 1990; Kazubowski-Houston 2010, 2011, forthcoming; Madison 2010). The interplay of dramatic text, image, and sound has also been seen as a means of documenting and representing research findings, and potentially facilitating a more engaging and accessible knowledge exchange (Allen and Garner 1995; Mienczakowski 1995). Importantly, storytelling is a form of social performance because meanings do not reside within the stories told, but rather, are co-created between storyteller and listener – or interviewee and interviewer – through verbal and nonverbal interactions, and are mediated by technique, audiences, and context (Benjamin 1973: 91; Cruikshank 1998).

Dramatic storytelling vs. interviews

Randia and Maria imagined futures differently in our interviews and our dramatic storytelling sessions. I suggest this is because the two research approaches facilitated different processes of knowledge construction. In the interviews, the women tended to tell stories in rather schematic and matter-of-fact ways, as if they were delivering a lecture. They often talked about the negative aspects of their lives: poverty, discrimination, violence, illness, loneliness and isolation. Another theme was the migration of their relatives, about which they always spoke favourably, expressing gratitude that family members were able to eke out a better existence abroad. Both Maria and Randia emphasized that they would never leave Poland: they did not want to burden their children; their health was too poor to relocate; and, as Randia put it, 'old trees shouldn't be replanted'.

In the interviews, they sometimes spoke about their mutual support as an important means of getting by, though they were more hesitant in general to talk about coping strategies. Generally, however, the women saw their lives as largely hopeless. They spoke about the future as being worse than the present, and much worse than the past. The futures were largely articulated within a logic of linear time: the past is what has already happened, the present, what is happening now, and the future, what is yet to come. While this logic rests on the hope that it is possible to progress from a worse past to a better present and an even better future, in their interviews, the women reversed this logic. This was evident when Maria remarked, 'There were better times before. We were all together, all Roma; there was more respect for the Roma tradition. Roma were real Roma. ... Things are hard for me now, but what can I expect? I'm old and nothing will change now.' The women construed themselves and others as largely 'flat' characters with 'flat futures' that 'never surprise us, never waver' (Mattingly 2008: 146).

But in our dramatic storytelling sessions, the women told stories in unpredictable ways, with an abundance of personal detail and emotional depth. For example, characters expressed anger at their children for failing to provide them with care in their old age, disrespecting them and even exploiting them monetarily. Indeed, in the play Randia created, the scenes portraying an idyllic family life – where loving children and grandchildren live together with parents and grandparents – simultaneously represent the elders as abandoned, depressed and angry. In one of Córka's soliloquies, she abruptly switches from anger at her migrant daughter, Hania, to asking her to make tea and set out biscuits for guests, as if Hania were there with her in the flesh:

Córka (to herself): She [Hania] won't call me anymore! I won't answer the phone! I won't! I had all these children – raised them on my own, fed them, and gave them whatever they wanted. They weren't deprived. And what was this all for? What for? (pause) I don't want to hear from her! ...

(Long pause)

Randia (to me): Now Córka addresses Hania.

Magda: But Hania is not around.

Randia: No, but Córka can hear her – like always, like normal.

Córka is addressing her imaginary daughter Hania.

Córka: Hania, make tea, won't you? And set out biscuits – those chocolate ones, my favourite. Yes, they're in the cupboard. Maybe someone will come today, someone must – it's Sunday. Do you think someone might come?

Similarly, while the women rarely discussed their coping strategies in the interviews, the characters of their plays sought to improve their well-being by, for example, taking on employment, pawning personal items or visiting their children abroad. Furthermore, the stories told in the interviews empha-sized the women's camaraderie, but the relationships between the elderly characters of their plays were more intricate. On many occasions, the elderly characters competed with one another over attention and resources, expressed jealously, bad-mouthed one another in front of neighbours or refused to help one another in times of need. In the following scene performed by Maria, Myca and her sister Roxana are bad-mouthing their elderly cousin Reza:

Roxana is visiting Myca. They are sitting in the living room, drinking tea.

Myca: Reza is very irresponsible; she constantly gets herself into debt. She wants a new sofa – what does she need it for? She complains her children don't help her out – what would she want from them? They give her enough. They have their own families to feed, not just her. But she's selfish. I'm telling you Roxana, I don't feel like visiting Reza. She always complains, but she has more things than we both combined.

Roxana: I know. She has more than we both ever could. Do you think she's truly blind? I've seen her do things she couldn't do if she were truly blind, no way!

A break with the real: Roving through space and time

As the dramatic storytelling sessions progressed, and the Roma women began employing elements of magic realism, their stories grew more unpredictable and ambiguous. Eventually, they started flouting the rules of the real by subverting common assumptions about time and space. The characters were rarely unified persons with fixed biographies, age or class for longer than a scene or two. Instead, they embodied different personhoods, living many lives simultaneously. In some scenes, Córka was the elderly protagonist of Randia's play, living in present Poland; in other scenes, she was the protagonist's cousin, sister-in-law, daughter or friend, from the past or the future. The characters simultaneously lived alone (depressed and abandoned) and with their children (happily looked after). As such, the characters were akin to Amazonian notions of personhood as 'uncertain and transitory ... caught in a continuous process of "Other-becoming"' (Rival 2012: 130). In Córka's soliloquy, she disparages her daughter Hania for leaving her behind, and then asks her to put out biscuits. Here, Hania's presence haunts, as Córka seems to summon her like a ghost from another place or time. Hania and Córka occupy realities where places and temporalities are 'tangled' (Schneider 2011: 3). In this scene, conse-quently, they (re)imagine time and space as something like circular essences (Crapanzano 2004: 34), rather than bound to linear progression and place. Their spatio-temporal framework is supported by how the characters' imagine presence (and absence) beyond the visual. This is evident when Randia explains that Córka is able to summon Hania to put out biscuits, not because Córka can see Hania, but because she can hear her; Córka (re)conceptualizes presence in auditory terms. Thus, one might argue that, at least in that particular scene, presence and absence, as are conventionally understood, are no longer part of the framework that defines Córka's world. What may seem absent is never absent, because all things are always here (and there). On one occasion, Randia remarked, 'I wish my mom were here – I wish I could speak with her – to get it all off my chest ... Sometimes, I wonder if she can hear me, because I know she's here – she watches, listens – I'd like to talk to her. I know one day I will. But not in this world. When I go over there'. In dramatic storytelling sessions, Córka was able to speak to her late mother, her daughter who lives abroad, and others who were no longer alive or nearby because, as Córka, she did not need to wait to go 'over there' to be able to hear them or to be heard. In these story-telling sessions, the past and the future sit at 'the very fingertips of the present' (Schneider 2011: 2), just as the 'over there' sits at the fingertips of the 'here.'

Subjectivity and storytelling

Why were there such differences in knowledge construction between the interviews and the dramatic storytelling? These disparities could be linked to the different ways in which the respective modes of research articulate subjectivity. In the interviews, the women's stories were more predictable, and evoked 'flat' chronological futures, because the women tended to tell them in terms of a fixed and unitary selfhood. I believe the women managed their portrayal of selfhood to address the politics of representation that defined our project, which were linked to the benefits and ends the women were trying to negotiate for themselves in and through my research.

They also knew that the excerpts from the interviews would be quoted verbatim in my published work, and thus might reach both their local community and a larger international audience. This may explain why they presented their stories in ways that could generate national and international interest in their plight. For example, following her first interview, Maria asked me, 'Do you think I spoke well? You know, I want people to know how we live here, that it's hard for Roma women – we have terrible lives. Do you think anybody will care?' This may also have been the reason why they presented their migrant relatives, as well as the relations between each other, in a positive light. One day Randia urged me, 'Tell people in Canada that the Roma stick together for each other. This is how it's always been. Let them know how Roma truly are!' The women also spoke about their lives with a certain emotional detachment, perhaps explained by Randia's worried comment: 'You don't think I said too much? Hmm? … I don't want to cry too much, or people will think that the Roma just whine, complain and want things for free.'

On the other hand, in the dramatic storytelling sessions, the Roma women told more unpredictable stories because they were able to construct – through the characters they created – their subjectivities as 'becoming' (Deleuze 1994). This is likely attributable to the interplay of a variety of factors. First, the characters, relations and locales in the dramatic scripts were fictional, which promised some level of anonymity. And, as such, it also mitigated some of the politics of representation that constrained the interviews. As Randia aptly put it in a storytelling session, fiction allowed her to 'say what [she] really want[ed] to say'. Maria also once remarked, 'I guess it doesn't matter if [the character] says she was stealing. It's a play after all, not a documentary – like the interviews. No one will know who Ana [the character] is.'

The storytelling sessions can also be seen as liminal – 'betwixt and between' (Turner 1982: 13) – spaces, where the women could express themselves as someone else and thus feel 'safe' to express what they would otherwise suppress. In our project, this anonymity was bolstered by the fact that the women participated individually in the storytelling sessions rather than together, and because the plays were not intended for public performances. As such, this liminal storytelling space can be seen as what Amira Mittermaier (2011: 30) defines as a barzakh – a space 'that shifts the attention from observable, material realities to the emergent, the possible, the prophetic, the visionary'.

On the other hand, the women may have constructed their subjectivities as 'becoming' because the storytelling sessions might have mobilized their interiority by tapping into its affective qualities differently than the interviews did. The interviews may have constructed ethnographic knowledge at the level of consciously experienced and acknowledged thoughts, feelings, emotions and desires, while the storytelling sessions might have drawn more on unarticulated, subliminal bodily sensations, and moods (Irving 2011; Massumi 2002). Improvising, the Roma women had to allow their stories, movements, expressions and emotions to arise with little time for rationalization. For Brazilian theatre director and theoretician Augusto Boal, working intuitively with the body allows actors to connect to their unconscious feelings and desires (Jackson 1992: xxiii). Working with fiction – which also opens a window onto the unconscious – might have contributed to this process. And while not every aspect of the women's inner lives was brought to the surface and rendered comprehensible, the process could have generated a spark, what theatre artist Jerzy Grotowski (1968) calls a physical 'impulse' – a push from the inside that fuels an actor's action (see also Richards 1995: 94–5) – that 'opened the way to discovery, something new, potential becomings, possible futures (Kumar 2013: 729). As such, it might have allowed the women to 'project [their] "fables" in a direction that does not have to reckon with the "evident universe"' (Crapanzano 2004: 19; Starobinski, cited in Crapanzano 2004: 19).

'I'll live like a lady one day!'

How is one to understand these imaginative breaks with the real? Were they merely an escape into fantasy? I suggest that rather than simple escapism, telling stories facilitated imaginative, embodied and affective 'agentic capacities' (Coole 2005: 124) in and through which the Roma women were able to re-envision their futures, turning them from dead ends to something alterable.

By creating characters whose lives both mimicked and departed from their own lives – acts of mimesis and alterity (Taussig 1993) – the women were able to watch inner dialogues they would have normally had only with themselves (or imaginary others) now play out before their own (and my) eyes, and be taken in new directions. They might have watched their less acknowledged feelings, sensations, moods and dreams rise to the surface and be articulated in surprising ways. Randia, while enacting Córka's frustration with Hania, might have been really enacting, and witnessing herself enact her own feelings of disappointment towards her daughter, Marta. This process may have either made her aware that she does in fact harbour those feelings or – if she was already aware of them – might have given her courage to confront Marta, just like Córka confronted Hania. Similarly, bad-mouthing Roxana as her sister Myca may have enabled Maria to realize, and want to act upon, her own acrimonious relationships with other Roma women. Indeed, the dramatic storytelling sessions did seem to impel the women to act in certain ways and renegotiate their relationships with others.

After storytelling sessions, Randia was able to alter – even if only temporarily – her relationships with her children. Following one session, she confided in me that she would no longer let her children take advantage of her. And then one day, when I was visiting her at home, she refused to answer a call from her daughter, brusquely remarking, 'It's Marta. I won't answer – she needs to know how it feels.' This took place following the storytelling session in which Córka asserts that she will not answer Hania's phone calls. And, while she never discussed this scene in connection to her relationship with her daughter, on several occasions when enacting this scene, Randia as Córka slipped and referred to Hania as Marta. Similarly, while Maria was normally reluctant to visit her daughter in England for monetary reasons, after recording a scene in which her character Reza planned to visit her children abroad for Christmas, Maria decided to visit her children for the holidays.

The storytelling sessions also impacted the women's relationships with others in the community. After scenes portrayed a contentious relationship between her elderly characters, Maria grew concerned about her own relationships with other Roma women, especially Randia. Another time, after narrating a scene in which her protagonist, Myca, was recounting her exploitative relationship with her employer, Maria noted, 'See, this is how it is for Myca – I'm also not going to work for [my employer] any longer. All these years and they haven't given me a single raise. I asked them once and they said they'd think about it, but that was it. They never mentioned it again'. In fact, Maria did take a few months' break from work. I recognize that Randia's and Maria's actions cannot be solely attributed to the dramatic storytelling sessions, as there were also other developments in their lives that were likely to have influenced how they acted. The fact that Maria's daughter bought her a ticket to travel to England certainly contributed to Maria's decision to take some unpaid leave from work. Nevertheless, I believe that the dramatic storytelling sessions served as a reference point against which the women were able to evaluate their lives and, consequently, act; on a few occasions, they even stated this themselves. Maria once observed that, as a result of one storytelling session, she decided not to relocate. Her original plan was to move to her daughter's vacant apartment and sublet her own. She explained that she decided against it because 'the play' had helped her 'think things through' and realize the risks inherent in 'letting someone else move into your home'.

The 'roving' spatio-temporal framework permitted in dramatic storytelling facilitated an important agentic capacity in our sessions. To even begin reimagining their futures as alterable, perhaps the women first needed to temporarily abandon the notion of the future as a linear what-is-yet-to-be. Once the future became a part of a roving temporal framework, where it could be imagined as both what-has-been and what-is-now, the women might have found it easier to conceive of a future that is better, more hopeful and, thus, worth trying for. The storytelling session transcript below demonstrates the ways in which Randia was able to intervene in the future by reworking the past. In this scene, Córka (played by Randia) was just telling Ela (played by me) about how she is afraid to live alone, without her children. Then she paused and said:

Córka (*to Ela*): What should I do, Ela? What should I do?

Ela: Uhmmm, I'm not sure. Maybe go and visit them [her children in England]? ... I'm sure they wouldn't mind!

Córka: No, they wouldn't mind! Sure, they wouldn't mind. You know what, Ela – I'll go! I'll go soon, before it gets cold. I'll go and live with them. I'll cook for the children! And maybe even find some fortune telling work ... help them out! Then I could put away some money for myself too! But I'll come back here one day. I'll buy myself a flat – my very own! With hot water and central heating! No more coal! Imagine that! I could even take a bath! I'm telling you, Ela, I'll live like a lady – like a lady one day!

Randia (*to me*): Now you, Ela, say: Work there!? What got into your head! [...] Where will you find fortune telling in England?! A lady!? A lady! When will you be that lady, huh?

I repeat the text suggested by Randia.

Córka: Just you watch, Ela! I'm telling you. I'll live like a lady one day. Yes! – When? When? Uhmmm, I'll tell you when – perhaps yesterday! Yes, let's see ...

Randia begins describing the subsequent scene.

Randia: So now we are in the living room. Hania, her husband and children are packing. They are leaving for England. It's 2008. The children are still young. They are asking Córka to go with them. She doesn't want to, but finally agrees. They leave early in the morning. She doesn't sell the house, because she knows she'll return. They go by bus and arrive in England in a couple of days. (*To me*) And what happens then?

Magda: Then they rent a small place. Córka is happy there. Her children look after her. Her health improves, she goes for walks, to church – has something to live for.

Randia: Yes! She has it good there! And she is fortune telling ... looking after her family...

Through the character of Córka, Randia constructed a subjectivity that could freely straddle the past, the present and the future, the here and the there. Following this storytelling session, Randia said to me, 'What if, what if, what could've been. But nothing to be done now. Nothing can change. … Only my cats and me. … There is no future.' But in Córka's world, nothing was finished, and time could always be turned back like a page in a book; the boundaries between the past, the present and the future were porous, things could still take place in the past, even if for some reason they no longer could in the present or the future.

Although the storytelling sessions encouraged the women to act in certain ways and renegotiate their relationships with others, some of these effects were short-lived. For example, when I returned to Poland a year later, Maria was still working, without a raise, for her exploitative employer. The agentic capacities of our storytelling sessions were not permanent, but rather, particular and situated – emerging in, and adjusting to, their immediate contexts (Coole 2005: 126). These capacities broke into smithereens in the outside world in unpredictable and unfinished ways. As such, they need to be understood as what Kathleen Stewart (2007: 2) defines as 'heterogeneous and incoherent singularities' that 'happen in impulses, sensations, expectations, daydreams, encounters, and habits of relating', working underneath larger systems and structures.

Intersubjectivity

As the women cast me as different characters alongside them, our dramatic storytelling sessions were not only about their break with the real, but also about my own. In that sense, the Roma women and I became spectators and actors, or – to borrow Boal's term (1979) – 'spect-actors' in our own and each other's lives. This term was coined to describe audience engagement in Boal's Forum Theatre – created in response to a particular group's oppression – where the spectators are invited to take the actors' roles and replace the play's protagonists, and improvise alternatives to the narrative underway. The Roma women and I were simultaneously actors and spect-actors, as we both performed and witnessed each other's performances. The dramatic storytelling sessions became the staging of all of our interior lives. For example, when I suggested to Randia that Córka visit her family in England, and that her life would be good there and that she could take walks to church, I (as Ela) was re-envisioning what my mother's life could have been like had she emigrated to Canada years ago. In retrospect, I realized that I was clearly referring to my mother, a practicing Catholic, as neither Córka nor Randia were churchgoers. Like the Roma women, I was breaking with the real to re-envision my mother's future in the space-time of the imaginary (Crapanzano 2004).

One can argue that it is in and through these practices of co-performing and co-witnessing that the agentic capacities of our storytelling sessions materialized. Even though inextricably linked to our individual affective interiorities, such agentic capacities need to be understood not as individualistic, but rather, as intersubjective processes 'that instantiate an inner world' (Coole 2005: 128). As Diana Coole notes, interiority needs to be understood as 'irreducibly interwoven with exteriority; individuality with sociability; subjectivity with intersubjectivity' (ibid.: 134); agents thus arise in and through lived experience as it unfolds onto 'a field of forces that incites, shapes, and constrains their development' (ibid.: 135). In our dramatic storytelling sessions, experience was converted into theatrical expression, and such 'a field of forces', with agency mobilized, was constituted through affective knowledge summoned between the performer and spectator (Kazubowski-Houston 2011: 179).

Yet why did the Roma women insist that I co-perform their stories? While I think it was a practical decision on their part – it would have been difficult to be always switching between different characters – it might have also been one of those intricate and unpredictable ways in which the agentic capacities of our storytelling sessions took on a life of their own, apart from the women's intentions. For it seems that these co-performances also constituted for the women yet another layer of protection in a world where, for the Roma, no public expression – not even a fictive one – is completely free of risk. When not only theirs, but also my interior thoughts, feelings, desires, hopes, dreams and fears were rolled out for scrutiny, we were finally in it together. As Randia once mused, 'This play of mine isn't too out there, is it? Or people will think I'm not there! Or even worse – but, ha! I guess you're in it as much as we are!'

So what does it mean to own the future 'in character', but then see no future outside of it? What does it mean to tell a story full of future but believe in no future for oneself? Following one session, Randia confessed, 'When I think of all the stories I've told you – what a life I had! A hard life, but I also think now, that maybe – maybe, despite everything, a life worth living?' Perhaps storytelling the future means to search for it, courageously and stubbornly, in a world that systematically and consistently takes that future away. And perhaps it means to take the anthropologist along on the search so she realizes what it might involve to both take and give that future back. And maybe, on the search through her own interior life, the anthropologist might imagine what a collaborative, deeply reflexive and engaged interventionist anthropology of futures might look like.

Notes

1 In this paper, I use the term Roma both as adjective and noun in accordance with the Oxford English Dictionary usage guidelines. While Romani or Romany can also be used as adjectives, my Roma participants favoured the adjectival form of Roma due to the ambiguity of the terms Romani and Romany, which can refer to both a Roma girl or woman, and to the Indo-Aryan language of the Roma people.

2 In psychological realism – an approach to acting defined by Russian theatre director/actor Konstantin Stanislavski (1863–1938) – actors invoke their own 'emotion memory' in order to faithfully represent the characters' emotions and intentions.

3 The term magic realism – coined by German art critic Franz Roh in 1925 – is used in reference to certain postcolonial literature, drama and performance that incorporate magical elements into otherwise realistic representations of life to subvert Western hegemony and dominant forms of representation (Ahmadzadeh 2011).

References

Ahmadzadeh, H., 2011. 'Magic Realism in the Novels of a Kurdish Writer, Bakhtiyar Ali'. *Middle Eastern Literatures* 14 (3): 287–99.

Allen, C. J. and N. Garner, 1995. 'Condor Qatay: Anthropology in performance'. *American Anthropologist* 97 (1): 69–82.

Appadurai, A., 2013. *The Future as Cultural Fact: Essays on the Global Condition.* London: Verso Books.

Benjamin, W., 1973. *Illuminations,* H. Zohn (trans.). Glasgow: Fontana/Collins.

Conquergood, D., 1988. 'Health Theatre in a Hmong Refugee Camp: Performance, Communication, and Culture'. *The Drama Review: A Journal of Performance Studies* 32 (3): 174–208.

Conquergood, D., 1991. 'Rethinking ethnography: Towards a critical cultural politics'. *Communication Monographs* 58 (2): 179–94.

Coole, D., 2005. 'Rethinking Agency: A Phenomenological Approach to Embodiment and Agentic Capacities'. *Political Studies* 53 (1): 124–42.

Crapanzano, V., 2004. *Imaginative Horizons: An Essay in Literary-philosophical Anthropology.* Chicago: University of Chicago Press.

Cruikshank, J., 1998. *The Social Life of Stories: Narrative and Knowledge in the Yukon Territory.* Vancouver: UBC Press.

Culhane, D., 2011. 'Stories and Plays: Ethnography, Performance and Ethical Engagements'. *Anthropologica* 53 (2): 257–74.

Deleuze, G., 1994. *Difference and Repetition.* London: Athlone.

Denzin, N. K., 2003. *Performance Ethnography: Critical Pedagogy and the Politics of Culture.* Thousand Oaks, CA: Sage.

Fabian, J., 1990. *Power and Performance: Ethnographic Explorations through Proverbial Wisdom and Theater in Shaba, Zaire.* Madison: University of Wisconsin Press.

Giddens, A., 2000. *Runaway World: How Globalization is Reshaping our Lives.* New York: Routledge.

Grotowski, J., 1968. *Towards a Poor Theatre.* New York: Simon and Schuster.

Hogan, S. and S. Pink, 2010. 'Routes to Interiorities: Art Therapy and Knowing in Anthropology'. *Visual Studies* 23 (2): 158–74.

Irving, A., 2011. 'Strange Distance: Towards an Anthropology of Interior Dialogue'. *Medical Anthropology Quarterly* 25 (1): 22–44.

Jackson, A., 1992. 'Translator's Introduction to the First Edition'. In *Games for Actors and Non-Actors*, xxvii. New York: Routledge.

Jasinska-Kania, A., 2009. 'Exclusion from the Nation: Social Distances from National Minorities and Immigrants'. *International Journal of Sociology* 39 (3): 15–37.

Kazubowski-Houston, M., 2010. *Staging Strife: Lessons from Performing Ethnography with Polish Roma Women.* Montréal: McGill-Queen's University Press.

Kazubowski-Houston, M., 2011. '"Don't Tell Me How to Dance!": Negotiating Collaboration, Empowerment and Politicization in the Ethnographic Theatre Project "Hope"'. *Anthropologica* 53 (2): 229–43.

Kazubowski-Houston, M., 2012. '"A Stroll in Heavy Boots": Studying Polish Roma Women's Experiences of Aging'. *Canadian Theatre Review* 151: 16–23.

Kazubowski-Houston, M., forthcoming. 'An elephant in the room: Towards an Awkward Anthropology'. *Anthropologica.*

Kumar, A., 2013. 'The Play is Now Reality: Affective Turns, Narrative Struggles, and Theorizing Emotion as Practical Experience'. *Culture, Medicine and Psychiatry* 37 (4): 711–36.

Madison, D. S., 2010. *Acts of Activism: Human Rights as Radical Performance.* New York: Cambridge University Press.

Massumi, B., 2002. *Parables for the Virtual: Movement, Affect, Sensation.* Durham: Duke University Press.

Mattingly, C., 2008. 'Reading Minds and Telling Tales in a Cultural Borderland'. *Ethos* 36 (1): 136–54.

Mienczakowski, J., 1995. 'The Theater of Ethnography: The Reconstruction of Ethnography into Theater With Emancipatory Potential'. *Qualitative Inquiry* 1 (3): 360–75.

Mienczakowski, J., 2001. 'Ethnodrama: Performed Research – Limitations and Potential'. In P. Atkinson, A. Coffey, S. Delamont, J. Lofland and L. Lofland (eds), *Handbook of Ethnography*, 468–76. London: Sage.

Mittermaier, A., 2011. *Dreams that Matter: Egyptian Landscapes of the Imagination.* Berkeley: University of California Press.

Miyazaki, H., 2004. *The Method of Hope: Anthropology, Philosophy, and Fijian Knowledge.* Stanford: Stanford University Press.

Myerhoff, B. G.,1980. *Number Our Days.* New York: Touchstone.

Nowotny, H., 1994. *Time: Modern and Postmodern Experience.* Cambridge: Blackwell Publishers.

Powiatowy Urząd Pracy w Elblągu: STOPA BEZROBOCIA 2010–2015. Available online: http://www.elblag.up.gov.pl/kategorie/248 (accessed October 2015).

Rapport, N., 2008. 'Gratuitousness: Notes Towards an Anthropology of Interiority'. *Australian Journal of Anthropology* 19 (3): 331–49.

Richards, T., 1995. *At Work with Grotowski on Physical Actions*. New York: Routledge.

Rival, L., 2012. 'The materiality of life: Revisiting the anthropology of nature in Amazonia'. *Indiana* 29: 127–43.

Robertson, L. and D. Culhane, 2005. *In Plain Sight: Reflections on Life in Downtown Eastside*. Vancouver: Talonbooks.

Roy, A. and A. Ong, 2011. *Worlding Cities: Asian Experiments and the Art of Being Global*. Malden: Wiley-Blackwell.

Saldaña, J., 2003. 'Dramatizing Data: A Primer'. *Qualitative Inquiry* 9 (2): 218–36.

Schneider, R., 2011. *Performing Remains: Art and War in Times of Theatrical Reenactment*. New York: Routledge.

Stewart, K., 2007. *Ordinary Affects*. Durham: Duke University Press.

Taussig, M. T., 1993. *Mimesis and Alterity: A Particular History of the Senses*. New York: Routledge.

Turner, V. W., 1982. *From Ritual to Theatre: The Human Seriousness of Play*. New York: Performing Arts Journal Publications.

White, A., 2011. *Polish Families and Migration since EU Accession*. Bristol: Policy Press.

WHO, *WHO | Poland* [Homepage of World Health Organization], [Online]. Available online: http://www.who.int/countries/pol/en/ (accessed August 2013).

Yeich, S., 1996. 'Grassroots Organizing with Homeless People: A Participatory Research Approach'. *Social Issues* 52 (1): 111–21.

Zwiazek Romow Polskich, 2012. 'Raport o sytuacji społeczności romskiej w Polsce-marzec 2012 r'. Available online: http://www.romowie.com/raport.pdf (accessed May 2013).

14

Remix as a literacy for future anthropology practice

Annette N. Markham

In 2014, I participated in generating the Future Anthropology Network manifesto, a document that boldly calls for transdisciplinary stances, interventionist attitudes, and other transgressive modes of being. These can be taken as tactics for figuring out how to grapple with the challenges of turning the anthropological gaze toward the future. In this article, I offer a framework whereby we can draw on the metaphor of remix as a way to enact these strategies.

Remix, a term long used to describe the process of rap or hip-hop music, now more broadly describes the everyday practice of cut/copy/paste in the digital and networked age. From fan fiction and internet memes to mashup videos, remix involves the creative recombination of cultural units of information for the purposes of comedy, parody, art or critique. As an even broader concept, remix can be seen as a primary way of everyday sense-making. Out of the endless swirl of stimuli around us every day, we somehow manage to create a relatively sensible understanding of our lived experience. This process certainly applies to researchers who spend their time making sense of the social worlds we live in.

Remix offers a dialogic and reflexive metaphor for thinking about future-oriented anthropology. The concept of 'remix methods' (Markham 2013) encompasses both the process of remixing and the product of remix. Adopted as a foundation or premise for ethnographic inquiry, remix highlights not only how inquiry actually happens but also how research functions in larger conversations. It offers an intriguing framework for resisting the typical labels associated with inquiry practices. Remixing in an Internet era is a playful and lively exchange of speculative, anticipatory, suggestive, critical, and interventionist arguments about cultural meaning.

The model of remix may seem far removed from the academic world, but it's a productive way to prompt a future-orientation. Remix doesn't just value experimentation and playful recombination of cultural units of information but also reminds us that our research products always exist within larger communities of remix. Whatever is created, is a temporary assemblage that will change almost immediately. In fact, the power of remix relies on the participation of others. The form of the remix will change over time as others remix it. Thus, anything we produce has the potential to grow in quality and cohesion over time through various iterations by others. Or, it might morph into something completely unrecognizable with very few elements to trace it back to the origin points (or like some memes that never flourish, it might wither and die from neglect). This view allows us to consider that quality emerges from how our work exists and functions in the larger sense, not simply from the manner in which it was conducted. Without abandoning rigorous criteria for quality, remix enables creative innovation for finding and honing practices and techniques that analyse what is not quite yet, what could be, or what ought to be.

I've used five terms over the past few years to describe a remix approach to studying complexity: Play. Borrow. Interrogate. Move. Generate.

When I use these terms, I deliberately imagine that these five activities comprise the entirety of the social research process, in any discipline across what we might call the social, human, and hard sciences. I don't make this claim blindly – I draw on remix theory, almost three decades of training and experience in interpretive ethnographic methods in organizational culture studies as well as a range of social science methods, and six years of giving talks and workshops on this topic. To allow myself to believe this whole-heartedly, I rely on the classic advice of rhetorical theorist Kenneth Burke, who places our role as thinkers directly in a larger, longstanding, and ongoing conversation:

> Imagine that you enter a parlor. You come late. When you arrive, others have long preceded you, and they are engaged in a heated discussion, a discussion too heated for them to pause and tell you exactly what it is about. In fact, the discussion had already begun long before any of them got there, so that no one present is qualified to retrace for you all the steps that had gone before. You listen for a while, until you decide that you have caught the tenor of the argument; then you put in your oar. Someone answers; you answer him; another comes to your defense; another aligns himself against you, to either the embarrassment or gratification of your opponent, depending upon the quality of your ally's assistance. However, the discussion is interminable. The hour grows late, you must depart. And you do depart, with the discussion still vigorously in progress. (Burke 1941: 111)

With this imaginary in place, I am allowed considerable freedom to rebuild an ethnographic practice to grapple with the demands of the specific context in which I find myself studying a phenomenon. In doing this, one doesn't abandon current tools or methods, but reconsiders how and why these are enacted. In this chapter, I discuss terms and concepts of a remix methodology to help readers consider the following: If these terms guide practice instead of traditional discipline-specific terminology, what is gained, highlighted or hidden through these terms? What is enabled and constrained?

To hint at some of the answers I would offer: This framework offers a way of thinking about methods as everyday practice, which can then be highly adaptable to complexities of twenty-first century technological mediations. A remix framework could be understood as a literacy focused on a set of critical strategies, skills and competencies for analysing, making sense of and communicating ethnographic knowledge about contemporary cultural phenomena. As a literacy, ethnographers in this emerging community of practice can explore ways of engaging in ethnography that foreground possibilities, critical speculation, anticipation, and uncertainty, all important considerations for future-oriented anthropology.

Remixing terminology of inquiry

By reconfiguring the terminology for 'what counts' as appropriate ethnographic method, researchers can explore what they actually do as they attend to notable features of the lived world, interpret these features or instances from some sort of stance, and then present accounts in particular forms for specific audiences. Deliberately dismantling what might be habitual in research practice allows one to rebuild and reframe – not necessarily reject or reinvent – practices. This is a matter of considering the focus and aims of our activities of sensemaking. If we take remix as an inspiration (and the five modes of playing, borrowing, interrogating, moving, and generating), we might notice that a remix approach

- enables a range of creative processes without privileging any single method,

- blends playful experimentation with critical interrogation,

- values the continual shifts in attitude and focus inherent in the activity of continually moving, borrowing, and generating,

- recognizes that quality is something found both in the making and the reception of the product,

- highlights the way that our activities are similar across disciplines, enabling us to work across contradictory or conflicting discipline-specific procedures,

- focuses attention on the unfinished or experimental mode of creating cultural knowledge with a keen awareness that one's individual products will and should be remixed by others, which will refine and improve the product, or transform it to be useful for other contexts,

- calls attention to the temporal qualities of knowledge, highlighting the way that ideas shift as they are used and mixed with other ideas, by communities both near and distant from the origin point.

These are attitudes that draw attention to certain values and relevant modes of action, most of which are commensurate with contemporary anthropological practice. If applied to considerations of what we might call 'futures', these ideas can strengthen the position of speculative or provocational forms and outcomes of inquiry, by framing these practices as typical and normal way of making sense of the world.

Such a reframing may seem unnecessary to those who already enact a contemporary postmodern anthropological stance. The point remains worthwhile if conducting transdisciplinary research, since discussions about methods would situate such a list of attitudes within an 'alternative' space. The symbolic pattern of qualifying one's approach as 'post-' or 'anti-' maintains and even reinforces some central or default position to which we are responding, or against which we are acting. To this tacit fetishism of positivism, we must add the explicit subjugation of nonpositivist scholarship to decades of modernist evaluation criteria. This has only worsened as funding sources dry up, increasing an academic's dependence on resources that privilege statistical findings over narrative accounts. For good reasons, taxpaying publics demand evidence-based impact with measurable results. I repeat a tired complaint when I say that these external forces constrain the ethnographic project at its very core.

Remix processes help break this pattern because the resulting products of research cannot be evaluated using traditional measures for the social sciences, such as replicability or validity – and here, 'cannot' means two things: 'should not' in the normative sense; and 'not possible', referring to the flaw of using illogical measures. Remix is not intended to produce anything that might be replicable because it creatively combines cultural information into a form designed for a particular purpose. If it has resonance with cultural members from whom the material is drawn, it is because it holds strong validity for that community. Like all interpretive creative scholarship, remix is also not necessarily intended to simply convey or transfer meaning from one context to another. Rather it is meant to build or encourage others to find new layers of meaning by shifting one's orientation slightly. Remix is always a future-oriented mode of reflexive inquiry that exchanges precision for projection, allowing for explorations of what could be.

Remix is already quite visible in the contemporary anthropological practices of pastiche, montage or bricolage, which help situate inquiry as particular and specific, situated and idiosyncratic. Engaging with these types of products is a constant reminder that ethnographers engage in a process of selecting, abstracting, editing and reimagining the world for others. Rather than obscuring the everyday practice of making, fashioning, and fabricating results of inquiry, remix becomes a reasonable and even apt way to describe how we enact and characterize ethnographic research even in the most classic sense. For when we deconstruct the activities of the researcher in situ, the strength of a great ethnographer lies in his or her ability to interpret, or write, culture. When we begin with the assumption that this activity is one of cutting and pasting various elements of the actual cultural experience into a new form that can be experienced by others, research becomes remix. Acknowledging that remix is already present as a dominant, if mostly obscured, practice, anthropologies of futures can reach in multiple directions outside typical disciplinary or institutional boundaries for inspiration and support. In this way, it becomes more possible to be, as the FAN Manifesto states, 'stubbornly transdisciplinary and transnational: we collaborate, hybridise, and compromise. We break boundaries and network without fear of incapacity or contamination'.

When we speak of anthropology of becoming or anthropology of possible futures, it is important to recognize the larger landscape within which ethnographic methods currently operate and to challenge the frameworks that keep it locked in a backward facing gaze. While ethnography may be known for its broad and flexible approach to the study of culture, the primary criteria for evaluation remain embedded in trends that deny the viability of inductive or exploratory processes of engagement and inquiry. This is a problem we can combat by shifting the terminology we use to talk about research practice. As Burke (1941) continues in his discussion of the larger scholarly conversation,

[A]ll these words are grounded in what Malinowski would call 'contexts of situation.' And very important among these 'contexts of situation' are the kind of factors considered by Bentham, Marx, and Veblen, the material interests (of private or class structure) that you symbolically defend or symbolically appropriate or symbolically align yourself with in the course of making your own assertions. (111)

Our literacies about what we might consider our methodological competencies are embedded in particular symbolic alignments or appropriations.

We can choose different alignments, which will foreground different sets of literacies, something that feminist and various post- scholars understand very clearly. At the most basic level, this is about changing our language about the processes and products of ethnographic research. Still, one should not presume that this discourse shift would erase or replace the general logics of social and scientific inquiry. Rather, it reimagines how and why inquiry is enacted and opens the door for greater possibilities.

Alongside rethinking our language around the *practice* of research, we can likewise rethink our terminology about the *purpose*. This is an active ethical shift. As we critically reflect on why we're doing research in the first place, we begin to reach beyond the prescriptive and somewhat entry-level purposes we find in basic textbooks: to describe, explain, predict and control. Simply by placing 'future' into the equation of inquiry, we orient ourselves differently – toward the project, the process and the outcomes. This orientation is an active turning toward some things versus other things, rather than a passive position in relation to some other agent that provides our orientation. A future orientated approach highlights one's role as maker, which is a label that goes well beyond the role of observer or documentarian.

Immediately upon when taking a 'future' and 'maker' approach, ethics become paramount. A future orientation allows us to consider the impact of our research. A mindset of intervention adds substance to the shape of this impact, which necessarily evokes a consideration of the ethics of our efforts. When we add 'remix' as a possibility for one's practice and approach, this framework – here, considered as an attitude more than a technique or product – can actually ease some of the anxieties associated with one's role as well as contribute to an overall understanding that the entire scientific enterprise is not a static or fixed enterprise.

The terminology we choose impacts the literacies we build. A remix literacy functions as an activist response to the contingencies of the early twenty-first century focus on data and datafication as well as recent shifts back to modernist criteria for evaluating the qualities and value of scholarship.

Below, I shift to a brief discussion of the elements characterizing remix and some of the many processes involved in remix(ing) methods. This both encapsulates and extends my previous work in this area (Markham 2013).[1]

Remix: Definition as praxis

One can take a product or process view of remix, although combining these most fully represents the intertwined qualities and functions. My own perspective draws on various authors who talk about different types of remix. Limor Shifman (2013), for example, highlights the process of memesis;

most recently, what might make particular vernacular videos on YouTube 'go viral' while others circulate only in small networks. Navas, in his work on the aesthetics of sampling as a foundational element of remix theory, uses practices common in hip-hop to describe different forms of remix, along a continuum of how they function in relation to the original(s) from which they are created (2012). Lessig's work critically explores what might happen to cultural innovation and development with narrow and strict regulations restricting what classically could be considered natural processes of remix. Whether one is using a cut/copy and paste technique to rethink cultural forms or creating novel forms through sharing and mixing various cultural expressions (2008) or creating interfaces through open source software (2004), Lessig argues that remix is is a fundamental element of cultural creativity and transformation. This point is illustrated across many contemporary examples by Ferguson in his video series and talks around 'Everything is a Remix' (2010).

Recent efforts to bring some of these ideas together with an online network of scholars and practitioners has resulted in robust development of remix theories, some of which are represented in the 2013 *Routledge Companion to Remix Studies*, where many of the prominent writers and thinkers of this topic are represented. As the concept continues to be defined in more nuanced ways, we find the emergence of a strong theory of praxis, which is where my own work has been situated. That is, a remix literacy for social research methods develops out of a need to address the future from an ethic of care, or, borrowing from actor network theorist Bruno Latour, shift from matters of fact to matters of concern. Praxis is a practical action based on simply on reflection but with a particular disposition about what constitutes the right or best action in the specific circumstance of one's action. We can use the imaginary of remix as a way of finding, rather than simply accepting methods most appropriate for engaging in anthropologies of futures.

I continue below with an introduction to remix elements and processes. This distinction highlights different ways remix might be operationalized in practice. These should be considered working points of reference rather than stable categories of meaning, in the spirit of remix thinking.

Remix elements

How can we recognize remix as remix? (How do we compare remix to bricolage, montage, improvisation, or pastiche?) *Remix elements* identify some of the outcomes of processes, which in some cases are processes themselves, but can be recognizable in almost every remix as an outcome (like systems theory, almost every element or process could be understood as both noun and verb, process and product, so this should not be considered inconsistent or confused, but dynamism, halted for a moment so we can look more closely at what is going on.)

Sampling is a key element in remix. Most simply, we can say that a sample is the outcome of picking some particulars and leaving others behind. From what we have selected, we make meaning, whether through examination or generalization. In music, sampling involves selecting bits and pieces from previous works, lifting them out of their original, and recombining them in different ways. When we look past the surface of this technical activity, we see a deeply dialogic exploration of meaning through connection. As Martin Irvine writes, remix uses sampling as a 'recursive combinatorial function for embedding constituent phrases as recognizable dialogically positioned units of "other's" expression'. If we follow Irvine's (2015) explanation, it becomes clear that sampling requires a strong understanding of the context in order to create meaning that is sensible to an audience. It involves at the very least:

(1) selecting syntactically possible units in contexts of prior symbolic relations and encyclopedic values (identifying and selecting 'answerable' combinable constituent units represent initial interpretive process for linking token to typed meaning), and (2) recontextualizing the selected unit by embedding it in the compositional structure of the new expression, a meaning environment that opens up additional encyclopedic meaning relations that were not active in the situation of the prior expression. (Irvine 2015: 29)

This interpretive and dialogic process of selection and recontextualization invokes and addresses already-existing – or to use the more precise term 'enyclopediac', offered by Irvine – symbolic meanings. His conclusion echoes that of many remix theorists, that '[s]ince we're born into a generative symbolic continuum already in progress, we always dialogically, collectively 'quote ourselves' to capture prior states of meaning as inputs for new interpretations in new contexts in materially reimplementable, remixable ways' (Irvine 2015: 33).

Sampling, defined as the continual and experimental selection and subsequent recombination of cultural meaning, is a prominent practice in social research; feminist, interpretive, and postmodern schools of thought have long understood the value of sampling in this sense. Geertz famously wrote, 'Doing ethnography is like trying to read (in the sense of "construct a reading of") a manuscript – foreign, faded, full of ellipses, incoherencies, suspicious emendations, and tendentious commentaries, but written not in conventionalized graphs of sound but in transient examples of shaped behavior' (1973: 10).

Indeed, if we look at the base strategies of social scientists and rap and hip-hop artists, we can see they draw on similar goals of drawing attention to or focusing on certain things versus others. The distinction between modernist social science and hip hop is in the overall point of sampling: the former is interested in explanation, whereas the latter is generally interested in generating resonant meanings. If we consider the practices of remix within a scholarly lens, it is clear that interpretive, feminist, and postmodern approaches sit more comfortably with the hip-hop artist. Purposive sampling has long been the suggested strategy for qualitative research. But this essential element of inquiry can get lost or misinterpreted, especially in disciplines that are haunted by the terminology of hypothetico-deductive science practice, where one is under significant external pressure to defend one's sample as being representative of some larger whole, generally called a population. Even in traditional qualitative research, at least as represented in most textbooks, one's sample is justifiable if it connects to larger methodological premises. For example, the difficulty of reaching participants in a new or unfamiliar situation can justify the practice of 'snowball' sampling. Alternatively, and here I refer to a common practice in grounded theory, when the context is novel or unfamiliar and therefore where theory is thin or absent, one can use systematic sampling to build a theoretical understanding. In anthropology, discussions of 'field boundaries' replace the word sampling. These determinations can be quite precise and even follow standard statistical parameters if the population is well defined. Or they can remain vague or unstated altogether, especially in situations where immersion and thick description takes precedence over cultural representativeness. In any case, *ending up with* a sample is far less likely than *using* a sample to add up to some ending. Put differently, we mostly use sample as a means rather than an end.

What happens, however, if we reverse this thinking and place the sample as the end or outcome? From this stance, the sample becomes a perspective or example that illustrates possibilities rather than probabilities. I come back to this later when I wrap this idea into a future anthropology mindset.

Hybridization is a term that encapsulates a thing or process that is between or both; neither one thing nor another. Taking parts of two or more different things, one can combine these elements into something new. This is such a natural practice in sensemaking it seems odd to examine it separately here using the term 'hybrid'. However, hybridization is a strong term in remix, indicating how new and creative things emerge from mixing previously understood elements. This is certainly the case in video mashups found mostly on YouTube, such as fake movie trailers. Readers may be familiar with how this works. Christopher Rule's 2006 remix, to take one example, combines the original visuals and the song *Stay Awake* from the 1960s

Disney film *Mary Poppins* with audio clips from the soundtrack of the film *An American Haunting* and stock music clips from iMovie. The resulting hybrid transforms a classic children's film into an advertisement for a contemporary horror film about *Scary Mary Poppins*.[2] The product that emerges is wholly dependent on the use of existing elements, but the meaning is unique (it can also be compelling and entertaining, but this is not dependent on the hybrid elements, but the rhetorical situation in which it is experienced).

Often, hybridization is seen retrospectively, as we reverse engineering the processes of thought and analysis that went into creating an account. If we consider the way that Christopher Rule uses precise and deliberate juxtaposition in this mashup movie trailer, we can notice how the hybrid performs and serves as an analysis of both prior elements. The strength of sampling as a process is startling when we can be convinced by the hybrid product. This also raises the point that unlike the sample, which is always simultaneously process and product, we can see hybridization most clearly as a form.

To illustrate how hybridization represents remix already well established as social science practice, we can look at the past three decades of interpretive sociology practices of analysis and representation, prompted not least by the edited collection *Writing Culture* by ethnographers Clifford and Marcus (1986). Carol Rambo-Ronai (1988), for example, published a nuanced and evocative sociological analysis of child sex abuse in what she called a 'layered account'. Her work is still heralded as a remarkable approach for sociology of sensitive or untouchable subjects, where it would be impossible to move beyond affect to understand from an interpretive perspective something like child sex abuse. Her account weaves samples from different moments in her own lifecourse, a practice adopted and developed into different forms by other scholars such as Lisa Tillmann-Healy, who through the pastiche of scientific literature, popular media accounts, and her own diaries presents a powerful rendering of the experience of bulimia within a larger culture of thinness (1996). I use similar techniques to discuss how 'fragmented narrative' is both a form of analysis and a style of destabilizing a single account 2005. There, I highlight a technique of analysis through proximal juxtaposition of contradictory or entangled data. In this experimental ethnography of an expression (inspired by Robin Clair, 1996), I sampled and arranged selections from my analytical findings and raw data as a process of piecing together a remixed account of the situation that would have resonance for particular audiences.

The outcome as well as the process of each of these cases highlights that samples are taken from cultural experience as analytical units, which are then (or simultaneously) combined with other samples to present possible accounts or conclusions. Each outcome comprises a partial account, but importantly, a hybridization of meaning that cannot be situated solely within the (auto)ethnographer, the analysis of materials drawn from fieldwork, or the findings. In other words, there is a strong acknowledgment in such work that there is not – and could never be – a 'whole' somewhere. Rather, these articles and arguments strive for multiplicity through deliberate juxtaposition of both the content and form through which a 'cultural reading' might be identified. This renders meaning precarious rather than partial. This work also tends to be deliberately vulnerable, to open the possibility for critique, reinterpretation, and the development of alternate meanings.

These efforts represent only a small part of a widespread paradigmatic conversation across multiple disciplines that emerged in force during the 1980s and 1990s. For some, the conversation was about dismantling traditional genres of academic writing by experimenting with new or mixed genres. For others, the conversation extended beyond genre to theory making. John Van Maanen writes about 'style as theory', emphasizing the need to reflect critically on how our theories are bound in the language we use to portray them to others. He questions, like many interpretive and postmodern scholars at the time, how we come to know the phenomena we study, how we represent what we know to others, and how our choices create particular versions of the world. In speaking of organizational theorist Karl Weick's use of a particularly confusing style of writing, Van Maanen notices that this style performs a particular kind of theorizing – one that keeps possibilities open through its continual 'assault on the unquestioned objectivity of our received notions of the world' (1995: 137). Weaving feminist theory into interpretive methods, then, long legacies of scholar repeat a strong message that our language around research methods should better fit current conceptions of how knowledge and theory are contingent, and our story-telling practices should be part of the reflexive process of conveying this contingency.

Recognizing and then working with hybrid forms is a way of highlighting that a) the form is meaningful but not necessarily stable and b) the story it presents is definitely not singular. This is very much how we experience internet memes, which present a particular hybrid of (generally) two or more distinctive ideas, such as image macros, where a picture of a cat is superimposed by some text that adds meaning to the image. The idea of a meme is that the original elements are separated and then put into new hybrid mixes, which transforms the meaning. The purpose of the hybrid is not to stand alone but anticipates that new hybridization will create new meanings.

Linkage Connecting previously unlinked elements or ideas is a hallmark of remix. The link, as simple as a loop in a chain, connects two things together. These two previously unconnected things then exist in some sort of relation. A linkage is therefore a causal element. It delineates the connection or relation, which might be a comparison, a juxtaposition, an interweaving, or some other type of relationship. Linking, or the resulting linkage, is interesting to specify as a key element of remix because it is through this tiny but necessary detail of sensemaking that the outcome of analysis is made relevant, meaningful, affective, or effective.

Linkages are nicely illustrated in internet memes, remixed movie trailers, fan vidding, and political video remix. One of the most prominent political video artists, Jon McIntosh, for example, generates strong cultural critique through his remixes of advertisements, films, and news. Sometimes juxtaposed or clashing, sometimes woven together seamlessly, McIntosh's critical pairings tend to transform the message of both elements being linked (Horwatt 2010: n.p.). There is most obviously a direct transformation of the media content of both original elements. One of his early works remixes an ad campaign for an oil and gas company promoting their social consciousness with news footage of the first war in Iraq. Through careful editing, McIntosh presents a convincing narrative of where the rancher's gasoline comes from as the stereotypical Texan stands next to his powerful pickup truck at the petrol station. We see oil running through pipelines and then blood streaming out of bodies. This is an example of a deliberate linkage.

This linking or connecting feature characteristic of remix distinguishes it from pastiche or bricolage, as these have been developed in relation to interpretive inquiry. In bricolage, the focus is more on the reflexive, recursive and consciously provocative processes involved in making or generating pastiche or collage. Remix is focused on making connections that generate innovative meanings. Because the comprehension of a remix is caught up in knowing something about the originals, these links may only be apparent to insider audiences who can therefore identify the new or revised meaning because there is a new connection being illustrated. This is illustrated in the remix *Queer Carrie*, a political video remix by Elisa Kreisinger that recombines original *Sex in the City* video clips with selective voiceovers from Carrie, the main character and narrator in the series. The resulting film trailer demonstrates in less than three minutes that the entire series is about LGBTQ issues and relationships. One would need to be armed with the knowledge that on the contrary, *Sex in the City* valorizes heterosexual relationships and marriage to recognize that this remix is making a strong critical point. By cutting and recombining particular elements, a specific link is made that would not exist otherwise, but which has meaning as an argument, in this case, a cultural critique. In this way, linkages can sponsor comparisons we wouldn't otherwise notice.

Applied to ethnographic practice in the most basic way, the element of linking simply rephrases and emphasizes the premise that when we see and identify anything in the world, as a phenomenon, a situation, or any part of a situation, we are making a connection between this and that. The symbolic interaction between elements in a research context lend themselves to considering what, how, and why we are making the connections we do.

Over time, these deliberate linkages become taken for granted connections, which can be both enabling and constraining. Take for example Goffman's links between theatre and everyday social behaviour. When he creates this particular linkage in his 1959 work *The Presentation of Self in Everyday Life*, it is to help him explain his case study. This linkage is so strong that decade after decade, once a scholar has read Goffman's allegory it is very difficult to find different words for the performance of identity, role adoption, or the frontstage and backstage moments of the performance of self. Although the internet in many ways defies this front and back stage metaphor, we have yet to unlink identity from Goffman's conceptualization. His deliberate linkages have become natural connections.

Linkage is such a powerful and normalized form of sensemaking, it seems redundant to mention it as a strong part of an anthropological research practice. But remixers are able to use the power of linkage more freely than scholars, for whom this remains an underlying assumption for how inquiry works rather than a tool for analysis or a form of critical representation. To determine how we might use linkage as a primary goal in analysis is only one of many challenges remix offers for academic research.

As we consider various possibilities for becoming, through a futures-oriented lens, the idea of linking becomes more active than passive, and of course it has strong ethical components. There's a great deal of power in making these connections. Memes that persist over time cannot be undone. The cat meme, for example, was the first and still considered the most robust of all memes. In recent years, we can watch a linkage between the internet and cats grow stronger or more fundamental. Whereas ten, or even five, years ago, not many would associate the internet with cats, now it is much more common to talk about how the internet is all about cats. While the combinations vary, the fundamental notion becomes normalized into a way of seeing the internet, or understanding its history.

Remix Processes

How do we know we're doing remix? What distinguishes remix from other processes of everyday practice? This framework focuses on five natural activities of everyday research practice: play, borrow, interrogate, move and generate. In the past few years, I have described these elements separately. Here, I want to talk in a more fluid way about how I believe these five activities can be powerful tools in anthropologies of futures.

Remix is a way of linking past to future possibilities. It is a way of reconnecting narratives of the past or present and shifting to a new narration/creation, which is a new way of describing the connection. This is, or could be, described as another narration of the past. This narration does not remain in the past, however, because it anticipates further remix.

Because remix anticipates remix, new trajectories are indicated. This suggestiveness is generative. Combined with an activist mindset or an ethic of future care, it supplies a critical playground for further interrogation. As the remixer tries out or plays with different combinations of samples drawn from current or past contexts, generative possibilities emerge. As Latour notes,

> Any given interaction seems to overflow with elements which are already in the situation coming from some other time, some other place, and generated by some other agency. This powerful intuition is as old as the social sciences. As I have said earlier, action is always dislocated, articulated, delegated, translated. Thus, if any observer is faithful to the direction suggested by this overflow, she will be led away from any given interaction to some other places, other times, and other agencies that appear to have molded them into shape. (2005: 166)

Remix is a way of following the overflow, the leaky boundaries, the spill of cause and effect that cannot be explained but noticed, interrogated and addressed. Rather than trying to sort it out, remix encourages us to stay with the trouble, in the way Haraway would recommend. This approach is neither random nor uncurated, but is certainly provocative through a recognition of multiplicity. Thus, it is interventionist.

As a provocation, remix carries ethical responsibility. It requires us, as creators, to consider what possibilities we are curating or sponsoring. Creating linkages and making associations will cause viewers/readers to consider these also, to respond to them, to resist, regress, or carry forward. The remix is therefore not just a description, illustration, or even an argument about what Geertz's faded manuscript might mean. It is an invitation and provocation.

As an invitation, remix leaves our space of play and moves elsewhere. It moves beyond us, taking a life of its own. But to exist as meaningful for others, it borrows from its origin points, a design influenced by the remixer. The cycle of playful encounter and continual remix demonstrates a distributed agency, in the best sense of the term and process. Our research can be an invitation to speak, providing a means for recombining new elements and morphing our remix into other forms. In a very simplified sense, we might see this as a process of conversation, whereby the product and content speaks, the origins speak. The maker speaks. The process of experiencing this remix in a situation where remix is indicated and desired is also allowed to speak. Multiple agencies are opened up by this entire endeavour.

Remix as an ethical literacy for anthropologies of futures

Remix as a methodological literacy takes well-known and developed tools and invites us to re-envision how and why inquiry happens in the first place. In this way, it opens what Ray Oldenburg called a 'third place', a space for supportive and friendly thinking between the private space of home life and the disciplined space of work life.

Enabling a third space within which we can playfully engage with innovative inquiry practice is an important response to recent and urgent calls to make our research matter in what Isabelle Stengers has called 'catastrophic times' (2009: 2015). A future interventionist approach to anthropology provides a strong and justifiable motivation for finding creative and playful environments outside the discipline(s) that influences our work. Of course, remix is not for everyone, or every situation. A remix idea does not preclude our ability to conduct different types of studies at different times of our careers or days of the week. We have different moments where different types of inquiry might be relevant and needed, and desired.

But the complexities of our futures demand we experiment with multiple ways of thinking, through a wide range of generative tools. This in turn demands that we continue to develop transdisciplinary literacies around methods. Remix places us in the midst of the creation process, and invites us to acknowledge that the products and processes of scientific inquiry are as temporary as contributions to a conversation that has been happening long before we arrived, and will continue long after we leave. Yet our efforts, terminologies, concepts, and interventions have impact

To build remix as a metaphor for anthropologies of futures is more attitudinal than formulaic. Emphasizing the generative and playful aspects of research, one can focus on these activities that produce mimetic materials. That is, the process and products are acknowledged as partial and experimental mashups of ongoing conversations. Remix is understood to be a constant work in progress. As remixes spread, they have the potential to function like memes, facilitating and encouraging further critical exploration and remixing by various others. The freedom associated with playful experimentation can open the door for critical interrogation, since it may be considered less risky to plant one's critical ideas if it's only as a contribution to a parlor conversation.

This can also work to encourage a methodological stance of uncertainty (Pink et al. 2015). Remix works beyond the level of the analytical. As an ethical and political practice, research that stubbornly refuses to provide certainty has certain benefits. This type of stance in ethnographic research leaves room for discussions and explorations of alternate trajectories and critique of future possibles. It also makes interventionist research more possible, by deliberately unfocusing attention from lingering positivist criteria of quality for social scientific research. More precisely, a remix method stance refocuses attention on the way that research can destabilize reductionist accounts and theorizing in complex sociotechnical contexts.

Notes

1 While I find these terms quite useful, and I have not in six years of workshops and conference presentations found anyone to add or replace a term, this is a generative tool to think with. Others might find more salient or powerful words to disrupt and rethink their own practices or products of research. It's meant to be creatively remixed for future use.

2 See https://www.youtube.com/watch?2T5_0AGdFic (accessed 20 October 2016).

References

Burke, K., 1941. *The Philosophy of Literary Form: Studies in Symbolic Interaction.* Baton Rouge: Louisiana State University Press.

Clair, R., 1996. *Expressions of Ethnography: New Approaches in Qualitative Practice.* Albany, NY: SUNY Press.

Clifford, J. and G. Marcus, 1986. *Writing Culture: The Poetics and Politics of Ethnography.* Berkeley: University of California Press.

Ferguson, K., 2015/10. 'Everything is a remix'. Video. Remastered complete version combining all three original parts. Available online: https://vimeo.com/139094998 (accessed 1 June 2016).

Geertz, C., 1973. *The Interpretation of Culture.* New York: Basic Books.

Goffman, E., 1959. *The Presentation of Self in Everyday Life.* New York: Anchor Books

Haraway, D., 2010. 'When species meet: Staying with the trouble'. *Environment and Planning D: Society and Space* 28: 53–5.

Horwatt, E., 2010. 'A taxonomy of digital video remixing'. *Scope*, 17. Available online: https://socialmediaecologies.wikispaces.com/file/view/Video%2Bremix%2BEli%2BHorwatt.pdf (accessed 1 June 2016).

Irvine, M., 2015. 'Remix and the Dialogic Engine of Culture: A Model for Generative Combinatoriality'. In E. Navas, O. Gallagher and X. Burrough (eds), *The Routledge Companion to Remix Studie*, 15–42. New York: Routledge.

Kreisinger, E., 2010. 'Queer Carrie'. Video series online. Available online: http://www.popculturepirate.com/videos/ (accessed 21 September 2016).

Latour, B., 2005. *Reassembling the Social: An Introduction to Actor Network Theory.* Oxford: Oxford University Press.

Lessig, L., 2004. *Free Culture.* New York: Penguin Press.

Lessig, L., 2008. *Remix: Making Art and Commerce Thrive in the Hybrid Economy*. London: Penguin Press.

Markham, A., 2005. '"Go Ugly Early": Fragmented narrative and bricolage as interpretive method'. *Qualitative Inquiry* 11 (1): 813–39.

Markham, A., 2013. 'Remix Culture, Remix Methods: Reframing Qualitative Inquiry for Social Media Contexts'. In N. Denzin and M. Giardina (eds), *Global Dimensions of Qualitative Inquiry,* 63–81. Walnut Creek, CA: Left Coast Press.

Navas, E., 2012. *Remix Theory: The Aesthetics of Sampling*. New York: Springer Press.

Oldenburg, R., 1989. *The Great Good Place*. Boston: Da Capo Press.

Pink, S., Y. Akama and contributors, 2015. *Un/Certainty*. eBook. Available online: http://d-e-futures.com/ (accessed 6 June 2016).

Rambo-Ronai, C., 1995. 'Multiple reflections of child sex abuse: An argument for a layered account'. *Journal of Contemporary Ethnography* 23 (4): 395–426.

Shifman, L., 2013. *Memes in Digital Culture*. Cambridge, MA: MIT Press.

Stengers, I., 2015. *In Catastrophic Times: Resisting the Coming Barbarism*. Luneberg: Meson Press.

Tillmann-Healy, L., 2003. 'A Secret Life in a Culture of Thinness'. In C. Ellis, C. and A. Bochner (eds), *Composing Ethnography: Alternative Forms of Qualitative Writing*. Walnut Creek, CA: AltaMira Press.

Van Maanen, J., 1995. 'Style as theory'. *Organization Science* 6 (1): 133–43.

Afterword: Flying toward the future on the wings of wind

Paul Stoller

An elder's words may appear to be jumbled in knots,
but in the end they gradually sort themselves out.
SONGHAY PROVERB

For many West African peoples, including the Songhay of Niger and Mali, time is not uniquely linear. It is often reckoned in a circular manner. The elder's talk may steer off on a tangent. Even so, by slowly following the side roads where one finds creative imagination, the elder eventually returns to the point of departure. In this circular way, the elder's talk can bring us powerful insight, perceptive knowledge and profound wisdom, enabling us to chart a path to the future.

Among the Dogon people of the Bandiagara Cliffs in northeastern Mali, time is imagined cyclically. Every sixty years, the Dogon stage a seven-year-long ritual called the *sigui*. During the first three years of the sigui, which begins in the village of Yougou, the theme is death. How did death come into the world and what are its ramifications? During the four succeeding years the sigui's theme is re-birth. In the shadow of death, how was the world regenerated? These questions are symbolically answered during the sigui's seven-year sequence, during which the sigui 'flies on the wings of wind' from east to west and from village to village. This journey restages the mythic trek of Lebe, a giant snake that is the Dogon's ancestor. Accordingly, every sixty years in each of the villages along the ritual route, Dogon carve a mythically sized Mother of Masks, the embodiment of Lebe. Kept in caverns above the Dogon villages, the Mother of Masks is displayed once during the sigui and then retired back to the cave never to be displayed again.

Every sixty years, this 'slow' seven-year ritual dramatically stages the reinvention of the world, which means that the Dogon are always focused on the future – on the next sigui, which begins in 2027. Flying on 'the wings of the wind' the Dogon will once again recreate their world and repeat the seven-year ritual sequence in 2087, in 2147 and in 2207 (see Griaule 1938; Rouch 1978; Echard and Rouch 1988; Fulchignoni and Rouch 1989; Stoller 1992).

What can this slow pattern of circular talk and cyclical worldmaking teach us about a future-oriented anthropology?

The papers in *Anthropologies and Futures: Researching Emerging and Uncertain Worlds* are strong, imaginative, diverse and prescient. They offer anthropologists and other social scientists concrete and innovative methods to unlock the imagination to wonder, ponder, anticipate and speculate about what might come to pass in the future. In the human sciences, as many of the contributors to this volume suggest, our frozen gaze has more often than not compelled us to look back on the past rather than to turn toward the future. As the Songhay of Niger and Mali like to say: 'If you walk forward while looking back, you'll eventually bump into a wall or fall off a cliff.'

In the introduction to the volume, Pink and Salazar write that the '... contributors are determined to refigure anthropology; beyond its reliance on documenting and analysing the past; its dependence on long-term fieldwork; and its tendency to close itself off in critical isolation. Such approaches have paralyzed the discipline in a world where the insights of creative, improvisational, speculative, and participatory techniques of a renewed anthropological ethnography have the potential to make a significant contribution in the making of alternative futures' (page 3). They also call for a more public anthropology in which future-oriented scholars become engaged world-makers who use the description of difference – in all of its iterations – to make a difference in the world.

In various and creative ways the wonderfully eclectic set of chapters in *Anthropologies and Futures* meet these important disciplinary challenges. Abram's essay on imagining fantasy futures considers how a future-orientation might felicitously affect urban planning. Several of the essays focus on how to explore the interior life in which human beings experience wonder, fear, love, hate and uncertainty. D'Onofrio writes about how creative practices – animation and storytelling exercises – trigger what Antonin Artaud would call 'cruel insights'. These insights enable Egyptian migrants in Italy, the subjects of her research, to tune into the internal frequencies of their lives. These discoveries give fuller shape to their identity, which, in turn, enables them to chart future courses of action. In the same vein, Kazubowski-Houston demonstrates how dramatic storytelling empowers her Polish subjects to explore their interior lives and ponder alternative futures. For his part, Sjöberg's method of 'ethno science fiction' demonstrates how improvisation and play can free the imagination of culturally-contoured disciplinary constraints.

Following the path of the late French filmmaker, Jean Rouch, Sjöberg's essay reminds us that to imagine the future we need to push hard against imposed disciplinary boundaries, which, of course, involves personal and professional risk.

The essays by Lanzeni and Ardèvol, Waltorp, Pink, Akama and Fergusson, and Salazar are fundamentally about how new methodological concepts and practices can generate future-oriented research in anthropology. Lanzeni and Ardèvol describe how design processes are driven by a necessary anticipation of complex futures in which technology-makers imagine what is to come when they engage in technological worldmaking. They suggest that future ethnographic research will reveal that there is no single master narrative that explains the complexities of the human condition. Waltorp also focuses on digital technologies. She demonstrates how the use of smart phones and video cameras supports the widespread representation of uncertainty and allows her research subjects, young Muslim women in Copenhagen, to speculate about their future. Pink, Akama and Fergusson write about how people can come to know about their present state and future potential through a blended research practice that combines ethnography, documentary video and design. They recommend that future research practices be collaborative and reflect a felicitous multi-disciplinary diversity. Such a mixed approach, they argue, can produce coherent stories that constitute a public anthropology in which the future is conceptualized as alterity. Markham also considers this kind of blended approach to research, calling it 'remixing'. In this method, the researcher utilizes montage, play, borrowing and sampling to destabilize our tendency to reduce the complexities of contemporary social life to a set of neat and clean explanatory principles. Remixing creates – at least for me – the creative and imaginary space of what Crapanzano (2004), following the twelfth-century Sufi wisdom of Ibn al-'Arabi, called the *barzakh*, the bridge that links two different entities. Such a liminal space inspires our creative imagination and compels us to think about the future. For his part, Salazar extends the methodological and conceptual focus of Pink, Akama and Fergusson. He argues for a reconfiguration of our thinking – about the future. How can scholars use 'speculative fabulation' to create, to borrow from Nelson Goodman (1978), 'ways of worldmaking'? How can we use film and fiction to make future worlds?

The future, of course, entails uncertainty. Using the results of long-term research on the social and cultural realities of disability in the US, Ginsburg and Rapp describe the erasure of disability in the ethnographic present and write about the uncertain future that people with disabilities face each and every day. They demonstrate how engaged public ethnographers, writers and filmmakers can help to produce a future in which disability is no longer considered a marginal element in the human condition. Irving uses a powerful narrative about HIV/AIDS, Uganda and 9/11 to discuss how contingencies, which are exponentially interconnected through digital technologies, can shape our social destinies. Choosing to walk left or right at the fork in the path can produce existential consequences that inexorably change a person's life. It is no wonder when we have to make a momentous decision many of us seek the advice of a diviner. Such uncertainty also weaves its way through Knight's essay on contested narratives about climate change. The dismal projections of climate scientists have compelled French environmental activists to advocate re-wilding programs that reintroduce predators into the eco-system of the French Pyrenees. Knight suggests that re-wilding environmental narratives stand in stark contrast to those of the local farmers. These competing narratives are ethnographic reminders that futures are uncertain, contingent and contested.

The chapters in *Anthropologies and Futures* underscore a set of themes that direct us onto the uncertain path that leads to the future. In what remains of this Afterword, I list these themes and comment on their importance.

1 **The future is contingent**. Contingency is usually quite stressful. It is not easy to move forward into uncertainty. Given the complexities of the future it is wise to adopt, as do all the contributors to the volume, an epistemological flexibility – having the capacity to change, to develop new ways of thinking and being in future worlds. Given our disciplinary histories, such flexibility presents many institutional challenges, which, through steadfast persistence, can be overcome.

2 **The future requires humility**. Much of our current take on the world devolves from the ongoing notion that we can conquer nature, that technology can solve our problems. It is much more insightful to confront the future with a dose of humility not unlike the great painter Paul Klee who approached the world with respect and humility. 'In a forest,' he wrote, 'I have felt many times over that it was not I who looked at the forest. Some days I felt that the trees were looking at me. I was there, listening … I think the painter must be penetrated by the universe and not penetrate it … I expect to be inwardly submerged, buried. Perhaps I paint to break out' (see Charbonnier 1959, cited by Merleau-Ponty 1964: 31). Humility is perhaps a special ingredient in the recipe for a future creativity.

3 **The future requires risk.** All the essays discuss the conceptual and institutional risks associated with anthropological futures. If concepts and methods push us onto institutional borderlands, we can expect institutional push back. Change is always associated with risk, and yet taking methodological, conceptual and representational risks is

also liberating. Why not follow the path of the late French filmmaker and anthropologist Jean Rouch, who took many methodological and representational risks in his work, and pose his famous question: 'Why not?'

4   **The future requires negative capability**. The philosopher John Dewey discussed negative capability in his classic work, *Art as Experience* (1934). He suggested that people who can tolerate the existential contradictions of life experience 'negative capability,' which makes them highly imaginative and creative. Dewey stated that Shakespeare and Keats possessed the capacity for 'negative capability'. Spaces of negative capability, which I, among others have called 'the between,' unleash the imagination and compel creative responses. Such a capacity is necessary for future worldmaking (see Stoller 2008: 2014).

5   **The future requires public anthropology**. Ethnographic practices that are oriented toward the future necessitate a public- oriented anthropology in which scholars (1) implicate themselves in the real-world problems of their subject populations and (2) produce works (ethnographies, films, novels, plays, installations and exhibitions) that connect with the general public. If we produce works that connect only with narrow and highly specialized audiences the anthropological impact on future worldmaking will be negligible.

Amid all the discussions about worldmaking, anthropologies of the unknown, and the impact of digital technologies on the future representation of social worlds there is one central theme that should not be overlooked or underestimated: the profound importance of stories and storytelling. In the 1980s, I had the rare privilege of attending a few film screenings in Jean Rouch's makeshift projection room above his office in the Musée de l'Homme in Paris. Rouch would routinely gather an eclectic group of people to chime in on a film's strengths and weaknesses. During those sessions, Rouch would invariably ask about the narrative character of the film:

Is the story a good one? Does it work?
Will the story connect with the audience?
If the story doesn't work, can a better one be imagined?

For me, our capacity to imagine, create, anticipate and speculate about the future emerges from a central source: the story. Does the narrative inspire? Does it make us think new thoughts and feel new feelings? Does it connect with the public and compel people to imagine the future?

We have much to learn from Songhay elders whose slow stories circle about the main point until they return to the beginning, inspiring us to know the place, to paraphrase T. S. Eliot, for the first time. We have much to learn from the Dogon who reconfigure their world every sixty years. During the sigui ceremonies they 'fly on the wings of the wind' to meet their future destiny. If we listen and are patient, we, too, can learn how to 'fly on the wings of the wind.'

References

Charbonnier, Georges, 1959. *Le monologue due peintre*. Paris: Julliard.

Crapanzano, Vincent, 2004. *Imaginative Horizons: An Essay in Literary-Philosophical Anthropology*. Chicago: University of Chicago Press.

Dewey, John, 1934. *Art as Experience*. New York: Putnam.

Echard, Nicole and Jean Rouch, 1988. 'Entretien avec Jean Rouch. A voix nu. Entretien d'hier à aujourd'hui'. Ten-hour discussion broadcast on France Culture, July.

Fulchignoni, Enrico and Jean Rouch, 1989. 'Conversation between Jean Rouch and Professor Enrico Fulchignoni'. *Visual Anthropology* 2: 265–301.

Goodman, Nelson, 1978. *Ways of Worldmaking*. Indianapolis: Hackett.

Griaule, Marcel, 1938. *Masques dogons*. Paris: Institut d'Ethnologie.

Merleau-Ponty, Maurice, 1964. *L'Oeil et l'esprit*. Paris: Gallimard.

Rouch, Jean, 1978. 'Le renard fou et le maître pâle'. In *Systèmes de Signes: Textes réunis en hommage à Germaine Dieterlen,* 3–24. Paris: Hermann.

Stoller, Paul, 1992. *The Cinematic Griot: The Ethnography of Jean Rouch*. Chicago: The University of Chicago Press.

Stoller, Paul, 2008. *The Power of the Between: An Anthropological Odyssey*. Chicago: The University of Chicago Press.

Stoller, Paul, 2014. *Yaya's Story: The Quest for Well Being in the World*. Chicago: The University of Chicago Press.

Index

The letter *f* after an entry indicates a page that includes a figure